The Paradox of Repression
and Nonviolent Movements

Syracuse Studies on Peace and Conflict Resolution
Robert A. Rubinstein and Çerağ Esra Çuhadar, *Series Editors*

SELECT TITLES IN SYRACUSE STUDIES
ON PEACE AND CONFLICT RESOLUTION

Civil Society, Conflict Resolution, and Democracy in Nigeria
Darren Kew

Democracy and Conflict Resolution: The Dilemmas of Israel's Peacemaking
Miriam Fendius Elman, Oded Haklai, and Hendrik Spruyt, eds.

Exploring the Power of Nonviolence: Peace, Politics, and Practice
Randall Amster and Elavie Ndura, eds.

Globalization, Social Movements, and Peacebuilding
Jackie Smith and Ernesto Verdeja, eds.

Humor and Nonviolent Struggle in Serbia
Janjira Sombatpoonsiri

Jerusalem: Conflict and Cooperation in a Contested City
Madelaine Adelman and Miriam Fendius Elman, eds.

Radical Pacifism: The War Resisters League and Gandhian Nonviolence in America, 1915–1963
Scott H. Bennett

Youth Encounter Programs in Israel: Pedagogy, Identity, and Social Change
Karen Ross

The Paradox of Repression and Nonviolent Movements

Edited by Lester R. Kurtz
and Lee A. Smithey

With a Foreword by Brian Martin

Syracuse University Press

Syracuse, New York 13244-5290

First Edition 2018

18 19 20 21 22 23 6 5 4 3 2 1

∞ The paper used in this publication meets the minimum requirements of the American National Standard for Information Sciences—Permanence of Paper for Printed Library Materials, ANSI Z39.48-1992.

For a listing of books published and distributed by Syracuse University Press, visit www.SyracuseUniversityPress.syr.edu.

ISBN: 978-0-8156-3564-2 (hardcover) 978-0-8156-3582-6 (paperback)
978-0-8156-5429-2 (e-book)

Library of Congress Cataloging-in-Publication Data

Available from the publisher upon request.

Manufactured in the United States of America

To the memories of our brilliant friend and colleague,
Dr. Gregory Maney,
who taught us compassion, determination,
and persistence, and
to Dr. Gene Sharp,
the pioneering scholar and educator
who established the study of strategic nonviolent action,
including political jiu-jitsu, the subject of this book.

Contents

Illustrations

Tables

Foreword

BRIAN MARTIN

Violence gets a good press. In school, children learn about armies and battles. National holidays salute the sacrifices of soldiers. In Hollywood movies, there is plenty of violence, and usually the violence of the good guys triumphs over the violence of the bad guys. Many video games involve fighting or shooting down enemies.

As a result of a cultural emphasis on violence, most people assume that the only way to counter violence is by superior violence, either stronger or smarter. In the aftermath of the 9/11 attacks, the US government launched an invasion of Afghanistan, based on the assumption that the way to respond to violence was by using even more violence.

In the United States the glorification of violence is especially strong, complementing a gross double standard. When opponent governments such as Iraq, Iran, or North Korea seek to obtain nuclear weapons, this is cause for massive alarm. Meanwhile, the thousands of US nuclear weapons seldom cause concern because "our" threat to annihilate enemies is for the purposes of defense, whereas "their" weapons are for attack. The US government uses drones to assassinate enemies in foreign countries. If foreign drones assassinated people in the United States, the response can be imagined.

The result of the valorization of violence is that alternatives are assumed ineffectual by comparison. Diplomacy is used regularly to

Thanks to Tom Weber for valuable comments on a draft.

resolve disputes, but is seldom lauded in history textbooks, Hollywood films, or videogames.

Then there is another alternative, nonviolent action, which includes rallies, strikes, boycotts, sit-ins, and a host of other methods of struggle. Nonviolent action is commonly conceived as social, political, or economic action that does not involve physical violence and that is nonstandard. Standard methods of political action include voting and campaigning. Boycotting an election or inauguration is nonstandard and can be a method of nonviolent action.

The term "nonviolent action" is awkward because it refers to a negative and is open to misinterpretation as referring to any action not involving violence. Various alternative terms have been proposed, including *people power*, *civil resistance*, and *satyagraha*, each with its own limitations.

Whatever the word, most people assume violence is always going to be victorious over nonviolent methods. Troops and police can use batons, tear gas, and rifles, if necessary, to quell an unruly crowd. The only scenario for nonviolent action succeeding is assumed to be when those in charge of violence are restrained in their use of it. This might happen in democratic countries, so the thinking goes, but will be hopeless against a seriously repressive government. It is at this point that Hitler is often invoked: nonviolent action wouldn't work against the Nazis. This is frequently taken as the definitive refutation of nonviolence.

In this context, the possibility that nonviolent action could triumph over well-armed and well-trained opponents is, for many people, inconceivable. That it could work against the Nazis (Semelin 1993) may be dismissed out of hand. That repression might be counterproductive, leading to a greater chance of success for challengers, thus is seen as a paradox.

Part of the problem is that nearly all attention has been on conflicts in which both sides use violence, including war as well as counterterrorism versus terrorism. When the focus is on these sorts of methods, the dynamics of nonviolent struggle are ignored.

History of an Idea

Over the past century, the features of the paradox of repression have gradually been recognized and better understood. The first person to name and try to explain the process was Richard Gregg, a US supporter of organized labor who saw the failure of strike campaigns in the 1920s. He went to India and studied Gandhi's methods. Mohandas Gandhi was the pioneer practitioner of nonviolent action as a strategy for social change. There had been major nonviolent campaigns previously; for example, the struggle by Hungarians against Austrian rulers in the mid-1800s and by the Finns against Russian oppressors from 1898 to 1905. The methods of nonviolent struggle were known, but Gandhi was the one who turned these methods into a conscious strategy. Gandhi rejected the previous name for these methods, *passive resistance* (Huxley 1990), and adopted the term *satyagraha.*

The pinnacle of Gandhi's efforts, the salt satyagraha of 1930, involved a twenty-four-day march to the sea and civil disobedience against the British salt laws by making salt from seawater (Weber 1997). After Gandhi had been arrested and imprisoned, his deputies continued the campaign. In a set piece made famous by the 1982 film *Gandhi*, satyagrahis (activists) calmly walked toward a saltworks. They were met by police who brutally beat them, and then they were carried away while a new group came forward.

The salt satyagraha was the turning point in the Indian struggle for independence, inflaming passions throughout India and triggering great support in Britain, the United States, and elsewhere. Gregg sought to explain how the struggle had been so powerfully invigorated by activists acquiescing in being cruelly beaten. In his 1934 book *The Power of Nonviolence* he presented the concept of "moral jiu-jitsu." Jiu-jitsu is a martial art in which the force of the opponent is used against them. By analogy, moral jiu-jitsu involves behaving in a way that morally destabilizes the opponent. Gregg (1966) hypothesized that by remaining nonviolent, satyagrahis caused psychological distress among the police who were beating them.

Over half a century later, Gandhian scholar Thomas Weber (1993) looked again at the salt march, traversing the route himself and examining archives about the response of the police. He discovered that the police were not affected in the way Gregg had hypothesized; instead, some of them became enraged by the nonresistance of the satyagrahis and became even more vigorous and cruel in their assaults. However, there was a jiu-jitsu effect that operated through a different medium: print. US press correspondent Webb Miller witnessed the beatings and wrote a moving account that was circulated by United Press and appeared in over a thousand newspapers, as well as reproduced in leaflet form with hundreds of thousands of copies. The brutality of beating unarmed and nonresisting protesters, as recounted by Miller, caused widespread outrage and a surge of international support for the Indian independence struggle.

Gene Sharp is widely acknowledged as the foremost researcher on nonviolent action. His magnum opus is *The Politics of Nonviolent Action*, published in 1973. It contains three parts. The first expounds Sharp's concept of power as a relationship, often called the "consent theory of power." The second part presents 198 methods of nonviolent action with documentation of the use of each one. The third and longest part, called "the dynamics of nonviolent action," presents a set of stages or elements in a nonviolent campaign: laying the groundwork, challenge bringing repression, maintaining nonviolent discipline, three potential roads to success, and the redistribution of power.

A key element in Sharp's dynamics framework he calls "political jiu-jitsu." Sharp broadened Gregg's concept of moral jiu-jitsu to include social and political processes, and he gave it a new name (Sharp 1973, 657–703). Political jiu-jitsu occurs when violence against nonviolent actionists is seen as so wrong or disturbing that it causes more people in the "grievance group" to become active, more third parties to become sympathetic, and even some opponents to change their minds or behavior. Sharp documented several cases of political jiu-jitsu, for example during the 1905 Russian revolutionary upsurge following the massacre of protesters on Bloody Sunday. Sharp is careful to say that political jiu-jitsu does not necessarily occur in every nonviolent campaign.

One of the requirements for political jiu-jitsu is maintaining nonviolent discipline: in the face of violence by police or soldiers, protesters must refrain from using violence themselves. The reason is so that the violence by authorities is seen to be unfair. When protesters, often under provocation, use violence themselves, it appears to justify the authorities' violence, which is typically far greater.

In the 2000s, I explored political jiu-jitsu further, prompted by noticing that there were many cases in which violence against peaceful protesters did not have a jiu-jitsu effect, such as massacres of civilians by Indonesian troops (Martin, Varney, and Vickers 2001). Why did political jiu-jitsu sometimes occur and sometimes not? This led me to look at methods perpetrators and their supporters could use to reduce the likelihood of popular outrage over an injustice. Five types of methods are commonly used: covering up the action, devaluing the target, reinterpreting the events (by lying, minimizing consequences, blaming others, and reframing), using official channels to give an appearance of justice, and intimidating and rewarding people involved (Martin 2007, 2012).

In the 1930 salt satyagraha, the British rulers used all these methods to reduce outrage from the brutal beatings of nonresisting satyagrahis. For example, they tried to prevent journalist Webb Miller's stories from being transmitted outside India (cover-up), denigrated the protesters (devaluation), claimed there was no brutality by the police and that protesters were faking their injuries (reinterpretation), offered Gandhi an opportunity to negotiate (official channels), and arrested protesters (intimidation). However, in this case these methods were inadequate to prevent a huge reaction to the beatings. It was a case of political jiu-jitsu (Martin 2007, 35–42).

I and others have documented the use of the same five methods in other sorts of injustices, including ones not involving violence or protesters. Examples include censorship (Jansen and Martin 2003), police beatings (Martin 2005), torture (Brooks 2016), bombing (Riddick 2012), and genocide (Martin 2009). To distinguish this model, with its five methods of reducing outrage and its application beyond the violence-versus-nonviolence format, I introduced the term *backfire*.

The framework might also be called the outrage management model (McDonald, Graham, and Martin 2010).

The model provides a guide for targets of injustice: counter each one of the methods for reducing outrage. The five resulting methods for increasing outrage are exposing the action, validating the target, interpreting the events as an injustice, mobilizing support (and avoiding official channels), and resisting intimidation and rewards. Preparing to use these countermethods—for example, to record and broadcast images of possible atrocities—can serve to deter attacks.

The backfire model includes two facets: backfire as a process (including the five methods of reducing outrage and the five countermethods) and backfire as an outcome. Backfire as an outcome is much the same as political jiu-jitsu, except that it can occur with a range of injustices such as censorship, torture, and genocide.

The paradox of repression, addressed in this book, primarily addresses backfire as an outcome. It is basically the same concept as political jiu-jitsu, though with slight differences in emphasis. In Sharp's framework of the dynamics of nonviolent action, political jiu-jitsu is a stage or facet of a nonviolent campaign triggered by violent attacks on protesters, dependent on the protesters not using violence themselves. The concept of the paradox of repression draws attention to the role of repression, suggesting it can be counterproductive, and opening the possibility that this dynamic may occur outside of an organized nonviolent campaign.

More to Learn

Whatever the nuances of the concepts—the paradox of repression, political jiu-jitsu, and backfire as an outcome—there is, no doubt, much to learn about them. This points to another contrast between nonviolent and violent struggle: the enormous discrepancy between the resources put into them, including research. The world's total military spending is well over a trillion dollars per year, a vast sum that covers everything from salaries to missiles. An important component of military budgets is research, including how to make bullets more deadly, how to design nuclear weapons, how to motivate soldiers to perform more reliably in battle, and how to control the media to serve military goals.

Given hundreds of billions of dollars spent each year on military research, it is perhaps surprising that nonviolent campaigns have been able to topple repressive regimes. These regimes seem to have all the advantages in terms of resources, including troops, weapons, and training. Their challengers are mostly ordinary citizens with minimal training, making use of tools readily available to them, such as phones and the Internet. Imagine that nonviolent campaigners had at their disposal massive resources to prepare the population to resist aggression and repression, with an entirely different set of policies for everything from communications to agriculture. This is a vision of a society organized for nonviolent struggle (Boserup and Mack 1974; Burrowes 1996; Martin 1993; Sharp 1990). Such a society would naturally want to rely on the best available knowledge—including about the paradox of repression.

However, nonviolence researchers are relatively few and receive very little support. There is no funding for major simulations or for developing communication systems designed for civil resistance. In this context, it is vital to learn as much as possible by analyzing previous struggles. This book is one outcome of researchers and activists seeking to develop and articulate insights about nonviolent struggle, with a focus on responding to repression.

The editors wisely decided not to insist on a particular definition of repression or the paradox of repression, thereby ensuring that the conceptual terrain is more open for exploration. Some of the possible areas for further exploration are canvassed by the editors in their chapters and by several of the other contributors. One of the most important contributions of this book is that it points to possibilities for future research and action.

One valuable approach involves databases and statistical analysis of campaigns, both violent and nonviolent. Erica Chenoweth and Maria Stephan's 2011 book *Why Civil Resistance Works* is the exemplar of this approach. It has had a huge impact on the field. In her chapter, Chenoweth points to insights gained from analyzing hundreds of antiregime campaigns. Undoubtedly there is much more to learn from such studies.

Case studies can provide insights about repression, as shown in the chapters by Williams, Ziada, and Satha-Anand. There are numerous additional case studies worth examining. I would like to see more study of cases of repression that did not backfire, namely when massive violence against activists and civilians did not lead to increased resistance. Unfortunately, there are untold numbers of such cases of nonbackfiring repression.

Then there are different domains. The canonical form of antiregime struggles involves large numbers of people protesting in public places. These at least are the most visible forms of resistance, given that strikes, boycotts, and occupations offer fewer opportunities for stunning visuals. As Beyer and Earl point out in chapter 5, struggles also occur online, and there are interactions between online and offline activism and repression. What other domains might be studied? Struggles inside organizations are one possibility, almost untapped in the nonviolence literature. If members of a dissident group within an army are attacked, could this generate greater support for the dissidents? And how should activists outside the military best interact with insider movements?

Many social analysts would like their studies to be useful to activists. There is much to learn from activists who reflect on their experiences, and on those of others. Lakey and Williams in their chapters approach repression issues from the perspective of activists, each with a special interest in how to overcome fear.

There are many other important insights in this volume, including MacNair's examination of the psychology of repressors (very useful for activists planning to fraternize) and Satha-Anand's surprising suggestion that locking up the leaders of a movement can open the door to more effective resistance.

There is little public information about whether and how authorities think of the possibility that repression can backfire. No doubt there is often an intuitive understanding, which is why they so often try to hide their actions, devalue targets, and frame their actions positively. But are authorities consciously calculating how best to control movements for greater freedom and justice? According to Baumeister (1997), those who perpetrate horrible actions such as torture and killing usually think they are victims or justified. So it may be unwise to think of repressors as consciously scheming to get their way: they may frame their actions as righteous and necessary, which means they may not act as instrumentally as imagined by resisters.

In their chapter on smart repression, the editors address some of the techniques used by sophisticated rulers. These techniques overlap with the methods of outrage management and with methods described in Dobson's 2012 book *The Dictator's Learning Curve*. The key point is that authorities with the capacity for repression can learn from experience, including experience interacting with nonviolent movements. They can also learn by reading about nonviolent movements and even from reading about the paradox of repression! In the long term, there is bound to be learning on both sides, with no final end point.

The one great advantage held by most nonviolent campaigners is that their methods cause limited harm. So while we might imagine military strategists studying the paradox of repression, they may not gain all that much from writings in the field because their mindsets cannot fully align with their role as repressors. Furthermore, convincing the rank and file to join in will remain a serious challenge for commanders.

Rulers and commanders are bound to make mistakes. As Shultziner shows in his chapter, some instances of repression can be transformative even when the circumstances do not seem all that favorable. If movements are prepared, then the chances of major change from repression are increased. In any case, it is important for activists to understand findings about the paradox of repression to stay one step ahead of their opponents.

References

Baumeister, Roy F. 1997. *Evil: Inside Human Violence and Cruelty*. New York: Freeman.

Boserup, Anders, and Andrew Mack. 1974. *War Without Weapons: Nonviolence in National Defence*. London: Frances Pinter.

Brooks, Aloysia. 2016. *The Annihilation of Memory and Silent Suffering: Inhibiting Outrage at the Injustice of Torture in the War on Terror in Australia.* PhD Thesis, University of Wollongong. http://ro.uow.edu.au/theses/4865/.

Burrowes, Robert J. 1996. *The Strategy of Nonviolent Defense: A Gandhian Approach.* Albany, NY: State University of New York Press.

Chenoweth, Erica, and Maria J. Stephan. 2011. *Why Civil Resistance Works: The Strategic Logic of Nonviolent Conflict.* New York: Columbia Univ. Press.

Dobson, William J. 2012. *The Dictator's Learning Curve: Inside the Global Battle for Democracy.* New York: Doubleday.

Gregg, Richard B. 1966. *The Power of Nonviolence*, 2d ed. New York: Schocken Books.

Huxley, Steven Duncan. 1990. *Constitutionalist Insurgency in Finland: Finnish "Passive Resistance" against Russification as a Case of Nonmilitary Struggle in the European Resistance Tradition.* Helsinki: Finnish Historical Society.

Jansen, Sue Curry, and Brian Martin. 2003. "Making Censorship Backfire." *Counterpoise* 7 (3) (July): 5–15.

Martin, Brian. 1993. *Social Defence, Social Change.* London: Freedom Press.

———. 2005. "The Beating of Rodney King: The Dynamics of Backfire." *Critical Criminology* 13 (3): 307–26.

———. 2007. *Justice Ignited: The Dynamics of Backfire.* Lanham, MD: Rowman & Littlefield.

———. 2009. "Managing Outrage over Genocide: Case Study Rwanda." *Global Change, Peace & Security* 21 (3): 275–90.

———. 2012. *Backfire Manual: Tactics against Injustice.* Sparsnäs, Sweden: Irene Publishing.

Martin, Brian, Wendy Varney, and Adrian Vickers. 2001. "Political Jiu-Jitsu against Indonesian Repression: Studying Lower-profile Nonviolent Resistance." *Pacifica Review* 13 (2): 143–56.

McDonald, Paula, Tina Graham, and Brian Martin. 2010. "Outrage Management in Cases of Sexual Harassment as Revealed in Judicial Decisions." *Psychology of Women Quarterly* 34 (2): 165–80.

Riddick, Brendan. 2012. "The Bombing of Afghanistan: The Convergence of Media and Political Power to Reduce Outrage." *Revista de Paz y Conflictos* 5: 6–19.

Semelin, Jacques. 1993. *Unarmed against Hitler: Civilian Resistance in Europe, 1939–1943*. Westport, CT: Praeger.

Sharp, Gene. 1973. *The Politics of Nonviolent Action*. Boston: Porter Sargent.

Sharp, Gene, with the assistance of Bruce Jenkins. 1990. *Civilian-Based Defense: A Post-Military Weapons System*. Princeton, NJ: Princeton Univ. Press.

Weber, Thomas. 1993. "'The Marchers Simply Walked Forward until Struck Down': Nonviolent Suffering and Conversion." *Peace & Change* 18 (3): 267–89.

Weber, Thomas. 1997. *On the Salt March: The Historiography of Gandhi's March to Dandi*. New Delhi: HarperCollins.

Acknowledgments

We wish first to thank our contributors, who shared their intellectual talents and expertise so generously. The quality and cohesion of this project was greatly enhanced by the support of the International Center on Nonviolent Conflict, Jack DuVall, Hardy Merriman, and Maciej Bartkowski, who made it possible to bring all of the contributors together for an authors' retreat to discuss their work and the core themes of this book. Jean Boucher provided early support as our research assistant. We have treasured the continuing interest and encouragement of Mary E. King, Pat Coy, Greg Maney, Sharon Nepstad, Stellan Vinthagen, Sarah Willie-LeBreton, and students in Lee's "Strategy and Nonviolent Struggle" course that contributes to the Global Nonviolent Action Database. We deeply appreciate the critical insight of anonymous reviewers. Our departments and colleagues at George Mason University and Swarthmore College continue to inspire and make us better scholars and teachers and have no doubt shaped this book in significant ways. Most importantly, we want to thank our families, who allow us to be professional lifelong learners. Finally, this book reflects the courageous work of many nonviolent activists, who overcome fear to experiment with truth.

The Paradox of Repression and Nonviolent Movements

1

Introduction

Nonviolent Strategy and Repression Management

Lee A. Smithey and Lester R. Kurtz

"It is not repression that destroys a movement," warns one of our contributors, George Lakey. "It is repression plus lack of preparation" (1973, 111). From Bull Connor's dogs and fire hoses attacking US civil rights demonstrators to the massacre at Amritsar in colonial India, the use of coercive force against dissidents often backfires, becoming a transformative event (Sewell 1996; Shultziner, chapter 3 in this volume) that can change the course of a conflict. Rather than demobilizing a movement, repression often ironically fuels resistance and undercuts the legitimacy of a power elite. Although a long scholarly tradition explores the unintended consequences of martyrdom and other acts of violence, more attention could be paid to what we call the paradox of repression, that is, when repression creates unanticipated consequences that authorities do not desire. Efforts by power elites to oppress movements often backfire, as Brian Martin (2007) calls it, mobilizing popular support for the movements and undermining authorities, potentially leading to significant reforms or even a regime's overthrow.

Our goal in this volume is to examine multiple aspects of the paradox of repression; in our own experience while exploring various social movements around the world and observing daily news reports, we now see this paradox in many spheres of life, historical epochs, and geographical regions of the world (see Kurtz 1986; Smithey and Kurtz

2003; Lyng and Kurtz 1985). In this chapter, we will introduce the concept and explore its relevance to empirical cases that this ensemble of authors has researched. In our conclusion (chapter 12), we discuss its possibilities and implications for future research. We have designed the volume to incorporate contributions from both scholars of social movements studies and practitioners of nonviolent civil resistance who have firsthand experience of repression and who have worked to manage it proactively through the careful and strategic use of nonviolent methods. Our purpose is to develop a better sense of the topography of the concept and discuss how it might enrich our studies of collective action, contentious politics, and social movements.

Repression and Its Paradoxes

In an asymmetrical conflict, when actors representing the status quo use force (psychological, physical, economic, or otherwise) to repress their opponents—especially those engaged in nonviolent movements—the use of coercion often backfires. As civil rights activist, clergyman, and author Will Campbell writes, "Of one thing I am certain: [the civil rights movement] was not destroyed by hooded vigilantes and flaming crosses. Nor by chains used on school children, dynamiting of churches and homes, mass jailings. All those things were an impetus to the Movement and brought determination to the victims" (1986, 198; cf. Durkheim [1893] 1984; Erikson 1966). Repressive coercion can weaken a regime's authority, turning public opinion against it. Paradoxically, the more a power elite applies force, the more citizens and third parties are likely to become disaffected, sometimes inducing the regime to disintegrate from internal dissent.

Repression involves efforts by people in power to demobilize dissent and social movements resisting a regime, corporation, or other influential institutions. Drawing upon Goldstein (1978), Christian Davenport (2007a, 1) observes that most scholars of repression define it as "actual or threatened use of physical sanctions against an individual or organization, within the territorial jurisdiction of the state, for the purpose of imposing a cost on the target as well as deterring specific activities and/or beliefs perceived to be challenging to

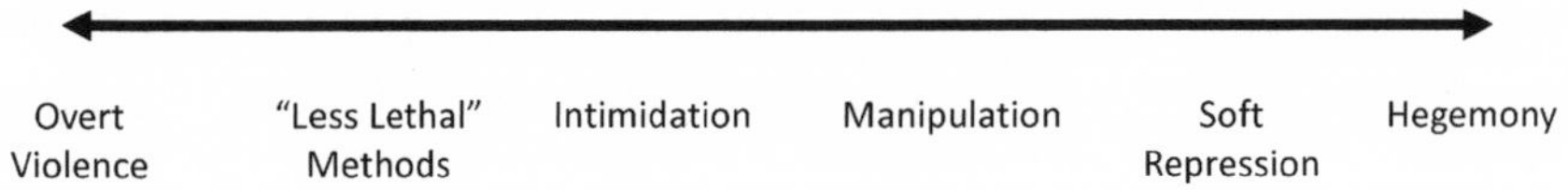

1.1. A Continuum of Demobilization (Source: Lee A. Smithey and Lester R. Kurtz)

government personnel, practices or institutions." We prefer to see repression as a much more complex phenomenon that goes far beyond physical threats or sanctions. As we discuss more fully in chapter 8, "'Smart' Repression," we find it conceptually helpful to place these methods along a continuum stretching from overt violence, on one end, to hegemony on the other (Figure 1.1). Viewing repression from this broad perspective helps to correct some of the narrowness of previous research, which Davenport and Inman (2012, 621) note has been "predominantly rationalist and structuralist in orientation, with cultural approaches being more recent and less mainstream."

Overt violence includes the actions we usually think of when we consider repression, such as beatings, torture, shooting unarmed demonstrators, and arrests. They are the repressive tactics most likely to cause moral outrage within the broader population and are, therefore, more likely to precipitate backfire. Because authorities are sometimes aware of the risks involved in using brute force, they may employ less-lethal methods such as pepper spray or "active denial systems" or simply intimidate activists with indirect threats, harassment, or surveillance. Soft repression, a concept developed by Myra Marx Ferree (2005) includes such actions as stigmatization of protesters and their movements, framing contests, and manipulative attempts to divide, divert, or distract social movement organizations or their pool of potential recruits. "The distinguishing criterion of soft repression," Marx Ferree explains, "is the collective mobilization of power, albeit in nonviolent forms and often highly informal ways, to limit and exclude ideas and identities from the public forum" (141). Although she develops the concept to explain gender-based movements, it is a strategy widely used by power elites to minimize the participation of movements and dissidents. Finally, the most effective demobilization technique used by authorities is the promotion of hegemony, in which dissidents censor themselves (for more details, see chapter 8).

Relational Nature of Conflict and Power

The paradox of repression functions more powerfully when challengers take advantage of the relational nature of conflict and the multiple sources of power posited in the work of scholars such as Georg Simmel ([1908] 1971), Mohandas K. Gandhi ([1945] 1967), Gene Sharp (1973, 2005), and Nancy Bell (2008). Conflict, as Simmel contends, is not the opposite of cooperation but of apathy or not knowing. That is, conflict is itself a form of interaction, a fundamental aspect of human nature that cannot be eliminated, but can be carried out by a variety of means along a spectrum from the most violent (e.g., thermonuclear war) to the most nonviolent (Kurtz 1992).

Repression is the expression of one type of power—often exerted under the assumption that it will crush the "powerless" or at least prevent or mitigate their insurgency. If, however, multiple sources of power are available to parties, and conflict is negotiated as a form of interaction, repression may not be accepted by its targets. Furthermore, bystanders may come to perceive a social movement's program and activities in a new light if they are repulsed by an elite's acts of repression against the movement; others outside of the local power elite may choose to take a role in questioning the authority of a regime.

Following Gandhi's lead in redefining power, Gene Sharp (1973; 2005) shows how insurgents can change their perspectives on power so that even political power is not seen as monolithic but is the result of multiple sources of power, the most important being the "consent" of the governed.[1] Nancy Bell's (2008) article on alternative conceptions

1. The term *consent* has become standard in the nonviolent action literature and refers to the simple proposition that large institutions, and states in particular, can only function because a sufficient number of people consent to cooperate in their functioning. Once participants begin to withdraw their participation, the institution necessarily weakens unless the disobedient can be easily replaced, requiring further mobilization for resistance. The word *consent* is perhaps an unfortunate choice as it

of power explores, in similar fashion, the difference between coercive "power over," on the one hand, and "power to," or cooperative empowerment, on the other (cf. Kurtz 2005). The former is "the traditional definition of power that focuses on power as domination, generally maintained through authority, force, or coercion," whereas the alternative perspective "focuses on power as 'empowerment,' ability, competence" (Bell 2008, 1703–4). Advocates of "power over" consider the accumulation of power a zero sum game, in which one side wins and the other loses. Conversely, "empowerment theories emphasize power relationships based on the assumption that the availability of power (as ability, competence, energy) is unlimited and that the dynamics of power relationships can be of the "both/and" or "win/win" variety. "In other words, power is potentially exercised by all people involved in an interaction, and an increase of power on one side does not necessarily lead to a lessening of power on the other" (1704).

Thus, empowerment theorists (often women) define power as an attribute rather than something one owns or commands (see French 1985); they view it instead as a process or an interactive dynamic, a communal phenomenon. This shift is especially helpful in looking at what are usually considered asymmetrical power relationships between the "weak" and the "powerful." Moreover, as Bell (2008, 1705) notes, "people in communities are held together by common interests, which serve as the catalyst for the exercise of 'power from below.' Power in this context is not seen as limited in quantity, but is rather a regenerative phenomenon." We join Bell in reconceptualizing power and locating it both within and between groups in relation (including opponents in conflict), not as a free-floating resource that can be accumulated and deployed by elites.

Similarly, Gandhi ([1945] 1967) contends, "Even the most despotic government cannot stand except for the consent of the governed,

---

could be interpreted to imply a conscious and willful agreement to participate in one's own domination. We believe *obedience* or *compliance* are better terms, as neither suggests approval of a corrupt elite.

which consent is often forcibly procured by the despot. Immediately the subject ceases to fear the despotic force, his power is gone" (313). When the "so-called master" attempts to force obedience, "You will say: 'No, I will not serve you for your money or under a threat.' This may mean suffering. Your readiness to suffer will light the torch of freedom which can never be put out" (313). When people are mobilized for noncooperation on a collective scale, as they were in the Indian Freedom Movement, the most powerful entities (such as the British Empire) may be unable to repress insurgents effectively because even their brutality becomes a starting point for increasing opposition.

With this sort of relational perspective on power and the possibility of noncooperation, the "weak," as Bell (2008, 1705) puts it, "are redefined as an important part of power interactions and their role becomes a primary focus of interest in alternative theories." Nonviolent activists do not simply absorb repression and accept it passively but anticipate it strategically as part of a sophisticated interaction, which they can shape (see Ackerman and DuVall 2000). Michel Foucault (1980, 116) calls this power at the grassroots level the "concrete nature of power"; that is, that which can be seen in daily struggles rather than in the state and other social institutions designed to create and maintain power from above (cf. Scott 1990). When mobilized, it can drive a resistance movement.

Thus, Sharp (1973, 2005) claims that nonviolent actionists, as he calls them, should not be dismayed or surprised at repression—it is, rather, a sign that their action constitutes a serious threat to the regime. If the protesters persist, the regime's problems may be aggravated:

> As cruelties to nonviolent people increase, the opponent's regime may appear still more despicable, and sympathy and support for the nonviolent side may increase. The general population may become more alienated from the opponent and more likely to join the resistance. Persons divorced from the immediate conflict may show increased support for the victims of the repression. Although the effect of national and international public opinion varies, it may at times lead to significant political and economic pressures. The

> opponent's own citizens, agents, and troops, disturbed by brutalities against nonviolent people, may begin to doubt the justice of his policies. Their initial uneasiness may grow into internal dissent and at times even into such action as strikes and mutinies. Thus, if repression increases the numbers of nonviolent actionists and enlarges defiance, and if it leads to sufficient internal opposition among the opponent's usual supporters to reduce his capacity to deal with the defiance, it will clearly have rebounded against him. This is political jiu-jitsu at work. (1973, 113)

Of course, nonviolent activists are not the only actors in a conflict trying to affect backfire and its effects. As Brian Martin asserts (2007, 2012, and in his foreword to this volume), people in power commonly use five types of methods to minimize backfire: "covering up the action, devaluing the target, reinterpreting the events (by lying, minimizing consequences, blaming others, and reframing), using official channels to give an appearance of justice, and intimidating and rewarding people involved." McDonald, Graham and Martin (2010) call this the "outrage management model."

Gandhi, Sharp, Gregg ([1938] 2007), and others have clearly established the fundamentals of the paradox of repression, but the circumstances in which it occurs, or how activists manage it, are less well understood. We turn now to a closer examination of the interaction between repression and resistance and attempts by nonviolent activists to take advantage of the paradox of repression.

Repression and Dissidence

The question of the relationship between repression and collective action is well worn but unsatisfactorily developed. Neither empirical studies nor theories of the impact of repression on social movements are conclusive, although statistical empirical evidence for the backfire effect is growing (e.g., Chenoweth and Stefan 2011; Sutton, Butcher, and Svensson 2014), confirming widespread case study and anecdotal support. In their review of "almost everything we know about state repression," Davenport and Inman (2012) note that the dominant research on repression assumes that political leaders calculate costs and benefits of coercive action and use a rational decision-making calculus to decide whether or not to employ repression. They contend that four findings in the study of repression are persistently important: first, "domestic factors such as democracy and political dissent generally outweigh the importance of international factors like trade dependence/globalization and the signing/ratifying of international human rights treaties. Second, we know that economic development measured by GNP per capita decreases state repression" (621).

A third finding, they contend, is more problematic: although previous studies show that democratic polities are less likely to repress, Davenport and Armstrong (2004) found that "democratic institutions have no impact on government coercive activity, but that above a specific threshold (e.g., above 0.8 on the Polity measure), democracy influences repression in a negative and linear manner as generally believed" (Davenport and Inman 2012, 622). Finally, studies of repression show that "when authorities are challenged with some form of conflict, they engage in some form of repressive action—simply, threatened governments normally respond with force" (622).

But what is the impact of repression on levels of resistance? That, Davenport and Inman assert, is more problematic; indeed, "repression has been found to have every single influence on behavioral challenges, including no influence" (2012, 624). One explanation for this conundrum is that "researchers generally ignore the fact that upon being repressed, dissidents could change tactics." In fact, a major goal of this volume is to explore repression management by social activists: How can those challenging a system anticipate, plan for, and shape, the consequences of repressive events? Looking at qualitative insights on the impact of repression, Davenport and Inman conclude that "repressive behavior is unable to curb challenging activity; however, the reasons for this influence vary significantly" (625).

As Opp and Roehl (1990) observe, "deprivation theory, resource mobilization theory, and the theory of collective action make different predictions about the effects of repression on political protest" (521). We do not presume to resolve that issue here. Clearly in some situations, repression works for the authorities, whereas in other situations it backfires. We have an insufficient number of empirical case studies to make any clear generalizations about the conditions under which repression actually promotes movement goals, although both theorists and researchers suggest a range of possibilities.

Some scholars emphasize ways in which repression may mitigate protest (see, for example, Oberschall 1973; Tilly 1978). Others, however, examine how it facilitates movement organizing (Gerlach and Hine 1970), while still others suggest that the relationship assumes an inverted U-shape (Gurr 1970) in which low levels of repression can be effective in undermining preliminary mobilization and very high levels of repression can demobilize or destroy a movement (e.g., Tiananmen Square). Once mobilization gains momentum, however, and has broad popular support, only high levels of repression can quench it. Some have asserted that regimes and opposition movements react to one another and reach a state of equilibrium (Francisco 1995, 1996; Gartner and Regan 1996). When Goodwin and Jasper (2012, 289) conducted a comparative analysis of fifty case studies of social movements to test political opportunity theory, they found unexpectedly that social movements were more likely to emerge under intense or increasing repression (nine of their fifty cases) than in situations where declining repression was a significant factor (seven of the fifty). Franklin (2015) found that in Latin America, repression filters out challengers that are less committed, so that repressive conditions lead to more persistent challengers.

Whereas most social movement scholars study repression from the point of view of the movement response to repression, Christian Davenport (1995) explored how fifty-three states responded to perceived threats from social movements in a time series analysis from 1948 to 1993, an issue that we will address in chapter 8.

We are particularly interested in those situations in which repression does serve paradoxically to strengthen social movements, and we seek to broaden our understanding of the factors contributing to this phenomenon. The resource mobilization perspective assumes that any society has enough discontent to fuel a social movement but that potential activists assess a risk-reward ratio before deciding to participate (McCarthy and Zald 1973, 1977; Oberschall 1978). Repression constitutes one potential cost of participation that will deter individuals from participating unless other rewards, such as those forthcoming from movement success, relationships with other activists, or a motivating sense of moral outrage, can compensate for the anticipated costs.

In the political process model, the prevalence of political and other opportunities external to the movement, such as divided elites within the regime, economic shifts, or the development of third party support, also influence assessments of the prospects for movement success and thus mobilization (Kriesi 2004; McAdam 1982). Emphasis on cost and opportunity, however, encourages scholars who approach the problem from the standpoint of the regime to ask which strategy or combination of repression and concession is most likely to shape an opposition movement's analysis of opportunities and thus pacify it (Goldstone and Tilly 2001). We believe it is equally important to examine mobilization processes, strategizing within movements, and how movements can create opportunities, even in the face of repression.

Opp and Roehl (1990) conducted one of the earliest up-close quantitative analyses of the paradox of repression. They studied attitudes toward protest before and after a major repressive event against an antinuclear power movement they studied in Germany. Indeed, they found that people were radicalized by the repression and became more motivated to participate in the movement. They concluded that repression interacts with movement micromobilization processes in which solidary incentives and cognitive liberation can compensate for high levels of repression.[2]

Similar results emerged from Marwan Khawaja's (1993) sophisticated multidimensional quantitative measurement of repression that

2. In social movement studies terminology, *solidary incentives* refers to the emotional psychological or other benefits accrued from personal relationships developed with other activists. *Cognitive liberation* refers to the dawning belief among individuals that a movement could be successful, encouraging them to participate.

looks at both collective and individual sanctions against Palestinians on the West Bank reported in a sample of Palestinian and Israeli newspapers between 1976 and 1985. Actions against individuals included "the use of tear gas, acts of beating, shooting, unlocking stores, threat of 'negative sanctions' against organizers or protestors (including threats to close schools), dispersion by force, and arrest" (55). Collective repression variables include the indiscriminate use of intimidating or provocative methods by the army, including curfews, closing schools or shops by military orders, military checkpoints, home-to-home searches, "invasions" of (or breaking into) places such as colleges, military "raids," and subsequent sieges on towns. "Provocations" involved actions such as the army's ordering bystanders or passersby to perform various kinds of physical actions, including standing on one foot against walls, sitting blindfolded on the floor for several hours, or removing stones from the streets (56). Although both relative deprivation and resource mobilization theory expect repression to decrease the level of collective action, most of the repressive measures against Palestinians—especially those directed against individuals—preceded increased collective action. Repression seems to have increased the ability of movement leaders to frame the regime in a way that encouraged the resolve of Palestinians and heightened their involvement in resistance.

Opp and Roehl's and Khawaja's findings suggest that decisions and strategies within social movement organizations bear on the impact of repression. William Gamson's (1975) analysis of authority-partisan interaction similarly suggests that the probability of collective action can be increased by movement strategies. Tarrow (1994, 88) points out that movement organizations can make new political opportunities by beginning to weaken the establishment, thus signaling the possibility of resistance by other organizations. In short, the methods and tactics social movement organizations deploy matter in the balance of power between regimes and challengers. Movement organizations can plan and execute strategies that enhance mobilization and influence the outcome of a struggle. Kurt Schock's (2005) groundbreaking book on unarmed insurgencies is perhaps the first to explicitly bridge the nonviolent action literature with the political process model, and while he rightly emphasizes the effects of complex opportunity structures on dissent, he also emphasizes the capacity of movements to use nonviolent tactics to take best advantage of opportunities and to resist even under high levels of repression.

Nonviolence and the Paradox of Repression

Certainly, opportunity structures change. Economic crises exacerbate grievances, and divisions within elites can embolden challengers, but the strategy and tactics of the movement interact with opportunity structures, the regime, and the public. To the extent that the movement can tailor its tactics to prevailing circumstances, it might shift advantage from the power elites.

Many activists are learning how to cultivate the right circumstances to take advantage of the paradox of repression. As Jonathan Schell (2003) eloquently asserts in *The Unconquerable World*, one of the most profound legacies within modernity has been the realization of popular nonviolent power. The last century produced a surge of innovation in nonviolent conflict strategies and methods, many of which have made effective use of the paradox of repression. (Violent insurgencies may also sometimes benefit from the paradox of repression, but their own use of violence can undermine and diminish support within their own communities and especially among third parties.)

Despite its ubiquity, the obscurity of the paradox of repression should not be particularly surprising. It is most apparent in conflicts in which one party employs strategic nonviolent strategy. However, it is only in the twentieth century that we witness the prodigious expansion of nonviolence corresponding with globalization and accelerating technological development. In a globalizing world where communications, travel, and arms technologies have become widely available, even small pockets of resistance have developed the capacity to challenge more traditionally powerful institutions, such as corporations and states.

Greater international interdependence requires economic and political cooperation across an increasingly complex network of cross-cutting alliances. The use of coercive force in this environment may offend or inconvenience mutual allies and neighbors and leave an aggressor isolated. The United States has experienced this dilemma in connection with the invasion of Iraq. Despite considerable support from the United Kingdom, the Bush administration encountered significant obstacles in cobbling together a coalition of smaller, less influential states. Larger states on the United Nations Security Council, such as France, Germany, and Russia, probably declined to participate in part because of significant economic interests in the region, but they were also under pressure from their own citizens who sympathized with the Iraqi people and considered the invasion unjustified aggression.

The structure of insurgent groups has also changed to take advantage of ever-emerging electronic communications technologies, such as fax machines, the Internet, cell phones, and instant messaging, while limiting the ability of authorities to repress resistance. Nonviolent direct action sometimes takes on the form of cell or affinity groups developed by non-state terror organizations to avoid repression. However, this trend may diminish the paradox of repression. As we will see shortly, the paradox of repression relies in large part not on avoiding repression but on enduring and sometimes provoking it.[3] In order for insurgents to invoke the sympathy and outrage of bystander publics, these publics must relate to and identify with the target of repression. Although affinity groups may make resistance groups appear shadowy and unrecognizable, much important organizing for nonviolent campaigns has taken place underground. The latter approach is more likely to prove effective in highly asymmetrical scenarios, where there is little ambiguity over public sympathies and the illegitimacy of a regime.

The paradox of repression is one manifestation of what the preeminent scholar of nonviolence, Gene Sharp (1973, 2005), calls "political jiu-jitsu." In the martial art of jiu-jitsu, one uses the weight and momentum of one's opponent to throw the opponent. Similarly, in

3. George Lakey warns against provoking repression because it "may alienate the revolutionaries from the people, brutalize the police, and even brutalize the demonstrators" (1973, 106).

strategic nonviolent action, one can use an opponent's resources, needs, and culture to one's own advantage. Thus, for example, arrests and imprisonment have always been a primary tool of governmental authorities against agents of social change. Nonviolent activists, however, have often prepared for arrest and willingly accepted or even sought incarceration in order to overload jails and strain government bureaucracies. The same dynamic can apply to the use of cultural resources to trigger the paradox of repression. Richard Gregg ([1938] 2007) first wrote about this dynamic as "moral jiu-jitsu," drawing on Gandhi's idea that self-suffering would induce conversion by an opponent, who, when confronted by a nonviolent resister, would lose "the moral support which the violent resistance of most victims would render him" (44).

As students and activists of nonviolence understand, the paradox of repression can be cultivated. True, in some cases, such as the ethnic cleansing of Native Americans, repression has been so complete as to overcome nearly all resistance. In other cases, however, where the relationship between opponents has been better integrated and where those traditionally considered less powerful have developed effective methods of resistance (such as cell structures and nonviolent collective action techniques), imperial and authoritarian states have found themselves unable to contend with grassroots opposition, often because the movement was able to rob the regime of some of its legitimacy. While the overtly systematic use of nonviolent collective action theory varies widely from case to case, training and strategic planning continues to spread. The cases we offer as illustrations do not always document an intentional preparation for the paradox of repression (though preparation is common, as we elaborate below) but indicate how challengers adopted collective action tactics that often both amplified and subverted attempts to repress and intimidate nonviolent activists.

Repression Management

We have set aside a portion of this volume to address what we call *repression management*, or the idea that social movement organizations can increase the likelihood of the paradox of repression occurring through preparation, mobilization, strategy, and tactical choice. Repression management might include preparing to withstand repression, temporarily avoiding repression, or choreographing confrontations with opponents in ways that are more likely to produce the disgust that can occur when nonviolent activists suffer repression. Framing (Snow et al. 1986; Benford and Snow 2000) or interpreting repression for publics through the media, social networks, and other communications outlets in such a way that it induces moral outrage is also important. We follow Kurt Schock in his book *Unarmed Insurrections: People Power Movements in Nondemocracies* (2005), in which he calls for social movement scholars to further explore "how the characteristics and actions of a challenge affects (*sic*) the repression-dissent relationships. Whether repression crushes dissent or promotes mobilization depends on a variety of conditions other than the level of repression, some of which may be at least within partial control of challenging groups, such as how the challenge is organized, movement strategy, the range of methods and mix of actions implemented, the targets of dissent, and communication within the movement and with third parties" (157). Several authors in this volume approach the paradox of repression from this pragmatic or strategic perspective.

Contributions of This Volume

The chapters in this book have two main goals: to gain a more nuanced understanding of how the paradox of repression works and when it has happened, on the one hand, and to examine how nonviolent activists have managed it, on the other, to enhance the extent to which it empowers movements and undermines unjust systems. We hope this volume will be valuable to scholars and activists alike, and we have recruited both scholars and activists as chapter authors (including several authors who are both). The first task of the contributors to this volume is thus to look at various aspects and cases of the paradox of repression to get a better sense of its topography beyond the isolated anecdotal cases diffused through the scholarly literature and activists' lore. We provide a conceptual and empirical overview and bring together quantitative and qualitative scholarship with activists who have experienced repression and experimented with its management. We begin with Erica Chenoweth's quantitative birdseye view of the phenomenon across the globe over half a century. Chapter 2, "Backfire in Action: Insights from Nonviolent Campaigns, 1945–2006," analyzes her large data set comparing 323 violent and nonviolent campaigns for major change to evaluate how backfire works and which movement features are most likely to provoke it.

Chenoweth identifies three critical factors facilitating a positive outcome from repression: (1) sustained high levels of campaign participation, (2) loyalty shifts among security forces and civilian leaders, and (3) the withdrawal of support from its foreign allies.

Doron Shultziner's conceptual chapter addresses a key aspect of the paradox of repression by delving into two historical cases. In chapter 3, "Transformative Events, Repression, and Regime Change," he focuses on the central tension between the parameters of opportunity structures and the agency of collective action. He explores the social psychological impact of "transformative events," which can sometimes suspend the habits and assumptions that normally underpin the political status quo and open up new opportunities for resistance. Transformative events that involve repression can thus operate as a causal mechanism or path to regime change and democratic outcomes. Shultziner focuses on cases such as the Soweto Uprising in South Africa and the Montgomery bus boycott to illustrate the relationship between repression and backfire as transformative events.

Elite defection has been identified as an important factor in the success or failure of nonviolent civil resistance campaigns, demanding that we delve into the ways in which agents of repression experience the repression they carry out. In her exploration of successful nonviolent revolutions, Sharon Erickson Nepstad (2011) found that defections by security forces were an important strategic factor. Nonviolent resistance has an advantage in managing and framing repression because it can create dilemmas for repressors.

Rachel MacNair reminds us in chapter 4, "The Psychology of Agents of Repression: The Paradox of Defection," that aggression and fear are not physical properties that people hold in their hands, but are psychological experiences. Agents of repression do not merely follow orders; they are caught up in complex psychological dynamics and risk suffering what she calls perpetration induced traumatic stress (PITS; see MacNair 2002 and chapter 4 in this volume).

In recent years, the nature of civil resistance has changed with the increased role of the Internet and social media in political processes. Jessica Beyer and Jennifer Earl bring their extensive expertise in this emerging field to bear in chapter 5, "Backfire Online: Studying Reactions to the Repression of Internet Activism." It is crucial to understand the ways in which online activism and the activists behind it interact with the state and other entities interested in silencing them. Drawing on recent cases studies, Beyer and Earl systematically present various forms of online repression and show how it has backfired on elites. They explore the affinities between different types of Internet activism and repressive tactics, identifying multiple levels of analysis of how backfire and deterrence can be differentiated according to the actors involved (individual versus group and public versus private).

A second major aspect of the book turns to repression management; that is, how nonviolent resisters—but also repressors—have attempted to shape the outcome of repression to their benefit. We begin with the firsthand experience of Jenni Williams, founder of the movement Women of Zimbabwe Arise (WOZA). In chapter 6, "Overcoming Fear to Overcome Repression," Williams emphasizes the importance of establishing a movement culture that prioritizes nonviolence and encourages empowerment through shared leadership and the creative use of traditional cultural themes to withstand and blunt repression. When WOZA transformed the traditional role of motherhood to scold and challenge the dictatorship of Mugabe, the activists were met with a brutal repression of their movement. By accepting and even courting arrest, Williams argues, the activists took away the regime's major weapon of repression, turning it instead into a source of empowerment for the movement and individual participants, increasing the costs of the regime's efforts to thwart them. They mobilized a campaign of "tough love," transforming a culture of fear into a culture of resistance and constructing a creative leadership structure that allowed them to be more flexible in their tactics than the rigid authoritarian police establishment bound by its limited repertoire.

Chapter 7, "Culture and Repression Management," focuses on the symbolic aspects of repression and its backfire. We conceptualize nonviolent struggle as a dance between an establishment and its dissidents, a regime and its insurgents, as they contest the frames used to make meaning of repressive events. This chapter explores proactive efforts by nonviolent activists to choreograph actions in ways that help to ensure the backfire effect of repression by clearly establishing the aggression of the agents of repression. In chapter 8, "'Smart' Repression," we address the growing efforts by elites to be more strategic about how they use repression, in order to mitigate the effects of its potentially backfiring. That chapter examines a relatively unexplored aspect of repression, the use of tactics that are deliberately crafted to demobilize movements while mitigating or eliminating a backfire effect.

Dalia Ziada gives us a participant's-eye-view of the Egyptian revolution of 2011 in chapter 9, "Egypt: Military Strategy and the 2011 Revolution," although she is also familiar with the literature on strategic nonviolent action. What she found most remarkable was that the army in some instances chose not to use violence during the citizen uprising, and ended up collaborating with the activists to oust President Mubarak, although they returned to the usual armed forces modus operandi after seizing power from Morsi and the Muslim Brotherhood in 2014. Ziada provides a firsthand account of the events of 2011 based on her own participation in the revolution and draws on her interviews with Egyptian and American military personnel.

In chapter 10, "Repression Engendering Creative Nonviolent Action in Thailand," Chaiwat Satha-Anand explores activist creativity following repression in Thailand. He argues that repression, such as the violent actions in 2010 of the Thai government against protesters in the Red Shirts movement, created space for new movement leadership and the introduction of creative nonviolent resistance. He calls this dynamic "the cleansing effect of violent repression." In this Thai case, Sombat Boonngamanong developed a series of highly symbolic and creative flash mob actions that drew on a history of nonviolent resistance in Thai society.

Finally, veteran activist, scholar, and trainer George Lakey concludes the volume by providing insights from decades of practical experience and reflection in chapter 11, "Making Meaning of Pain and Fear: Enacting the Paradox of Repression." According to Lakey, nonviolent activists create narratives that provide meaning for their risks, injuries, suffering, and losses, helping them to transform pain and fear into opportunities for mobilization. These stories in turn have consequences for the tactics and strategies they choose and help to trigger the paradox of repression. Activists use these stories to prepare in advance for repressive events by training and shaping confrontations.

By weaving together these case studies, scholarly analysis, and activists' reflection, we aim to shed light on how the paradox of repression works in multiple contexts and how activists have managed repression to enhance its potential to backfire and empower resistance.

Repression as Relational Conflict

Nonviolent resistance is based in large part on the strategic harnessing of relational power. We focus on one subform in this volume: the strategic cultivation of the paradox of repression. Sometimes, when one party takes coercive action that violates basic norms, its ability to rally support and cooperation—its legitimacy—is undermined, threatening its capacity to meet its own goals. The contributors to this volume present cases in which authorities or elites used intimidation, coercion, and sometimes violence in attempts to crush dissident movements; but in each case, intimidation and physical force were seen to violate norms of proportionate response and helped to mobilize movement recruits. Elites' efforts rebounded on them, undermining their legitimacy and diminishing their ability to govern as they wished.[4]

4. These unintended consequences may occur without any framing by opponents, and as the case of the Catholic modernist movement demonstrates, repression can activate a movement that did not exist previously (Kurtz 1986).

Moreover, activists can rhetorically frame the actions of their opponents or can choreograph their own actions in ways that draw attention to repression by opponents. By adopting nonviolent tactics, activists can generate a striking contrast between their own actions and the "unfair" tactics of their opponents. The dissonance that gap creates can, in turn, provoke a moral outrage that increases the support and involvement of local and third parties. Such a contrast can also cause factions to develop among a movement's opponents as some withdraw their cooperation and refuse to participate in further repression. When repression does occur against nonviolent civilians, it may serve as a deterrent to other regimes, as when Gorbachev (1996) took note of the negative consequences worldwide of the Tiananmen Square massacre and decided not to back communist states across Eastern Europe with force when they faced nonviolent uprisings a few months later (see Smithey and Kurtz 1999).

Activists may also draw on local indigenous cultural resources to sensitize potential recruits and sympathetic publics to acts of repression (Sørensen and Vinthagen 2012). Legacies may be framed that perpetuate the paradox of repression long after the immediate crisis has passed. Dissidents in Czechoslovakia in 1989 commemorated the death of a young student, Jan Palach, who self-immolated in response to the 1968 invasion of Prague by Warsaw Pact troops two decades earlier. Similarly, the legacy of the British Army's killing of civilians on Bloody Sunday in 1972 continues to influence Northern Ireland politics today, more than forty years after the event. Figuring out how to harness cultural resources requires indigenous creativity or what James Jasper (1997) has called "artfulness" in developing effective tactics. The ability of activists to design effective nonviolent collective action creatively that mitigates repression or induces it to backfire may develop out of rational strategizing, but it will often emerge instinctively from the habitus, the intimate, unspoken, and inarticulable perception of relations that is uniquely local. This creativity is the source of agency, which complicates cost-benefit paradigms since it is elusive and difficult to measure, and yet can significantly enhance the power potential of groups who might otherwise be considered susceptible to repression.

In short, although the paradox of repression is a phenomenon that is widely glossed over in both policy and academic circles, it seems an obvious and ubiquitous fact in twenty-first century political culture and a key element in the history of successful nonviolent movements. We hope that this collection of studies will enhance understanding by reconceptualizing repression as an interaction between conflicting parties, by expanding our scope of the spheres in which repression occurs, by delving into the social, psychological, and cultural dimensions of repression, by thinking more closely about the costs of repression among agents of repression, and by introducing repression management to explore ways in which strategic nonviolent activists become powerful agents within repressive contexts.

References

Ackerman, Peter, and Jack DuVall. 2000. *A Force More Powerful: A Century of Non-Violent Conflict*. New York: St. Martin's Press.

Bell, Nancy. 2008. "Power, Alternative Theories of." In *Encyclopedia of Violence, Peace, and Conflict*, 2d ed., edited by Lester R. Kurtz, 1703–9. Oxford: Academic Press.

Benford, Robert D., and David A. Snow. 2000. "Framing Processes and Social Movements: An Overview and Assessment." *Annual Review of Sociology* 26: 611–39.

Campbell, Will D. 1986. *Forty Acres and a Goat: A Memoir.* Atlanta: Peachtree.

Chenoweth, Erica, and Maria J. Stephan. 2011. *Why Civil Resistance Works: The Strategic Logic of Nonviolent Conflict*. New York: Columbia Univ. Press.

Davenport, Christian. 1995. "Multi-Dimensional Threat Perception and State Repression: An Inquiry into Why States Apply Negative Sanctions." *American Journal of Political Science* 39: 683–713.

———. 2007a. "State Repression and Political Order." *Annual Review of Political Science* 10: 1–23.

———. 2007b. *State Repression and the Domestic Democratic Peace*. New York: Cambridge Univ. Press.

Davenport, Christian, and D. A. Armstrong II. 2004. "Democracy and the Violation of Human Rights: A Statistical Analysis from 1976–1996." *American Journal of Political Science* 48 (3): 538–54.

Davenport, Christian, and Molly Inman. 2012. "The State of State Repression Research since the 1990s." *Terrorism and Political Violence* 24 (4): 619–34.

Davenport, Christian, Hank Johnston, and Carol McClurg Mueller. 2004. *Repression and Mobilization*. Minneapolis: Univ. of Minnesota Press.

Durkheim, Emile. (1893) 1984. *The Division of Labor in Society*. New York: Free Press.

Erikson, Kai T. 1966. *Wayward Puritans: A Study in the Sociology of Deviance*. New York: Macmillan; Collier Macmillan.

Foucault, Michel. 1980. *Power/Knowledge: Selected Interviews and Other Writings, 1972–1977*. Edited by Colin Gordon. New York: Pantheon Books.

Francisco, R. 1995. "The Relationship between Coercion and Protest: An Empirical Test in Three Coercive States." *Journal of Conflict Resolution* 39: 263–82.

———. 1996. "Coercion and Protest: An Empirical Test in Two Democratic States." *American Journal of Political Science* 40: 1179–1204.

Franklin, James. 2015. "Persistent Challengers: Repression, Concessions, Challenger Strength, and Commitment in Latin America." *Mobilization: An International Journal* 20 (1): 61–80.

French, Marilyn. 1985. *Beyond Power: On Women, Men, and Morals*. New York: Summit Books.

Gamson, William A. 1975. *The Strategy of Social Protest*. Homewood: Dorsey Press.

Gandhi, Mohandas K. (1945) 1967. *The Mind of Mahatma Gandhi*. Edited by R. K. Prabhu and U. R. Rao. Ahmedabad: Navajivan.

Gartner, S. S., and P. M. Regan. 1996. "Threat and Repression: The Nonlinear Relationship between Government and Opposition violence." *Journal of Peace Research* 33: 273–88.

Gerlach, Luther P., and Virginia H. Hine. 1970. *People, Power, Change: Movements of Social Transformation*. Indianapolis: Bobbs-Merrill.

Goldstein, R. J. 1978. *Political Repression in Modern America: From 1870 to the Present*. Cambridge, MA: Schenkman.

Goldstone, Jack A., and Charles Tilly. 2001. "Threat (and Opportunity): Popular Action and State Response in the Dynamics of Contentious Action." In *Silence and Voice in the Study of Contentious Politics*, edited by R. Aminzade, J. A. Goldstone, D. McAdam, E. Perry, W. H. Sewell Jr, S. Tarrow, and C. Tilly. Cambridge: Cambridge Univ. Press.

Goodwin, Jeff, and James M. Jasper. 2012. *Contention in Context: Political Opportunities and the Emergence of Protest.* Stanford, CA: Stanford Univ. Press.

Gorbachev, Mikhail Sergeyevich. 1996. *Memoirs.* New York: Doubleday.

Gregg, Richard B. [1938] 2007. *The Power of Non-Violence.* Ahmedabad: Navajivan. https://archive.org/details/mkbook080omkga.

Gurr, Ted Robert. 1970. *Why Men Rebel.* Princeton: Princeton Univ. Press.

Jasper, James M. 1997. *The Art of Moral Protest: Culture, Biography, and Creativity in Social Movements.* Chicago: Univ. of Chicago Press.

Khawaja, M. 1993. "Repression and Popular Collective Action: Evidence from the West Bank." *Sociological Forum* 8: 47–71.

Kriesi, Hanspeter. 2004. "Political Context and Opportunity." In *The Blackwell Companion to Social Movements,* edited by D. A. Snow, S. A. Soule, and H. Kriesi, 67–90. Malden, MA: Blackwell.

Kurtz, Lester R. 1986. *The Politics of Heresy: The Modernist crisis in Roman Catholicism.* Berkeley: Univ. of California Press.

———. 1992. "Nonviolent War: An Idea Whose Time Has Come?" *Gandhi Marg* 14: 450–62.

———. 2005. "Rethinking Power: Its Sources and Our Options." *Ahimsa Nonviolence* 1 (Jan.–Feb.): 9–15. http://works.bepress.com/lester_kurtz/40/.

Lakey, George. 1973. *Strategy for a Living Revolution.* San Francisco: W. H. Freeman.

Lyng, Stephen G., and Lester R. Kurtz. 1985. "Bureaucratic Insurgency: The Vatican and the Crisis of Modernism." *Social Forces* 63: 901–22.

MacNair, Rachel M. 2002. *Perpetration-Induced Traumatic Stress.* Westport, Connecticut: Praeger.

Martin, Brian. 2007. *Justice Ignited: The Dynamics of Backfire.* Lanham, MD: Rowman & Littlefield. http://www.bmartin.cc/pubs/07ji/ji-all.pdf.

———. 2012. *Backfire Manual: Tactics against Injustice.* Sparsnäs, Sweden: Irene Publishing. http://ro.uow.edu.au/artspapers/1312/.

Marx Ferree, Myra. 2005. "Soft Repression: Ridicule, Stigma, and Silencing in Gender-Based Movements." In *Repression and Mobilization,* edited by Davenport, Christian, Hank Johnston, Carol McClurg Mueller, 138–55. Vol. 21 of *Social Movements, Protest, and Contention.* Minneapolis: Univ. of Minnesota Press.

McAdam, Doug. 1982. *Political Process and the Development of Black Insurgency, 1930–1970.* Chicago: Univ. of Chicago Press.

McCarthy, John D., and Mayer N. Zald. 1973. *The Trend of Social Movements in America: Professionalization and Resource Mobilization*. Morristown, NJ: General Learning Press. https://web.archive.org/web/20180313170452/https://deepblue.lib.umich.edu/bitstream/handle/2027.42/50939/164.pdf?sequenc.

McCarthy, John D., and Mayer N. Zald. 1977. "Resource Mobilization and Social Movements: A Partial Theory." *American Journal of Sociology* 82: 1213–41.

McDonald, Paula, Tina Graham, and Brian Martin. 2010. "Outrage Management in Cases of Sexual Harassment as Revealed in Judicial Decisions." *Psychology of Women Quarterly* 34 (2): 165–80.

Nepstad, Sharon Erickson. 2011. *Nonviolent Revolutions: Civil Resistance in the Late 20th Century*. New York: Oxford Univ. Press.

Oberschall, Anthony. 1973. *Social Conflict and Social Movements*. Englewood Cliffs, NJ: Prentice-Hall.

———. 1978. "Theories of Social Conflict." *Annual Review of Sociology* 4: 291–315.

Opp, K. D., and W. Roehl. 1990. "Repression, Micromobilization, and Political Protest." *Social Forces* 69: 521–47.

Schell, Jonathan. 2003. *The Unconquerable World: Power, Nonviolence, and the Will of the People*. New York: Metropolitan.

Schock, Kurt. 2005. *Unarmed Insurrections: People Power Movements in Nondemocracies*. Minneapolis: Univ. of Minnesota Press.

Scott, James C. 1990. *Domination and the Arts of Resistance: Hidden Transcripts*. New Haven: Yale Univ. Press.

Sewell, W. H. 1996. "Historical Events as Transformations of Structures: Inventing Revolution at the Bastille." *Theory and Society* 25 (6): 841–81.

Sharp, Gene. 1973. *The Politics of Nonviolent Action*. Three Volumes. Boston: Porter Sargent.

———. 2005. *Waging Nonviolent Struggle: 20th Century Practice and 21st Century Potential*. Boston: Porter Sargent.

Simmel, Georg. (1908) 1971. "Conflict." In *On Individuality and Social Forms: Selected Writings*, edited by D. N. Levine, 70–95. Chicago: Univ. of Chicago Press.

Smithey, Lee, and Lester R. Kurtz. 1999. "We Have Bare Hands: Nonviolent Social Movements in the Soviet Bloc." In *Nonviolent Social*

Movements, edited by S. Zunes, L. Kurtz, and S. B. Asher, 96–124. Malden, MA: Blackwell.

———. 2003. "Parading Persuasion: Nonviolent Collective Action as Discourse in Northern Ireland." *Research in Social Movements, Conflicts and Change* 24: 319–59.

Snow, David A., Jr., E. Burke Rochford, Steven K. Worden, and Robert D. Benford. 1986. "Frame Alignment Processes, Micromobilization, and Movement Participation." *American Sociological Review* 51: 464–81.

Sørensen, Majken Jul, and Stellan Vinthagen. 2012. "Nonviolent Resistance and Culture." *Peace and Change* 37: 444–70.

Sutton, Jonathan, Charles R. Butcher, and Isak Svensson. 2014. "Explaining Political Jiu-Jitsu Institution-Building and the Outcomes of Regime Violence against Unarmed Protests." *Journal of Peace Research* 15 (51): 559–73.

Tarrow, Sidney G. 1994. *Power in Movement: Social Movements, Collective Action and Politics*. New York: Cambridge Univ. Press.

Tilly, Charles. 1978. *From Mobilization to Revolution*. Reading, MA: Addison-Wesley.

2

Backfire in Action

Insights from Nonviolent Campaigns, 1946–2006

Erica Chenoweth

Introduction

The use of violence to subdue dissent is quite common, even as human rights organizations have sought to end it. In fact, Christian Davenport (2007) argues that one of the most stable and predictable patterns in global politics is that when people dissent, the state meets such dissent with coercion. Davenport calls this the "law of coercive responsiveness." Since this pattern is close to a "law," he explains, we can expect that any form of dissent will be met with some form of coercion. What varies are (1) the form of dissent; (2) the form, scope, and intensity of the coercion; and (3) the consequences of the coercion.

This chapter is concerned with the third form of variation—that the political effects of coercion do not fall neatly into any particular pattern. As noted by Davenport (2007) and by Smithey and Kurtz in the introduction to this volume, scholars have long puzzled over the fact that repression often seems to embolden even more dissent or challenge the legitimacy of the regime, thereby threatening its very existence, in a number of different ways.

I gratefully acknowledge detailed suggestions provided by the coeditors and anonymous reviewers, useful comments from Hardy Merriman at the International Center on Nonviolent Conflict, and helpful observations from participants at a workshop at George Mason University. Remaining errors are my own.

Previous research has found complex and ambiguous relationships between repression and subsequent mobilization. Conventional wisdom suggests that repression reduces mobilization—particularly nonviolent mobilization—by lowering the perceived opportunities for unarmed action. Some researchers have found support for a linear, negative association between repression and protest (Oberschall 1973; Jenkins and Perrow 1977; Tilly 1978). A different school of thought suggests that repression has a positive-negative curvilinear (inverted U-shape) association with mobilization, suggesting that at very low levels and very high levels of repression, there is very little mobilization (Gurr 1969). This is because at low levels of repression, would-be agitators are more or less satisfied with the status quo; at very high levels of repression, on the other hand, mobilization is perceived as far too costly. In middling regimes, however, where the level of repression is just high enough to provoke outrage and just low enough to make mobilization appear feasible and potentially productive, scholars expect levels of mobilization to be at their highest. Some have argued that repression has a positive and linear effect on mobilization, with a sense of injustice and outrage overriding fears of further repression (Gerlach and Hine 1970; Martin 2007). Still other scholars find no significant, general association between repression and mobilization (Davenport 2007).

There are a few limitations to the current literature. First, many of the works attempting to establish general theoretical expectations are based on only a few cases of repression and dissent, meaning that their findings are difficult to generalize. Second (and perhaps as a consequence of the latter point), findings are inconclusive and—at times—completely contradictory. And third, much of the literature examines dissent or mobilization in general but does not distinguish which form of mobilization is underway, or which kind of actors are mobilizing. Specifically, an important omission from the current literature is the effect that the method of mobilization—namely strategic nonviolent action—may have on the association between repression and mobilization. Finally, many studies emphasize the political environment—such as the level of democracy or the level of repression—and downplay the extent to which movement features—such as movement size, structure, and nonviolent discipline—may affect the propensity for backfire.

Indeed, nonviolent mass campaigns tend to defy many expectations. Contrary to previous literature on mobilization, such campaigns are often set on in highly repressive contexts (Chenoweth and Stephan 2011). Even though state repression tends to increase the risks involved in nonviolent action, recent research suggests that repression does not always doom these movements. Instead, unarmed civilians have achieved ambitious political and social goals through nonviolent action in the face of brutality (Chenoweth and Stephan 2011). Often, but not always, such changes have been brought about by backfire—a process in which dissidents render counterproductive a state's repression and subsequent attempts to justify it (Hess and Martin 2006; Martin 2007). In other cases, repression has effectively crushed nonviolent campaigns without backfiring at all.

Why do some campaigns succeed at making repression backfire, while others do not? In this chapter, I draw on the Nonviolent and Violent Campaigns and Outcomes (NAVCO) data set to better understand how participation, internal organization, media coverage, and nonviolent discipline affect five indicators of backfire as an outcome, including (1) domestic condemnation (like denunciations by prominent politicians); (2) international condemnation and sanctions (such as the broad sanctions and divestments directed toward the offending regime); (3) an ally's withdrawal of support for the target regime (such as the refusal of a patron to continue providing political, diplomatic, or security guarantees to the regime); (4) security force defections (such as noncooperation or disobedience by police or other state agents); and (5) future domestic mobilization in support of the campaign (such as large rallies held in response to atrocities committed against smaller protests).

The results raise a number of interesting issues. First, I find evidence that international condemnation is more likely to result when nonviolent campaigns experience a high degree of repression captured by international media outlets. However, the presence of a violent radical flank[1] increases the likelihood that the campaign achieves international media coverage, thus suggesting a moral hazard effect[2] in which oppositionists can elicit international attention and subsequent condemnation of the regime by (1) adopting violent flanks and (2) provoking higher levels of repression against civilians. These results provide support for similar arguments about moral hazard by Alan Kuperman, who has argued that the international community tends to mobilize direct support for rebels who use violence to accelerate humanitarian emergencies (Kuperman 2008).

Second, I find that erstwhile state allies of the regime—such as the United States as it supported Ferdinand Marcos in the Philippines—are much more likely to withdraw support from the regime when a nonviolent campaign achieves a high level of international media coverage and when it possesses a more hierarchical structure as opposed to a more decentralized one.

Third, I find that condemnation by domestic actors is more likely to occur when repression is high and when domestic media outlets have widely reported the repression. However, neither campaign size nor the presence of a radical flank influences the degree to which domestic elites condemn the repression, indicating that any positive radical flank effect is limited to the international level.

1. *Positive radical flanks effects* are those in which small amounts of violence benefit an otherwise nonviolent social movement, either by providing them with higher levels of disruptive capacity, attention, leverage, recruits, financing and third-party support, or bargaining space through perceptions that the nonviolent elements of the movement are more "moderate" or "reasonable" (see, for instance, Haines 1984). *Negative radical flank effects* are those in which small amounts of violence undermine an otherwise nonviolent movement by reducing participation, increasing repression, reducing popular sympathy for the movement, and alienating potential third-party supporters. Little systematic empirical research exists evaluating which of these effects—positive or negative—is most common across cases. See Chenoweth and Schock (2015) for a recent attempt.

2. A moral hazard is a situation in which an actor is willing to take higher risk because she knows that any potential costs will be borne by others.

Fourth, I find that campaign size is positively correlated with defections by key state elites and/or security forces, and that widespread participation is the most important factor in increasing the likelihood of defections when controlling for a variety of other factors.

Fifth, I find that increased mobilization is largely influenced by prior levels of mobilization and levels of repression. Unsurprisingly, campaigns with high mobilization are likely to stay relatively large, but this is especially true when they face lower levels of repression.

The data also reveal that not all five indicators of backfire are equally important in bringing about the success of nonviolent campaigns. I find, strikingly, that the most influential backfire outcomes are those in which erstwhile foreign allies withdraw support from the regime, campaign participation increases, and state elites defect from the regime. Domestic and international condemnation and sanctions have very little effect on success, suggesting that although campaigns often expend resources—and even increase their acceptance of violence—in seeking these outcomes, they do not necessarily provide them with sufficient leverage to achieve change. The fact that international condemnation and sanctions are not highly correlated with campaign success further undermines support for a positive radical flank effect.

The conclusions we can draw from these findings are threefold. First, sustained campaign participation—in terms of both size and diversity—is among the most important elements in understanding whether domestic and international audiences mobilize in support of the campaign when it is repressed. In other words, for successful backfire, participation is paramount. This is true whether or not the campaign maintains nonviolent discipline, although prior research has shown that nonviolent campaigns are much larger than violent ones to achieve mass participation (Chenoweth and Stephan 2011).

Second, a hierarchical organization seems to increase the likelihood of an ally's withdrawal of support for the opponent regime. More decentralized campaigns, moreover, are no more likely to increase subsequent year participation, induce loyalty shifts within regime elites, or bring about domestic or international condemnation. This finding challenges the commonly held view that decentralized structures are better suited than more hierarchical organizations to achieving success.

Third, international media coverage also appears crucial to put pressure on regime allies to withdraw their support. Thus movements seeking to produce these outcomes should likely invest in international media strategies to shed light on the repression to produce these outcomes.

This chapter proceeds in three sections. First, I identify five different backfire outcomes and lay out different arguments emerging from the existing literature concerning the impact that movement features may have in influencing these backfire outcomes. Second, I conduct an exploratory analysis using the NAVCO 2.0 data set to identify which movement attributes affect different forms of backfire, as well as which forms of backfire are most influential in the outcomes of the campaign. And finally, I lay out some implications of these findings.

A Theory of Backfire

As Smithey and Kurtz note in the introduction to this volume, scholars of civil resistance adopt a relational concept of power involving three basic claims. First, power is not monolithic. Instead, every power holder is totally dependent on the cooperation, obedience, and help of people who reside in the so-called pillars of support—the security forces, civilian bureaucrats, state media, economic and business elites, religious authorities, workers and organized labor, consumers, and educational elites. When people who work in these pillars stop obeying, the regime's grip on power dissolves (Sharp 1973; Nepstad 2011). Second, power is based on consent, not force. True power comes from voluntary obedience, not coerced obedience. In fact, a power holder's use of violence to compel compliance is paradoxically a sign of weakness rather than strength (Arendt 1970). Third, power is impermanent and must be constantly replenished (Arendt 1970). This is because power is fundamentally based on legitimacy—a fluid and ever-changing process that depends entirely on the population's agreement that the state is righteous and justified in its actions, expressed through the people's voluntary acquiescence to the regime's right to govern (Sharp 1973).

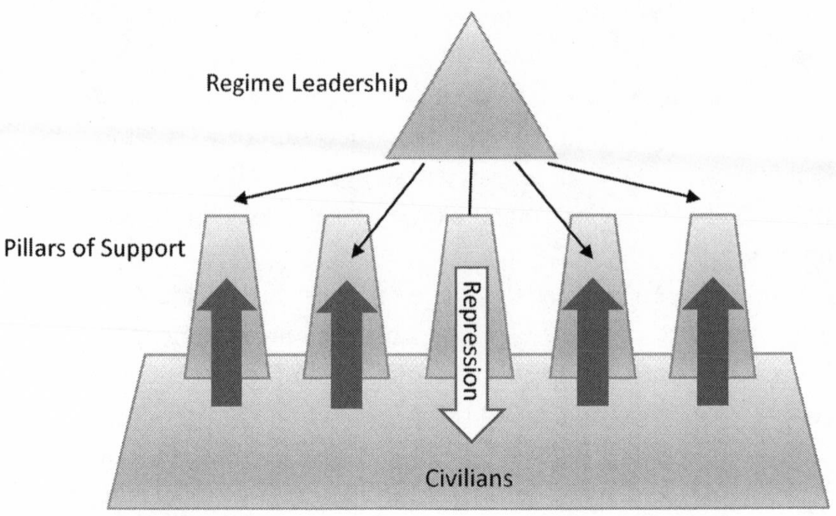

2.1. Traditional Civil Resistance Model (Source: Erica Chenoweth)

Typical theories of civil resistance therefore rightfully emphasize the domestic sources of leverage in civil resistance, conceptualizing the technique as a civilian-led form of struggle, whose object is to pull the pillars of support away from the power holders (Figure 2.1).

Yet we know that no regimes exist in isolation from others, and that often they enjoy the patronage of powerful allies resulting in impunity from their actions toward their own population. Moreover, even within the pillars of support, people may have varying degrees of sensitivity to the international implications of their continued recalcitrance in the face of nonviolent mass mobilization. In Egypt, for example, some have made the argument that the Egyptian army shifted its loyalty away from Hosni Mubarak to the January 25 revolutionary movement in large part because of concern about the economic implications of continued instability, which would have threatened many of the army elite's investments. Similar patterns unfolded in El Salvador, where routine labor strikes in the 1980s threatened foreign direct investment, and in South Africa where the international divestment campaign and black South Africans' boycotts of white businesses in the early 1990s had near-catastrophic effects on the economy. In both of these cases,

2.2. A Multilevel Model of Civil Resistance (Source: Erica Chenoweth)

economic and business elites pressured incumbent governments to negotiate with oppositionists to protect their own business interests from mounting international economic pressure (Wood 2000).

In this chapter, I argue that the different pillars of support are engaged in a multilevel game, and that these pillars are sensitive to both domestic *and* international costs of violent suppression of dissent. The basic framework from which this chapter proceeds is visualized in Figure 2.2.

Fundamental to my argument is the assumption that repression is usually politically costly and risky. Every time regime leaders issue an order to their subordinates to repress unarmed civilians, they risk insubordination, loss of domestic legitimacy, and the possibility of renewed mobilization. Regimes that attempt to suppress popular uprisings also risk painful consequences at the international level, with the possibility that the international media will publicize the abuse, powerful allies will part ways, and international organizations will wield sanctions against them. This might create even more divisions within regime elites, further sowing the seeds of insubordination, internal collapse, or insurmountable domestic opposition.

Knowing Backfire When We See It: Five Potential Indicators

Backfire is often defined as an outcome in which one's actions have the opposite effect of what was intended. That definition of backfire requires us to make defensible assumptions about the perpetrator's intentions. The problem is twofold—first, we seldom know the intentions that state elites have when they make decisions and, moreover, actors often revise their stated intentions after events seem to move away from their interests, suggesting that they planned for the latest developments all along. This problem is conceptually important because regimes might reinterpret their past intentions and behavior according to current events. For example, the Egyptian regime under General al-Sisi might today argue that the massacre at Rabaa Mosque on July 27, 2013, was a deliberate attempt to provoke Muslim Brotherhood activists into staging a sit-in (which they did in early August) where they would be highly vulnerable to regime repression. However, at the time of the massacre, the al-Sisi regime's intentions may have been quite different. The massacre may have been an attempt to crush the Muslim Brotherhood on site, a function of insubordination among a particular group of anti-Islamist security forces—or even a mistake.

As a consequence, scholars interested in repression and dissent usually make assumptions about what the regime's intentions were when the repression occurred. In this chapter, I argue that we can safely assume that factors favoring a nonviolent campaign are probably not viewed as favorable to the regime. In general, the purpose of repression is to punish those who would rise up against a government and to deter others from doing so in the future. Additionally, repression is intended to minimize the political costs to the regime of either maintaining the status quo or improving its political position both domestically and internationally.

Based on these assumptions, we can infer that any outcome that increases the costs to the regime of maintaining the status quo, reduces the regime's international or domestic political position, or threatens the regime's very survival should be viewed as an indicator of backfire.

We can assume that many regimes generally find it unfavorable for their behavior to be condemned by the international community, draw sanctions from international actors, and/or lead a patron to withdraw its support from the regime. Although international condemnation is less severe than, say, a patron's withdrawal of support, any reasonable leadership would usually prefer not to confront these scenarios if possible and would see them as costs rather than assets.

The same applies to domestic conditions. Because the intention of repression is usually to stop behavior from continuing, increased mobilization would be a quite direct indicator that the repression had backfired. Condemnation among powerful political figures and loyalty shifts from security forces or regime elites would be especially disastrous for the regime.

Some might argue that provoking a nonviolent campaign into even more extreme, violent action would be another indicator that repression had backfired. I am not so sure about that. Scholars and practitioners of nonviolent action have long suggested that repression is more likely to backfire when activists maintain nonviolent discipline (Ackerman and Kruegler 1994; Merriman 2010; Hess and Martin 2006; Martin 2007; Chenoweth and Stephan 2011). The reason is that a necessary requisite for political jiu-jitsu to occur is that repression generates moral outrage—a process more likely to occur when repression is directed at unarmed people (Martin 2007). Indeed, Chenoweth and Stephan find that when campaigns are overwhelmingly nonviolent, their success rates are more than double those of primarily violent campaigns (2011). Because provoking an erstwhile nonviolent campaign to use violence may actually benefit the regime more than the campaign, a campaign's use of violence probably does not undermine the regime. In fact, if we accept the fundamental assumptions put forth by Arendt (1970) and Sharp (1973), it may be precisely what the opponent regime hoped for all along. Indeed, adopting a violent flank might undermine the campaign's ability to elicit other backfire outcomes—a hypothesis I submit to testing in this chapter. Next, I turn to an exploratory, empirical investigation of how movement features might impact the probability of the five outcomes of backfire.

An Exploratory Study: Insights on Backfire from the NAVCO 2.0 Data Set

The NAVCO 2.0 data set project is a campaign-year database that catalogues 250 major nonviolent and violent resistance campaigns around the globe from 1946 to 2006 (Chenoweth and Lewis 2013). The data set compiles annual data on mass movements to bring about a maximalist social change; that is, to remove incumbent leadership, remove a foreign military occupation, or secede. NAVCO 2.0 also includes features of each campaign, such as participation size and diversity, the behavior of regime elites, repression and its effects on the campaign, support (or lack thereof) from external actors, and progress toward the campaign outcomes.

The data set includes one hundred major nonviolent campaigns, which form the basis of this study. Since the unit of analysis in the data set is the campaign-year—and since many of these campaigns lasted longer than one year—the data on nonviolent campaigns constitutes a total of 342 observations.

The data set defines a *campaign* as a "series of observable, continuous, purposive mass tactics or events in pursuit of a political objective" (Chenoweth and Lewis 2013, 416). A campaign is a coordinated sequence of observed tactics that lasts anywhere from days to years, distinguishing it from spontaneous one-off events, riots, or revolts.

Our inclusion criteria are based on observed participation, goals, and level of coordination between events. We considered a campaign to set on when we observed a series of multiple, coordinated, contentious collective actions with at least one thousand observed participants.[3] Once observed participation during associated events drops below one thousand, the campaign has effectively concluded. Second, we include

3. To read more about the data construction process, see Chenoweth and Lewis 2013.

only campaigns that claimed "maximalist" goals of irregular change in incumbent leadership, secession, or the removal of a foreign occupier. Actions that never do more than call for policy change or canvas for a candidate during a democratic election would not meet these criteria because they do not possess system-changing goals. Third, the contentious events had to be linked together rather than merely coincide. Campaigns often have discernable leadership or names, which helps to identify the continuity and coordination of different tactics like otherwise discrete protests.

We collected the data using a multitiered process. First, I assembled an earlier version of the data based on an extensive review of the literature on nonviolent conflict and social movements (Chenoweth 2011). The main sources were various encyclopedias, case studies, and a comprehensive bibliography on nonviolent resistance put together by Carter, Clark, and Randle (2006). I corroborated cases using various news sources, a study of civic-led democratic transitions by Karatnycky and Ackerman (2005), and a summary list of revolutions provided by Schock (2005). I then validated the data by circulating them among approximately a dozen experts in nonviolent conflict. I asked these experts to assess whether I had properly characterized the cases as primarily nonviolent, whether I had properly characterized their outcomes, and whether I had omitted any notable cases (particularly failures). Where the experts suggested additional cases for inclusion, I then triangulated their recommendations through additional source material. In updating the data for NAVCO 2.0, research assistants further revised and refined the data through a thorough, year-by-year study of each campaign. In this process, researchers used archival sources to confirm onset and end dates, confirm characterization of each campaign-year as nonviolent, violent, or mixed, and add new detail to each observation about intracampaign dynamics, campaign strategy, and international and domestic support.

In Table 2.1, I describe the indicators I use in this chapter. For more details, see the NAVCO 2.0 codebook available at the NAVCO website (www.navcodata.org). Data and replication files are also posted there.

TABLE 2.1 Variable Descriptions

Backfire Outcomes

Variable Name	*Description*	*Coding*	*Notes*
International Condemnation/ Sanctions	Publicly stated disapproval of politically relevant states (defined as major allies of the target regime) or international organizations, and/or international sanctions targeted the regime for its behavior vis-à-vis the resistance campaign	2=condemnation and sanctions; 1=condemnation or sanctions; 0=neither	Combines international sanctions and international backlash variables in NAVCO 2.0
Ally Withdraws Support	Whether prominent allies of the target regime withdraw their support	1=other states have withdrawn support for regime; 0=otherwise	
Domestic Condemnation	Prominent individuals or organizations within the country not directly associated with the campaign publically express disapproval of repressive state tactics	1=yes; 0=otherwise	
Regime Loyalty Shifts	A dummy variable that looks at whether security forces, police, or civilian leaders associated with the state break with it to publically announce their support for the opposition movement	2=security force and civilian regime defections; 1=security force or civilian regime defections; 0=no known defections	Combines regime_defect and state_defect in NAVCO 2.0
Subsequent Year Campaign Size	Campaign size at t+1	0=1–1000; 1=1000–10,000; 2=10,000–100,000; 3=100,000–500,000; 4=500,000–1 million; 5= >1 million	

TABLE 2.1 Variable Descriptions *(continued)*

Campaign Characteristics and Processes

Variable Name	*Description*	*Coding*	*Expected Effect on Backfire Outcomes*
Campaign Size	Approximate number of people taking part in the opposition campaign	0=1–1000; 1=1000–10,000; 2=10,000–100,000; 3=100,000–500,000; 4=500,000–1 million; 5= >1 million	+
Repression	Measures the most repressive episode or activity perpetrated by the state in response to campaign activity	0=no repression; 1=mild repression; 2=moderate repression; 3=extreme repression	-
International Media Coverage	Measures the degree to which the international traditional media covered the campaign	0=little to none; 1=moderate; 2=high	+
Radical Flank	Codes whether or not there is a "radical flank" in a movement that is otherwise nonviolent. A radical flank is defined as a group that adopts violent strategies to pursue their goals. They represent a faction within the broader opposition movement.	0=primarily violent campaign; 1=no radical flank; 2=radical flank	-
Hierarchical Campaign Structure	Analyzes the structure of campaign organization and leadership, in particular the extent to which there is a clear hierarchical structure to campaign decision-making	0=diffuse, consensus-based and participatory campaign structure; 1=centralized and hierarchical command and control campaign structure	+

(continued)

TABLE 2.1 Variable Descriptions *(continued)*

Campaign Characteristics and Processes

Variable Name	*Description*	*Coding*	*Expected Effect on Backfire Outcomes*
Domestic Media Coverage	Measures the degree to which domestic traditional media sources covered the campaign	0=little to none; 1=moderate; 2=high	+

Source: Erica Chenoweth

For ordinal dependent variables, I employ ordinal logistic regression models. For dichotomous dependent variables, I employ a logistic regression. All models include robust standard errors clustered around the campaign to account for cross-sectional heteroskedasticity and autocorrelation. For the purposes of this chapter, I focus exclusively on movement-level features, including campaign size, structure, nonviolent discipline, and domestic and international media attention. In all models, I also account for the level of repression directed at the campaign, as hypothetically the intensity of repression should increase the probability of all five backfire outcomes. Although further research might also evaluate characteristics of the domestic and international environment in which these campaigns operate, I am most interested in seeing which movement features manifested in campaigns shape movement outcomes (Ackerman 2007). Table 2.2 reports the findings of all five backfire outcome models.

In Model 1, I evaluate factors that might elicit international condemnation, including sanctions. Campaign size has no effect on international condemnation, while repression, international media coverage, and radical flank have positive and significant effects. This finding suggests that the more lethal the repression, the more likely are international sanctions and condemnation. Moreover, international media coverage has a strong impact on this outcome, providing support for Martin's (2007) notion that publicity of abuses is a necessary condition of backfire. Finally, the possession of a radical flank

TABLE 2.2 Factors Associated with Different Forms of Backfire

		International Effects		**Domestic Effects**	
	Model 1	*Model 2*	*Model 3*	*Model 4*	*Model 5*
	DV: International Condemnation/ Sanctions	DV: Ally Withdraws Support	DV: Domestic Condemnation	DV: Regime Loyalty Shifts	DV: Subsequent Campaign Size
Campaign Size	-.189 (.159)	-.023 (.167)	.017 (.179)	.187* (.169)	2.000*** (.446)
State Repression	.872*** (.212)	.529 (.479)	1.414*** (.241)	.066 (.482)	-.471*** (.171)
International Media Coverage	1.679*** (.401)	.775*** (.300)		.228 (.257)	
Radical Flank	.796* (.471)	.253 (.606)	-.105 (.485)	-.008 (.470)	.229 (.374)
Hierarchical Campaign Structure	.131 (.528)	.958** (.461)	-.334 (.480)	.116 (.482)	.352 (.332)
Domestic Media Coverage			1.419*** (.539)	.543* (.413)	.072 (.164)
Constant		-5.268*** (1.272)	-4.911*** (1.178)		
N	280	280	275	273	178
Wald chi2	56.77	15.88	51.67	6.87	43.51
Pseudo R2	0.2390	0.0977	0.2928	0.3335	0.0000
Prob > chi2	0.0000	0.0072	0.0000	0.0560	0.3127

Source: Erica Chenoweth

* p < .10; ** p < .05; *** p < .0

leads to a heightened probability of international condemnation and sanctions. In other words, when a nonviolent campaign has a violent flank, it is more likely to elicit an international response condemning the repression. Perhaps this is because radical flanks help campaigns obtain international media attention, which in turn provides them with the publicity needed to elicit this response.

Model 2 explores the factors that are correlated with an external ally withdrawing support from the power holders. This is a situation wherein a longtime patron of the country—like the United States in the Philippines under Marcos—expresses that it will no longer provide diplomatic, material, or verbal support for the regime—as did Ronald Reagan in the final days of Marcos's rule. As with Model 1, the higher the level of international media coverage, the higher the probability that a patron withdraws support for the power holders. Moreover, campaigns that have a more hierarchical structure—usually indicating some sort of central or umbrella leadership organization—have a higher association with an ally's withdrawal of support than leaderless resistance campaigns. Perhaps this is because regime allies see organized campaigns as more viable and therefore more threatening to the regime's stability than more diffused campaigns, while also giving those allies a credible sense of who their potential new partners would be after the country has made a transition. Importantly, the size of the campaign, the degree of repression against the campaign, the presence of a radical flank, and domestic media coverage seem to have no significant influence on whether a regime ally withdraws its support.

Model 3 identifies several key variables correlated with the condemnation of repression against unarmed persons. State repression is positively associated with domestic condemnation. I interpret this as suggesting that more intense repression (e.g., moving from arrests and beatings to lethal repression and/or torture) is more likely to elicit outrage among domestic observers. Contrary to theories that expect an inverted-U association to repression and subsequent dissent, this finding points to a positive and linear association between a state's use of repression and domestic opposition.[4] Importantly, this indicator of domestic opposition is essentially a verbal one, which may not necessarily translate into actual protest activity. Nevertheless, it is important to note that even the highest levels of repression are not without political costs and risks. The other factor that is highly correlated with domestic condemnation is, unsurprisingly, domestic media coverage. It is perhaps an obvious point that repression must go noticed in order to be condemned.[5] Campaign size, structure, and the presence of a radical flank have no significant effect on domestic condemnation.

Model 4 identifies factors that correlate with defections among security forces and high-ranking civilians within the opponent government. The only movement-based factors that have effects are campaign size and domestic media coverage, which are positively associated with loyalty shifts within the regime. This corroborates the findings reported in Chenoweth and Stephan (2011), wherein the authors find that as nonviolent campaign size increases, the probability of security force defections likewise increases. When a significant proportion of the population is involved in resistance, security forces and civilian elites may want to jump from what appears to be a sinking ship. And, as mentioned above, domestic media coverage is more likely to signal to these elites that their fellow citizens are watching. International media coverage, repression, radical flank, and campaign structure appear to have no significant effect on loyalty shifts.

And finally, Model 5 evaluates the factors that correlate with large campaigns in subsequent years. In this model, the dependent variable is the campaign size the next year (at t+1).[6] Two factors are statistically

4. Note that this analysis does not consider inverted-U or other nonlinear effects, which are beyond the scope of the present study.

5. There may be, of course, some downsides to coverage in mainstream media. For an example, see Gitlin 1980.

6. Note the smaller *n* for this model. This is due to the fact that several dozen campaigns lasted less than one year and therefore had only one observation associated with them.

significant: campaign size in the current year, and repression. It is intuitive that a large campaign in the current year would be highly correlated with campaign size in the following year, so this is not too surprising. However, it is notable that the intensity of repression in the current year has a negative effect on campaign size in the following year. This means that the higher the intensity of repression, the smaller the campaign in the subsequent year. This finding contradicts that of Model 3, which finds that the intensity of repression increases domestic condemnation of the regime. Although outrage and political opposition may increase with high levels of repression, it also appears that high levels of repression diminish the number of people who are willing to engage in nonviolent action as well. Domestic media coverage, the presence of a radical flank, and campaign structure have no significant effect on campaign size in the following year.

Which of these five backfire outcomes are most influential in achieving success? In Table 2.3, I use the outcome of the campaign (i.e., success or failure) as the dependent variable, and I use the five backfire outcomes as covariates. Campaign success is defined as a dichotomous variable identifying whether the campaign achieved 100 percent of its stated goals within a year of the peak of activities, with clear signs that the outcome would not have occurred without the campaign's influence.[7] The variable is coded 1 if the campaign was a success and 0 if otherwise. I employ a logistic regression with robust standard errors clustered around the campaign.

Importantly, in Model 6 neither domestic nor international condemnation or sanctions is associated with increased chances of campaign success. This finding suggests that when it comes to winning a civil resistance campaign, talk is cheap—both at the domestic and international levels.

7. Some campaigns' goals were achieved years after the "peak" of the struggle in terms of membership, but the success was a direct result of campaign activities. When such a direct link can be demonstrated, these campaigns are coded as successful.

TABLE 2.3 Effects of Backfire on Nonviolent Campaign Success

	Model 6 DV: Campaign Succeeds
Campaign Size	.398***
	(.147)
Domestic Condemnation	-.306
	(.481)
International Condemnation/Sanctions	-.193
	(.303)
Regime Loyalty Shifts	1.096***
	(.246)
Ally Withdraws Support	.858*
	(.512)
Constant	-2.974***
	(.676)
N	283
Wald chi2	43.63
Pseudo R2	0.1756
Prob > chi2	0.0000

Source: Erica Chenoweth
*p < .10; ** p < .05; *** p < .01

Equally importantly, Model 6 demonstrates that campaign size, loyalty shifts among security forces and regime leaders, and the withdrawal of support from an ally are the most influential factors in explaining campaign success. The joint effects of these three variables are startling. In the smallest campaigns, where only one thousand people are participating, defections among regime elites do not occur, and foreign allies remain loyal to the regime, the model estimates less than 4 percent chance of success. However, among the largest campaigns (more than one million participants), where regime elites defect and foreign allies withdraw their support from the regime, the estimated

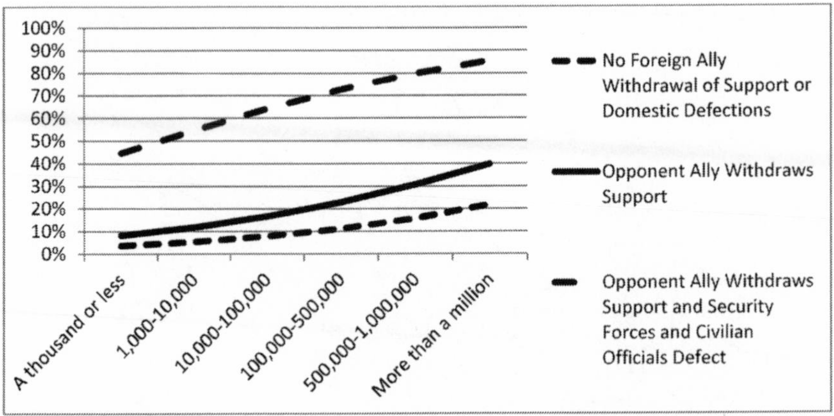

2.3. Estimated Effects of Campaign Size, Regime Ally Withdrawal of Support, and Security Force/Civilian Defections on Viability of Nonviolent Campaign Success (Source: Erica Chenoweth)

probability of success is over 85 percent—an extraordinary increase based on a small number of covariates.

Figure 2.3 illustrates the substantive effects of these three covariates on the probability of success, calculated following Model 6 using the prtab command in STATA.[8] We can see that even without the withdrawal of support from a regime ally or domestic defections, the chances of success for a nonviolent campaign increase by over 20 percent from the smallest to largest campaigns. But critically, once a regime ally does withdraw support, the chances for success among the largest campaigns double to over 40 percent. Add domestic security force loyalty shifts and elite defections, and the chance of success rockets up to about 45 percent for the smallest campaigns and 85 percent for the largest campaigns. These results suggest that people power is a critical factor in explaining the success of nonviolent campaigns. But the influence of the regime's international and domestic pillars

8. This is a set of commands developed by J. Scott Long and Jeremy Freese. For details about its application, see Long 2009.

of support in determining whether such people power translates into true leverage is crucial to the outcome of the campaign.

Conclusion and Implications

The empirical picture presented above is instructive in several key ways, lending some insights for scholars and activists about which movement features may be most effective in eliciting the types of backfire outcomes that are most likely to yield successful campaigns.

First, and most obviously, if campaign size, loyalty shifts among security forces and civilian leaders, and allies' withdrawal of support from the regime are the critical backfire outcomes, then campaigns would be better served by spending more time eliciting these results and less time seeking domestic and international condemnation or international sanctions. This begs the question: what kind of movements best elicit these three backfire outcomes? In Models 2, 4, and 5, we see that large, hierarchical campaigns that obtain international media coverage are most likely to provoke a foreign ally to withdraw support for the regime, most likely to provoke defections within the regime, and most likely to remain large the following year.

Importantly, the intensity of repression was negatively associated with subsequent year campaign size, but not significantly correlated with loyalty shifts or the withdrawal of an ally's support. This suggests that campaigns that wish to benefit from political jiu-jitsu should, paradoxically, avoid the most intense kinds of repression as much as possible. It is important to note that repression is not directly and significantly correlated with campaign success. But to the extent that higher intensity repression reduces the size of campaigns in subsequent years—and yields no strategic benefits when it comes to provoking domestic or international defections—the most intense kinds of repression could have indirect, negative effects on the chances of campaign success.

Another key insight yielded from these findings is the absence of a positive radical flank effect. It is true that radical flanks appear to be positively correlated with international condemnation and sanctions against the opponent regime. Activists would do well to note, however, that international sanctions are not the most influential backfire outcome, and that instead campaign size, loyalty shifts among regime functionaries, and the removal of support for the regime by an erstwhile ally are more influential processes leading to campaign success. Radical flanks have no apparent benefits on any of these three most important backfire outcomes, contradicting earlier findings that using small amounts of violence benefits the strategic position of nonviolent campaigns (Haines 1984).

Third, sustained campaign participation is among the most important elements in understanding whether domestic and international audiences mobilize actionable support of the campaign. In other words, for repression to result in backfire in any meaningful sense, participation is crucial.

Fourth, a hierarchical organization seems to increase the likelihood of an ally's withdrawal of support for the opponent regime. And more decentralized campaigns were no more likely to increase subsequent year participation, induce loyalty shifts within regime elites, or bring about an ally's withdrawal of support for the regime. This finding contests the oft-touted view that a decentralized structure—or "leaderless resistance"—is better suited than more hierarchical organizations to achieving success, providing further support to scholars like Bob and Nepstad who argue in favor of "administrative" leadership over "symbolic" leadership (2007).

Finally, international media coverage is vital to raising awareness and putting pressure on regime allies to withdraw their support. Movements seeking to produce this particular outcome should invest in strategies to publicize abuses to international media sources such that foreign allies are forced to reckon with these revelations. Domestic media coverage may also be important in heightening the effects of widespread popular participation on the calculations of domestic elites. Future research could focus on these important media dynamics—which types of media, which types of outlets, and which types of coverage are most influential in affecting these outcomes.

The results in this exploratory study should not be taken as the last word. The quantitative study of civil resistance is still a relatively new trend, and as more data sets become available with which to examine such questions, scholars can subject different findings to robustness and validity checks. In particular, further research should likely examine how contextual factors—such as regime features, demographic characteristics, and international system features—affect these findings. Moreover, due to the nature of the data structure, it is only possible to identify correlation, not causation. Future research should employ careful case study analysis and quasi-experimental designs to test causal claims about these statistical associations.

In the meantime, however, the findings in this chapter suggest that the paradox of repression is often as much a paradox for the regime as it is for the campaign. Repression is always risky and costly and can have both domestic and international effects, the most pronounced of which is the disintegration of internal and external lifelines upon which the regime has relied to maintain power all along.

References

Ackerman, Peter. 2007. "Skills or Conditions: What Key Factors Shape the Success or Failure of Civil Resistance?" Paper delivered at the conference on Civil Resistance and Power Politics, St Antony's College, Univ. of Oxford, Mar. 15–18.

Ackerman, Peter, and Christopher Kruegler. 1994. *Strategic Nonviolent Conflict: The Dynamics of People Power in the Twentieth Century*. Westport, CT: Praeger.

Arendt, Hanna. 1970. *On Violence*. Boston: Harcourt.

Bob, Clifford, and Sharon Erikson Nepstad. 2007. "Kill a Leader, Murder a Movement? Leadership and Assassination in Social Movements." *American Behavioral Scientist* 50 (10): 1370–94.

Carter, April, Howard Clark, and Michael Randle. 2006. *People Power and Protest since 1945: A Bibliography of Nonviolent Action*. London: Housmans.

Chenoweth, Erica. 2011. *The Nonviolent and Violent Campaigns and Outcomes (NAVCO) Dataset*, v. 1.1. Univ. of Denver.

Chenoweth, Erica, and Orion A. Lewis. 2013. "Unpacking Nonviolent Campaigns: Introducing the NAVCO 2.0 Dataset." *Journal of Peace Research* 50 (3): 415–23.

Chenoweth, Erica, and Kurt Schock. 2015. "Do Contemporaneous Armed Challenges Affect the Outcomes of Mass Nonviolent Campaigns?" *Mobilization: An International Quarterly* 20: 427–51.

Chenoweth, Erica, and Maria J. Stephan. 2011. *Why Civil Resistance Works: The Strategic Logic of Nonviolent Conflict*. New York: Columbia Univ. Press.

Davenport, Christian. 2007. "State Repression and Political Order." *Annual Review of Political Science* 10: 1–23.

Gerlach, Luther P., and Virginia H. Hine. 1970. *People, Power, Change: Movements of Social Transformation*. Bobbs-Merrill.

Gitlin, Todd. 1980. *The Whole World Is Watching: Mass Media in the Making and Unmaking of the New Left*. Berkeley: Univ. of California Press.

Gurr, Ted R. 1969. *Why Men Rebel*. Princeton, NJ: Princeton Univ. Press.

Haines, Herbert. 1984. "Black Radicalization and the Funding of Civil Rights: 1957–1970." *Social Problems* 32 (1): 31–43.

Hess, David, and Brian Martin. 2006. "Repression, Backfire, and the Theory of Transformative Events." *Mobilization* 11 (1): 249–67.

Jenkins, Craig T., and Charles Perrow. 1977. "Insurgency of the Powerless: Farm Worker Movements (1946–1972)." *American Sociological Review* 42 (Apr.): 249–68.

Karatnycky, Adrian, and Ackerman, Peter, eds. 2005. *How Freedom Is Won: From Civic Resistance to Durable Democracy*. Washington, DC: Freedom House.

Kuperman, Alan. 2008. "The Moral Hazard of Humanitarian Intervention: Lessons from the Balkans." *International Studies Quarterly* 52 (1): 49–80.

Long, J. Scott. 2009. *The Workflow of Data Analysis using STATA*. College Station, TX: STATA Press.

Martin, Brian. 2007. *Justice Ignited: The Dynamics of Backfire*. Lanham, MD: Rowman and Littlefield.

Merriman, Hardy. 2010. "The Trifecta of Civil Resistance: Unity, Planning, and Discipline." *OpenDemocracy*, Nov. 19. http://www.opendemocracy.net/hardy-merriman/trifecta-of-civil-resistance-unity-planning-discipline.

Nepstad, Sharon. 2011. *Nonviolent Revolutions: Civil Resistance in the Late 20th Century*. Oxford: Oxford Univ. Press.

Oberschall, Anthony. 1973. *Social Conflict and Social Movements*. Englewood Cliffs, NJ: Prentice Hall.

Schock, Kurt. 2005. *Unarmed Insurrections: People Power Movements in Nondemocracies.* Minneapolis: Univ. of Minnesota Press.

Sharp, Gene. 1973. *The Politics of Nonviolent Action*, vol. 1–3. Boston: Porter Sargent.

Tilly, Charles. 1978. *From Mobilization to Revolution.* Reading, MA: Addison-Wesley.

Wood, Elisabeth Jean. 2000. *Forging Democracy from Below: Insurgent Transitions in South Africa and El Salvador.* New York: Cambridge Univ. Press.

3

Transformative Events, Repression, and Regime Change

Theoretical and Psychological Aspects

Doron Shultziner

This chapter develops the proposition that a focus on *events* is a useful (and possibly more accurate) way to understand why and how regime change occurs when it does compared to theories that rely on macro factors and political opportunities alone. Of particular interest is how *repressive events* can paradoxically become transformative points that either change the conflict dynamics between a social movement and power holders or bring movements to life. Repression can backfire and lead to significant changes or even the demise of the power structure. Transformative events can serve as emotional and cognitive triggers with important consequences for regime power, collective action, and shifts that favor resistance movements.

I explore the political and psychological impacts of dramatic events involving repression and their relation to regime change, while building on the work of political sociologists (McAdam and Sewell 2001; Sewell 1996), political scientists (Bunce and Wolchik 2007, 2010), and my own prior research (Shultziner 2010, 2013; Shultziner and Tetreault 2011).

In order to understand the paradox of repression, it is helpful to explore the impact of events on the emotions, goals, and behavior of affected groups, as well as on the political process and time scales that lead to regime change. In this chapter, I focus on the inherent potential in events to serve as solutions to problems of collective action, and I elaborate on the psychological meaning of these events and how they affect regime power and authority. I also examine the relationship between explanations of regime change that are based on events and those based solely on macro-level explanations that emphasize political, economic, and other conditions that are favorable or unfavorable to insurgencies.

Transformative Events

Structural-political transformations, such as transitions to democracy and other regime changes, are often set in motion by dramatic, unusual, and unexpected events. These types of transitions are not normally smooth. They are characterized by bursts of mass participation and sometimes violence, and by nonlinear and drastic departures from old patterns of political behavior, norms, and power configurations (Berman 2007; Sewell 1996; see also Chenoweth's chapter in this book), although sometimes these transitions are also preceded by gradual structural changes (Capoccia and Ziblatt 2010). As William Sewell argues, "What makes historical events so important to theorize is that they reshape history, imparting an unforeseen direction to social development and altering the nature of the causal nexus in which social interactions take place. For this reason, a theoretically robust conception of events is a necessary component of any adequate theory of social change" (1996, 843).

Following Sewell's approach to sociopolitical change, I focus here on the importance and characteristics of *transformative events*. Transformative events are dramatic-symbolic events that substantially change the degree and sense of injustice and motivation for resistance in the population. A major type of transformative event could be further classified as *transformative repressive events*, because they are caused and characterized by repressive regime actions that come to the attention of many affected citizens within a short span of time and lead to cognitive, emotional, and behavioral changes that eventually challenge power holders.

The events themselves are usually followed by temporary suspension or change of political power configurations, and often political instability. Ruling elites may eventually contain this instability, but the rupture and protests may also lead to structural changes (Sewell 1996). Doug McAdam and William Sewell observe that "the key feature of transformative events is that they come to be interpreted as *significantly disrupting, altering, or violating the taken-for-granted assumptions governing routine political and social relations*" (2001, 112; original emphasis). Transformative events change attitudes of complacency or possibly even agreement with nondemocratic systems or practices into widespread attitudes of dissatisfaction and rejection among the oppressed. As such, transformative events "can produce radical turning points in collective action and affect the outcome of social movements" (Morris 2000, 452). These events constitute a departure from previous patterns of political thinking, behavior, and levels of radicalization. Transformative events can also be seen as tipping points (Gladwell 2000) in which the political environment is irreversibly transformed and radicalized. These events are different from "dynamics of struggle" and "cycles of protest"[1] both in their magnitude and their causal importance, in the sense that transformative events affect the political outlook and emotional energies of masses of people in a very short period of time.

Transformative events are important to movement mobilization, regime change, and democratization. They affect the ways in which struggles for political change often begin unexpectedly and the nonlinear fashion in which resistance activity against incumbent regimes develops. Transformative events can occur on various levels: transformation of a small community due to the mistreatment of one or more of its members; the transformation of several communities following

1. *Dynamics of struggle* are the ongoing interactions between activists and their targets. *Cycles of protest* are the sequences of escalating protest activity that spread through society and in which the speed of contention is the outcome of interactions between protest movements (Tarrow 1994; Snow and Benford 1992; Tilly 2007).

an inspiring local struggle; and the transformation of people in one state due to a dramatic event in another state. Such examples are common in many cases of regime change and constitute a recurrent pattern in otherwise highly complicated and almost chaotic processes leading to regime change and to democracy.

Repression and Transformative Events

Many transformative events develop out of confrontations between the regime and its opponents within the political system. Typical examples include the mistreatment, killing, or humiliation of a member or members of a group. Such incidents must come to the attention of the group's members and potentially external audiences in order to have an effect, making media exposure highly important (see more examples in Martin 2007). For example, the news and picture of fatally wounded schoolboy Hector Peterson in Soweto on June 16, 1976, generated anger in regions of South Africa and beyond. News about the arrest of Rosa Parks in Montgomery, Alabama, produced similar outrage and mobilization within the civil rights movement in the United States (Shultziner 2010, chapters 4–6).

Incidents of repression that cause widespread moral shock and public outrage in an oppressed group can backfire against governmental regimes domestically, internationally, or both (Hess and Martin 2006; Keck and Sikkink 1998; Martin 2007; Sharp 2003). Typical examples of positive (or inspiring) incidents are successful or symbolic domestic challenges to the regime that encourage and increase motivation to mobilize for political change. The framing of repression by effectively linking it to the regime and communicating this to the relevant public are key in converting an event into a dramatic turning point against a regime or its policies (Hess and Martin 2006; Martin 2007).

When a dramatic incident of abuse comes to the attention of the population and international media, it can create moral shock and anger and lead to a wave of protest that the ruling elite may not be able to withstand. All other factors in the system may be constant or least favorable to unrest (e.g., economic improvement, strong military discipline, ruling elite cohesion), and yet the sudden shift in public opinion and resistance against the regime can emerge due to dramatic repressive events. In fact, autocratic regimes can collapse when they are at the height of their power (Davidheiser 1992) and feel secure in their position and thus abuse their power most. The Arab Spring in the Middle East, for instance, emerged under several regimes that appeared powerful, and social scientists were working to explain their robust stability (Gause 2011). There seems to be little dispute that the *events themselves* radicalized and inspired Arab citizens across borders, from Tunisia to Egypt and beyond.

Links between repression, transformative events, and regime change appear to be important given that democracy rarely emerges without bottom-up pressures that force unelected ruling elites to initiate political change, to step down, or to be forcefully removed from power altogether (see, for example, Chenoweth's discussion on the importance of campaign participation in chapter 2). Repression is one important type of transformative event that can contribute to regime change and often to democratic outcomes.

External Transformative Events and Elections

External transformative events are incidents that emerge outside of a political system, and yet they can affect the actions of the oppressed and the ruling elite in remarkable ways. The most well-known example of multiple external transformative events is probably the collapse of the Eastern European Soviet bloc in 1989 (Smithey and Kurtz 2007). The democratic revolutions of 1989, which began in Poland, spilled over into Hungary, West Germany, the former Czechoslovakia, Bulgaria, and Romania, and they eventually led to a revolution in Russia itself and to the formal collapse of the Soviet Union (Beissinger 2009; Kramer 2009; Smolar 2009). These events invigorated or created democratic movements in other parts of the world and also led to regime replacements, some of which did not end in democracy. Political scientists have used various terms to describe this phenomenon: contagion, diffusion, emulation, domino effects, snowballing, or demonstration effects (Huntington 1991, 100). The phenomenon is essentially the same, whatever term is chosen: a sudden direct experience (positive or negative) within one country can generate political contention in other locations because people are significantly shocked and angered, inspired and encouraged, or suddenly come to believe that the time to rebel has come because liberation is possible and imminent. The domestic configuration of the system in terms of power relations, economic factors, and other structures may have been constant for many years, and yet the external effect directly changes people's political values, goals, aspirations or calculations. A recent example of this phenomenon could be seen in the way the escape of Tunisian President Ben-Ali quickly inspired and motivated Egyptians to organize protests against President Mubarak.

Apart from external transformative events, elections should also be highlighted in the context of repression, transformative events, and regime change. In nondemocratic countries, elections are normally means of hegemony in the sense that power holders rely on elections to maintain at least an appearance of legitimacy, both domestically and internationally (Bunce and Wolchik 2007, 2010; McAdam and Tarrow 2010; Schedler 2002; Teorell and Hadenius 2008). Almost all nondemocratic elites hold elections. Many elections are only a show, most are rigged, and some reflect popular will to an extent. Elections can, and increasingly in recent decade have, become events that enable political mobilization and hence create effective paths to replace authoritarian regimes, especially in former communist states and in Africa. As Bunce and Wolchik (2007, 6) put it, elections "are in many ways ideal as catalysts, because they take place within a circumscribed period of time; they ask for political engagement; they address directly the distribution of political power; and they have visible political results—which everyone learns about at the same time and which serve as a concise summation of both where things stand and where they are likely to go in the future."

Events of this sort can bring about regime change and democracy when an attempt to falsify election results is revealed and paradoxically becomes the opposite of what the regime intended. In other words, the very attempt to gain legitimacy from the people can reveal the truth about the regime's or ruler's lack of legitimacy. Of course, it depends on whether and how activists manage to turn these events into a symbolic and actual rallying point for action against the regime, as was done in Serbia to remove Milosevic (Vejvoda 2009), in Georgia to oust Shevardnadze in 2003 (Jones 2009), in Ukraine in the 2004 removal of Yanukovych (the first of two) (Wilson 2009). If devised successfully, a mass scheduled event can also become a transformative event, depending on activists' actions and the regime's reactions (Bunce and Wolchik 2007; Hess and Martin 2006).

Events and Backfire Effects as Collective Action Problem Solvers

Two major related challenges to mobilization against nondemocratic regimes are coordination and collective action problems. Unelected authoritarian elites actively seek out and suppress civic organizations that have potential for antiregime mobilization. They use repression, various state resources, and manipulation tactics (including control of the electoral process) to make collective action against the political system as difficult as possible (Schedler 2002; Tarrow 1994; Tucker 2007).[2] Citizens thus face daunting obstacles and sometimes grave risks in challenging such regimes, especially when they act alone or in a small groups.

The regime can more easily handle small-scale resistance. The costs of repression are also lower when the regime handles smaller groups because it does not need to exploit or overuse its material resources, nor must it jeopardize whatever popular legitimacy it commands. Suppressing smaller groups does not test and erode the loyalty of its human resources, such as specialists and law enforcement agents (Sharp 2003, 2007; Stephan and Chenoweth 2008). Furthermore, even if unrest exists, this does not necessarily mean that citizens are aware of the extent to which others share their problems and grievances or that there is consensus that the time to challenge the regime is ripe

2. See Smithey and Kurtz's continuum of regime tactics for demobilizing movements in chapter 8 in this volume.

(Kuran 1995). It may be the case that the ruling elite is weak, but so is civil society; or it may be that no one takes the initiative to coordinate resistance (Bunce and Wolchik 2010, 49; see also Chenoweth's findings in chapter 2 about how the level of participation is a significant factor in predicting whether repressive events will backfire).

The costs of repression during dramatic events are higher for small groups. It is relatively easy to shut down communication of small groups, but it is very difficult, costly, and arguably impossible to do so when large segments of the population suddenly begin communicating politically. Under such conditions, the attempt to block all formal and informal channels of communication (ranging from technological to social) is likely to be ineffective and counterproductive for the regime (see Beyer and Earl's discussion of the technological aspects of repression in chapter 5).

Events that affect the population in a narrow timeframe create opportunities for coordination, mobilization, and collective action in a way that helps to overcome the daunting routinization of oppression and power of nondemocratic regimes. Events can be the problem solvers of coordination and collective action (Tucker 2007). A dramatic event changes the normal routine of politics under repression. It can temporarily or permanently change the configuration of power in the sense that new spaces for communication are opened; new norms about how the regime may or may not use its power are introduced; the risks of individual citizens' participation without being caught are reduced; and generally new opportunities for coordination and mobilization are created and enable effective pressure on the regime. Dramatic events also help activists tap into sources of influence through alliances with players in the international community, including sympathizing citizens, nongovernmental organizations, and the media (Keck and Sikkink 1998).

During dramatic events that draw widespread attention, it is also more costly and dangerous for the regime to use its military and police forces to quell widespread popular resistance. The backlash effects can mobilize additional segments of the population and international allies, further restraining the capacity of the regime to act (Hess and

Martin 2006; Keck and Sikkink 1998). Furthermore, the use of law enforcement agents against civilians during mass events can lead to the undermining of discipline in the military and police and may lead to defections, splits, and abandoning the ruling elite. This is especially the case when the protesters use nonviolent methods and when the army and police are not part of the ruling ethnic elite and have less to lose (Stephan and Chenoweth 2008).

In sum, dramatic events that attract wide attention help collective action as channels of communication open and provide people with new information about their society and its governance. They can compel people to withdraw cooperation from the regime, to cooperate with other citizens who want to protest, and to vent their frustrations and hopes. Such events create an atmosphere of change in which people are more easily mobilized to protest and the target is clear. Concrete alternative policies are not always offered during dramatic events, nor are they necessary. The alternative policies and visions of tomorrow may not even be agreed or consistent among the groups that call for political change. The important point is that the event helps to bring many different individuals and groups together for a concentrated effort in a relatively short period of time with a shared objective of changing the regime.

The Psychological Aspects of Transformative Events

The importance of transformative events lies in the fact that they are essentially a psychological phenomenon that affects the regime's power and authority. The events themselves are of course unique in each case, but there is a general similarity in their impacts on political consciousness and political behavior, which consequently undermine the regime. In this section, I review several psychological characteristics based on my research of two transformative events: the first official day of the Montgomery bus boycott (December 5, 1955) and the first day of what became the Soweto uprising in South Africa, June 16, 1976 (Shultziner 2010). Both of these events involved backlash following an act of repression.

The first psychological characteristic of transformative events is that they indeed, as McAdam and Sewell note, "come to be interpreted as *significantly disrupting, altering, or violating the taken-for-granted assumptions governing routine political and social relations*" (2001, 112). The emergence of resistance activity is the result of a dramatic cognitive change in how people evaluate themselves in relation to longstanding practices of oppression, often in relation to the political system itself. In transformative events, people's fear about the regime is reduced. Elsewhere in this volume, Jenni Williams (chapter 6) and George Lakey (chapter 11) address measures activists take to overcome fear. However, the events themselves also enable activists, and the population more generally, to overcome the regular fear of political engagement and to experiment with new modes of politics (e.g., Sewell 1996, 867). With their new collective awareness, people no longer feel powerless and complacent regarding their situation or their ability to achieve political change. In other words, people gain a new sense of self-efficacy (Bandura 1977) and high self-esteem regarding their collective ability to reform the system and change their lives for the better.

A second characteristic of transformative events is that people come to identify with the movement and stake their self-esteem on struggle goals. People's positive and negative feelings become affected by whether they are doing something about their oppression (as Lakey describes in chapter 11). Self-esteem is a powerful motivator for action. Once a person admits that his or her predicament is directly due to the regime (or its indirect structures of oppression), it becomes hard to disassociate from the negative and positive feelings intertwined with inaction or action, respectively. This compulsion could arguably be stronger when that person has experienced injustice through an act of direct repression (e.g., being beaten in a demonstration). Transformative events can thus create a drastic turning point as people begin to feel satisfaction and generate positive self-evaluations of themselves by actively resisting, or not cooperating with, nondemocratic regimes, and vice versa. The domain that had caused humiliation for so many people seems suddenly amenable to change or even under their control. In such situations, people will not easily give up this new sense of power, autonomy, and positive self-esteem.

The ability to continue protesting becomes in itself a pivotal goal and a source of joy. By continuing to defy the regime, citizens are gaining recognition, restoring their damaged sense of self-esteem, or simply enjoying their new freedom to act and express themselves. In other words, resistance becomes a source of pride or even a form of therapy. Taking pride in action becomes an emotional benefit and can facilitate and maintain long-term resistance activity (see, for example, Wood 2001). The protest itself is a sort of demand for recognition, a demand more basic than the immediate demands that may be placed on the ruling elite (Shultziner 2010). Furthermore, for some citizens, it becomes more difficult to stop defying and resisting the regime after they experience the system through confrontation, violence, or moral shock, all of which can make them see the system in a new way.

A third psychological characteristic of transformative events pertains to politicizing and radicalizing people's outlooks and undermining the regime's authority. The coming together of ordinary citizens in mass meetings, and through other new political spaces (physical or online) that suddenly open up in dramatic events, impacts the ways people understand their own problems. The sudden union of masses of people enables them to freely communicate and convey new information to each other (perhaps even new channels of communicating with the agent of the regime, such as police and army). For many, this will be their first experiences as activists, given the harsh penalties that nondemocratic regimes impose on such political acts during "normal days" of repression and close surveillance by security forces. Dramatic events compel citizens to rethink basic premises governing their lives and to redefine their values and hopes for the future; or in other words, to decide on a new "vision of tomorrow." This sudden break with the habits of normal politics can have far-reaching political consequences. Personal experiences suddenly become reframed and contextualized as collective experiences. The participants then realize the extent to which their personal problems were in fact a collective problem (Evans 1980; Gamson 1992a, 1992b). A significant number of people who unite to protest become a "visible verdict on such critical questions as the size of regime support, the very right of the regime to rule, and, more generally, the quality of democratic life" (Bunce and Wolchik 2007, 6).

Moreover, by coming together for the first time in large numbers and for a political purpose, the participants are introduced to political goals that most of them did not even dream were possible to achieve. The creation of new spaces and mass meetings injects new meaning, perspective, and points of reference to citizens' lives and even to the concepts they use (Sewell 1996, 861). It situates their personal experiences within a new and far more politicized worldview. The realization that "politics as usual" is suspended and that significant segments of the public are in a different political mindset (e.g., moral shock, anger, new hopes for liberation) generates the opportunity for collective action; or rather, this realization itself *is* the opportunity. Normally, habitual beliefs in the ability and authority of the government to rule are basic and key elements of political power (on habit as a source of legitimacy and authority, see Shively 2014, 13–17). By undermining habits and life routines, transformative events essentially undermine the authority and legitimacy of the government.

A related characteristic of transformative events is the creation of a new group identity and heightening of solidarity among those who resist. Due to a transformative event, a person comes to see that he or she has issues, interests, and/or sympathies in common with other individuals whom they may have previously perceived as dissimilar or possibly even disliked. In such contexts, new personal experiences, social interactions, and information generate group (or social) identity. Individuals either begin to see themselves as part of a group for the first time, or their existing group identity gains new meanings. Social identity theorists argue that group identity formation is rooted in the human desire to maintain positive self-esteem (Horowitz 1985; Tajfel and Turner 1979; Turner 1982). Thus, a related process of identity formation during transformative events is the attempt to change negative meanings that may be associated with the individual's relevant social category and self-conception and to ascribe new positive meanings to that category.

For example, in South Africa and the modern US civil rights movement, popular slogans involved generating pride in being black (e.g., Biko and Stubbs 1978; King [1958] 1965, [1963] 2000), and in Egypt during the Arab Spring, citizens enthusiastically told media reporters that they finally felt proud to be Egyptians (Contenta 2011). In other words, following transformative events, people begin to take pride in and profess their political and social identities.

Events, Repression, and Macro Factors

Regime change and the success or failure of dramatic events leading to democracy are poorly predicted by the economic performance and characteristics of a regime on both region-specific (Bunce and Wolchik 2010, 56–57) and worldwide scales (Przeworski and Limongi 1997; Teorell and Hadenius 2006). Theories of regime change and democratization have tended to ignore events, including responses to repression, as major *causes*. When the impact of events, such as repression, could not be ignored, they were normally conceptualized as mere triggers that led to the explosion of deeper existing unrest. The unrest itself is usually seen as the result of macro factors and processes pertaining to the state economy, government and military relations, social inequalities, or international factors. While there is no necessary contradiction between macro-level explanations and those based on events, the two approaches can yield very different explanations about the source of unrest and regime change (Shultziner 2014). I illustrate this point with two examples, which also illuminate the centrality of repressive actions by law enforcement and social interactions between state authorities and resistance groups.

South Africa: The Soweto Uprising

A common argument is that the Soweto uprising and those that quickly followed it in many parts of South Africa were caused by macroeconomic factors, principally the deterioration of material conditions in schools and poverty due to an economic world recession (Price 1991;

Lodge 1983, 325–28; Marx 1992, 61–62; Sisk 1995, 63). However, interviews with participants and historical process tracing reveal a different empirical reality. The schoolchildren who took to the streets did not develop their anger due to worsening material conditions, and in fact many of them were not particularly angry over material conditions before June 16, 1976, the first day of the Soweto uprising. Material conditions were relatively constant, and many schoolchildren felt privileged and happy to be able to attend school, not least because most young black Africans could not afford to do so and because many dropped out of school. The initial reason that schoolchildren took to the streets in Soweto was because they were forced to learn several hard subjects in the Afrikaans language. As some of them were failing their exams they organized a protest *only* against this unfair policy. However, the unprepared and aggressive police forces that encountered the schoolchildren reacted with live fire, killing many of the young protesters. It was this violent police reaction, and the picture of fatally wounded sixteen-year-old Hector Peterson carried in the arms of an older student, that caused the critical moral shock and anger, and spurred the widespread uprising in South Africa (Shultziner 2010, chapter 6).

The events of June 16, 1976, and the cycle of violence that ensued in the next few weeks in South Africa transformed the 1976 generation's (and others') worldview about social injustices. From a limited protest *within* the apartheid system, June 16 turned the protest into a struggle against the whole system. The causes of this event, however, cannot be reduced to or explained by macro-level factors. As Kane-Berman explains, "Any attempt to answer [the causes of the uprising] must assign overwhelming weight to the shooting itself. It instantly transformed a protest which might otherwise have been confined to the Afrikaans issue and to Soweto into a generalised nation-wide revolt against the total situation in which black South Africans find themselves. Thereafter, inevitably, events gained a momentum of their own" (1981, 48). That is, a meaningful explanatory role must be given to the *event* of June 16 and its brutal repressive nature, which had immediate implications for the ensuing clashes (see also Shultziner 2010, chapters 6 and 7).

Montgomery, Alabama: The Bus Boycott

The Montgomery bus boycott offers a different example of a reaction to a repressive event that led to prolonged and highly complex collective action mostly by adults within their daily lives and responsibilities. In this case, frustration and unrest built up due to increasing humiliation of black bus riders by white bus drivers in the two years preceding the struggle (Shultziner 2013). The causes for this increasing humiliation, however, were related to bus drivers and the bus system, not to rising expectations on the part of black bus riders or other macro-level processes (e.g., McAdam 1982, 2004, 2009; Morris 1984, 2000; Shultziner 2013).

Instead, Rosa Parks's arrest for refusing to give up her bus seat on December 1, 1955, was widely perceived as an act of cruel repression that generated outrage and resistance in the black community in Montgomery. Parks was known in the community as tender, kind, and nonconfrontational, and news of her arrest quickly spread by word of mouth due to the quick publicity work of Jo Ann Robinson and her peers in the Women's Political Council (Robinson and Garrow 1987). Black Montgomerians had been increasingly humiliated by their treatment on the buses, and Parks's arrest appalled and angered them, enabling community leaders to manage and channel this anger into a one-day boycott on December 5, 1955. That the buses were almost completely empty on that day surprised everybody in Montgomery, including the organizers of the boycott (King [1958] 1965).

December 5 was a transformative day for the community for two reasons. First, black Montgomerians realized at once the scope of their shared humiliation on the buses. Second, the mass meetings on the evening of December 5 brought the black Montgomery community together for the first time, physically in the same church, for a shared struggle. The community collectively redefined the way it perceived the bus system in their city. They shared personal stories of humiliation, and the collective problem emerged in full clarity. Furthermore, the participants realized that they could actually do something effective to respond to the discrimination they experienced. Their willingness to struggle against the long-standing injustices on the buses was born and cemented on that day (Shultziner 2010, chapters 4 and 5), and at this point, the story becomes more familiar. The community entrusted its leadership to coordinate the struggle and establish specific goals and tactics through a new organization that was set up for this purpose (the Montgomery Improvement Association, led by Dr. Martin Luther King Jr.; see King [1958] 1965).

The events of December 5, 1955, in Montgomery cannot be explained by macro-level factors alone (Shultziner 2014). The cognitive and emotional changes that occurred on that day were not gradual but a radical departure with the past and thus stand out as independent causes of the community's mobilization. From that point on, a majority within the black community decided to stay off the buses as an act of reaffirming their self-esteem and gaining recognition from the world. They persisted until the bus segregation system was abolished.

In both of the cases above, the importance of repression and transformative events becomes even more evident when we consider that these radical turns in political consciousness and action took place while there was relative stability in macro-level factors and processes. In South Africa, the world recession was not felt by schoolchildren by the time of the Soweto uprising. In Montgomery, the economic situation also had not significantly changed. Thus, it appears the outbreak of civil resistance can occur when there is relative stability in terms of the macro configurations of the economy and institutions.

To be clear, I do not argue that dramatic events necessarily result in regime replacement and democratic progress. The argument is that regime change and democratic progress are *more likely* to occur as a result of repression or other transformative events. In fact, democratic change is often the end result of a chain of events beginning with a dramatic event.

Conclusions

Events are important, not as triggers for broader macro factors and processes but as important factors that raise (but do not solely determine) the likelihood of regime change: systems that maintain stability and power over many years suddenly collapse; rulers that appear (and arguably are) at the height of their power are suddenly ousted; radical turning points in public opinion occur despite minimal or no changes in important socioeconomic parameters, and these changes in public opinion are often not gradual but drastic and concentrated in a very short period of time. These sudden and rapid breakdowns of regimes are often related to excessive repression that backfires.

Transformative events are powerful factors in regime change because they enable radical departures from old ways of thinking about the system, new opportunities, suspension of longstanding power configurations and authority, and sudden unexpected pressures on the ruling elite. Chains of events may begin from a repressive event within the system, such as the killing or humiliation of a citizen. They may also begin from the inspiration and hopes gained from a mass movement elsewhere in the region or beyond. Dramatic events that involve moral shock, widespread public outrage, and emotions that are conducive for collective action raise the chances of repression backfiring against a regime (Martin 2007). Dramatic events involving repression shake the political system, generate emotional energy, and create opportunities for collective action, often suspending existing power relations and undermining acceptance of government authority. Whether a regime can withstand the crumbling of the status quo depends on many factors and involves a high degree of contingency and chance. It is very difficult, and arguably impossible, to forecast which dramatic event will lead to regime change and transition to democracy. The timing of regime change depends on highly complex social and political processes, as well as framing and media coverage. Yet certain patterns do emerge from this preliminary study that warrant further attention and exploration. Repression is a common theme in dramatic events, and this should draw more research attention to the special nexus between repression, transformative events, and regime change.

References

Bandura, Albert. 1977. "Self-Efficacy: Toward a Unifying Theory of Behavioral Change." *Psychological Review* 84 (2): 191–215.

Beissinger, Mark R. 2009. "The Intersection of Ethnic Nationalism and People Power Tactics in the Baltic States, 1987–91." In *Civil Resistance and Power Politics: The Experience of Non-violent Action from Gandhi to the Present*, edited by Adam Roberts and Timothy Garton Ash, 231–46. Oxford: Oxford Univ. Press.

Berman, S. 2007. "Lessons from Europe." *Journal of Democracy* 18 (1): 28–41.

Biko, Steve, and Aelred Stubbs. 1978. *I Write What I Like*. London: Bowerdean Press.

Bunce, Valerie J., and Sharon L. Wolchik. 2007. "People Power and Democratizing Elections: Post-Communist Europe and Eurasia." Unpublished paper. https://web.archive.org/web/20151227192640/http://vjbunce.weebly.com:80/uploads/3/2/9/3/3293465/bunce_wolchik_people_power_icnc_final_july07l3.doc.

———. 2010. "Defeating Dictators: Electoral Change and Stability in Competitive Authoritarian Regimes." *World Politics* 62 (1): 43–86.

Capoccia, G., and D. Ziblatt. 2010. "The Historical Turn in Democratization Studies: A New Research Agenda for Europe and Beyond Introduction." *Comparative Political Studies* 43 (8–9): 931–68.

Contenta, Sandro. 2011. "'We Got Rid of the Pharaoh'." *The Star*, Aug. 15. https://www.thestar.com/news/world/2011/02/12/we_got_rid_of_the_pharaoh.html.

Davidheiser, Evenly B. 1992. "Strong States, Weak States: The Role of the State in Revolution." *Comparative Politics* 24 (4): 463–75.

Evans, Sara M. 1980. *Personal Politics: The Roots of Women's Liberation in the Civil Rights Movement and the New Left*. New York: Vintage Books.

Gamson, William A. 1992a. *Talking Politics*. New York: Cambridge Univ. Press.

———. 1992b. "The Social Psychology of Collective Action." In *Frontiers in Social Movement Theory*, edited by A. D. Morris and C. M. Mueller, 53–76. New Haven: Yale Univ. Press.

Gause, Gregory F. 2011. "Why Middle East Studies Missed the Arab Spring: The Myth of Authoritarian Stability." *Foreign Affairs* 90 (4): 81.

Gladwell, Malcolm. 2000. *The Tipping Point: How Little Things Can Make a Big Difference*, 1st ed. Boston: Little, Brown.

Hess, D., and B. Martin. 2006. "Repression, Backfire, and the Theory of Transformative Events." *Mobilization* 11 (2): 249–67.

Horowitz, Donald L. 1985. *Ethnic Groups in Conflict*. Berkeley: Univ. of California Press.

Huntington, Samuel P. 1991. *The Third Wave: Democratization in the Late Twentieth Century*. Norman: Univ. of Oklahoma Press.

Jones, Stephen. 2009. "Georgia's 'Rose Revolution' of 2003: Enforcing Peaceful Change." In *Civil Resistance and Power Politics: The Experience of Non-violent Action from Gandhi to the Present*, edited by Adam Roberts and Timothy Garton Ash, 317–34. Oxford: Oxford Univ. Press.

Kane-Berman, John Stuart. 1981. *Soweto: Black Revolt, White Reaction*. Johannesburg: Ravan Press.

Keck, Margaret E., and Kathryn Sikkink. 1998. *Activists beyond Borders: Advocacy Networks in International Politics*. Ithaca, NY: Cornell Univ. Press.

King, Martin Luther, Jr. [1958] 1965. *Stride toward Freedom: The Montgomery Story*. New York: Harper.

———. [1963] 2000. *Why We Can't Wait*. New York: New American Library.

Kramer, Mark. 2009. "The Dialectics of Empire: Soviet Leaders and the Challenge of Civil Resistance in East-Central Europe, 1968–91." In *Civil Resistance and Power Politics: The Experience of Non-violent Action from Gandhi to the Present*, edited by Adam Roberts and Timothy Garton Ash. Oxford: Oxford Univ. Press.

Kuran, Timur. 1995. "The Inevitability of Future Revolutionary Surprises." *American Journal of Sociology* 100 (6): 1528–51.

Lodge, Tom. 1983. *Black Politics in South Africa since 1945*. Johannesburg: Ravan Press.

Martin, Brian. 2007. *Justice Ignited: The Dynamics of Backfire*. Lanham, MD: Rowman & Littlefield.

Marx, Anthony W. 1992. *Lessons of Struggle: South African Internal Opposition, 1960–1990*. New York: Oxford Univ. Press.

McAdam, Doug. 1982. *Political Process and the Development of Black Insurgency, 1930–1970*. Chicago: Univ. of Chicago Press.

———. 2004. "Revisiting the U.S. Civil Rights Movement: Toward a More Synthetic Understanding of the Origins of Contention." In *Rethinking Social Movements: Structure, Meaning, and Emotion*, edited by J. Goodwin and J. M. Jasper, 201–32. Oxford: Rowman & Littlefield.

———. 2009. "The U.S. Civil Rights Movement: Power from Below and Above." In *Civil Resistance and Power Politics: The Experience of*

Non-violent Action from Gandhi to the Present, edited by Adam Roberts and Timothy Garton Ash, 58–74. Oxford: Oxford Univ. Press.

McAdam, Doug, and William H. Sewell Jr. 2001. "It's About Time: Temporality in the Study of Social Movements and Revolutions." In *Silence and Voice in the Study of Contentious Politics*, edited by R. Aminzade, 89–125. Cambridge: Cambridge Univ. Press.

McAdam, Doug, and Sidney Tarrow. 2010. "Ballots and Barricades: On the Reciprocal Relationship between Elections and Social Movements." *Perspectives on Politics* 8 (2): 529–42.

Morris, Aldon D. 1984. *The Origins of the Civil Rights Movement: Black Communities Organizing for Change*. New York: Free Press.

———. 2000. "Charting Futures for Sociology: Social Organization—Reflections on Social Movement Theory: Criticisms and Proposals." *Contemporary Sociology—A Journal of Reviews* 29 (3): 445–54.

Price, Robert M. 1991. *The Apartheid State in Crisis: Political Transformation in South Africa, 1975–1990*. New York: Oxford Univ. Press.

Przeworski, Adam, and Fernando Limongi. 1997. "Modernization: Theories and Facts." *World Politics* 49 (2): 155–83.

Robinson, Jo Ann Gibson, and David J. Garrow. 1987. *The Montgomery Bus Boycott and the Women Who Started It: The Memoir of Jo Ann Gibson Robinson*. Knoxville: Univ. of Tennessee Press.

Schedler, A. 2002. "The Nested Game of Democratization by Elections." *International Political Science Review* 23 (1): 103–22.

Sewell, William H. 1996. "Historical Events as Transformations of Structures: Inventing Revolution at the Bastille." *Theory and Society* 25 (6): 841–81.

Sharp, Gene. 2003. *There are Realistic Alternatives*. Boston: Albert Einstein Institute.

———. 2007. "The Politics of Nonviolent Action and the Spread of Ideas about Civil Resistance." Paper read at Conference on Civil Resistance and Power Politics, Mar. 15–18, St. Antony's College, Oxford Univ.

Shively, Phillips W. 2014. *Power and Choice: An Introduction to Political Science*, 14th ed. Singapore: McGraw-Hill.

Shultziner, Doron. 2010. *Struggling for Recognition: The Psychological Impetus for Democratic Progress*. New York: Continuum Press.

———. 2013. "The Social-Psychological Origins of the Montgomery Bus Boycott: Social Interaction and Humiliation in the Emergence of Social Movements." *Mobilization* 18 (2): 117–42.

———. 2014. "A Multi-Stage Approach to Social Movements." *Mobilizing Ideas*, Aug. 4. https://mobilizingideas.wordpress.com/2014/08/04/a-multi-stage-approach-to-social-movements/.

Shultziner, Doron, and Mary Ann Tetreault. 2011. "Paradoxes of Democratic Progress in Kuwait: The Case of the Kuwaiti Women's Rights Movement." *Muslim World Journal of Human Rights* 7 (2): 1–25.

Sisk, Timothy D. 1995. *Democratization in South Africa: The Elusive Social Contract*. Princeton, NJ: Princeton Univ. Press.

Smithey, Lee, and Lester R. Kurtz. 2007. "'We Have Bare Hands': Nonviolent Social Movements in the Soviet Bloc." In *Nonviolent Social Movements: A Geographical Perspective*, edited by Stephen Zunes, Lester R. Kurtz, and Sarah Beth Asher, 96–124. Malden, MA: Blackwell.

Smolar, Aleksander. 2009. "Towards 'Self-limiting' Revolution: Poland 1970–89." In *Civil Resistance and Power Politics: The Experience of Nonviolent Action from Gandhi to the Present*, edited by Adam Roberts and Timothy Garton Ash, 127–43. Oxford: Oxford Univ. Press.

Snow, David A., and Robert D. Benford. 1992. "Master Cycles and Cycles of Protest." In *Frontiers in Social Movement Theory*, edited by A. D. Morris and C. M. Mueller, 133–55. New Haven: Yale Univ. Press.

Stephan, Maria, and Erica Chenoweth. 2008. "Why Civil Resistance Works: The Strategic Logic of Nonviolent Conflict." *International Security* 33 (1): 7–44.

Tajfel, Henri, and John C. Turner. 1979. "An Integrative Theory of Intergroup Conflict." In *The Social Psychology of Intergroup Relations*, edited by W. G. Austin and S. Worchel, 33–47. Monterey, CA: Brooks-Cole.

Tarrow, Sidney G. 1994. *Power in Movement: Social Movements, Collective Action, and Politics*. Cambridge: Cambridge Univ. Press.

Teorell, Jan, and Axel Hadenius. 2006. "Democracy without Democratic Values: A Rejoinder to Welzel and Inglehart." *Studies in Comparative International Development* 41 (3): 95–111.

———. 2008. "Elections as Levers of Democracy: A Global Inquiry." *QoG Working Paper Series* 2008: 17, University of Gothenburg, Sweden.

Tilly, Charles. 2007. *Democracy*. Cambridge: Cambridge Univ. Press.

Tucker, Joshua A. 2007. "Enough! Electoral Fraud, Collective Action Problems, and Post-Communist Colored Revolutions." *Perspectives on Politics* 5 (3): 535–51.

Turner, John C. 1982. "Toward a Cognitive Definition of the Social Group." In *Social Identity and Intergroup Relations*, edited by H. Tajfel, 15–40. Cambridge: Cambridge Univ. Press.

Vejvoda, Ivan. 2009. "Civil Society versus Slobodan Milosevic: Serbia, 1991–2000." In *Civil Resistance and Power Politics: The Experience of Non-violent Action from Gandhi to the Present*, Eds. Adam Roberts and Timothy Garton Ash. Oxford: Oxford Univ. Press.

Wilson, Andrew. 2009. "Ukraine's 'Orange Revolution' of 2004: The Paradoxes of Negotiations." In *Civil Resistance and Power Politics: The Experience of Non-violent Action from Gandhi to the Present*, edited by Adam Roberts and Timothy Garton Ash, 335–53. Oxford: Oxford Univ. Press.

Wood, Elizabeth Jean. 2001. "The Emotional Benefits of Insurgency in El Salvador." In *Passionate Politics: Emotions and Social Movements*, edited by J. Goodwin, J. M. Jasper and F. Polletta, 267–81. Chicago: Chicago Univ. Press.

4

The Psychology of Agents of Repression

The Paradox of Defection

Rachel MacNair

Introduction

A major insight of nonviolent resistance is that power is not a physical property that people hold in their hands but is instead a *psychological* experience. If people perceive leaders as legitimate and cooperate with their rule, then the rulers have power, and the system will be strong and stable. If people perceive leaders as illegitimate but nevertheless cooperate for reasons such as fear or apathy, then the rulers still have power, but it will be unstable and weak—vulnerable to resistance whenever that fear or apathy is overcome (Johnstad 2012).

Repression happens when rulers who have not gained the confidence of their populations need to induce more fear. Though being competent at governing and avoiding corruption would be a much more stable way of ensuring the needed cooperation, people who think in terms of repression do not grasp this basic point. They have had positive experiences with getting the behavior they want through fear.

Repression requires police, soldiers, death squads, or similar people to carry it out. If a dictator orders repression and its agents do not follow the orders, then the ruler's power is lost right there, before even considering the reaction of the repressed population. Since police and soldiers are often recruited out of the population and have friends and family members there, this refusal to follow orders does actually occur at times—especially when there is a trigger, such as a clearly stolen election, signaling that the time has come for those who are prepared to act to do so, knowing that others will act in concert. At other times, police and soldiers will continue to understand themselves to be on the side of order and against the forces of chaos, and this perception will allow them to engage in horrific acts of repression.

The potential for atrocity is especially high when portions of the population disagree with rebels concerning the legitimacy of the rulers or when the agents of repression have property interests they wish to protect. That is to say, some agents sincerely believe in the justice of what they are doing and feel a patriotic duty, while others are corrupt themselves, with no pretense to actual justice. In either case, it is a matter of basic psychology that they will usually rationalize to themselves that they are serving the public good and are entitled to their booty.

There is a practical question for the nonviolent revolution: How can we best encourage these agents of repression to defect and join noncooperation with the ruler? Psychological studies on successful attempts to psychologically disarm agents of repression are hard to come by, but a couple of historical studies illustrate the potential for repression management.

Cascio and Luthans (2013) focused on the experience of Nelson Mandela and several other South African political prisoners, who were held in abusive conditions at Robben Island from the mid-1960s until the end of apartheid in 1991. The authors drew from the prisoners' and guards' accounts, showing that Robben Island changed from a traditionally repressive institution into "one where the positively oriented prisoners disrupted the institution with a resulting climate of learning and transformation that eventually led to freedom and the end of apartheid" (51). The assertively friendly interactions the prisoners offered the guards had their effect.

A study of the 2000 Serbian movement to oust Milosevic and the 2004 Orange Revolution in Ukraine looks at how organizers developed strategies to undermine the willingness of the agents of regression to commit violence against them (Binnendijk and Marovic 2006). There was no major crackdown in these two cases, and the strategies used contributed to that outcome—or perhaps were entirely responsible for it. Military personnel in both cases had lost pay and prestige under the regime, so activists could advocate for better treatment of military personnel and assert that helping the revolution was better serving the country.

To better understand the psychological underpinnings of repression and its management, we will first look at the ways that people can be induced to become agents of repression. Then we will examine the traumatizing impact this actually has on them. These investigations can help us understand the psychology of otherwise puzzling behavior and should offer major insights into how to deal with repression.

Experiments on How to Make Agents of Repression

How do rulers get soldiers, police, and others to engage in repression, and how can those crucial actors be persuaded to defect? Although this aspect of nonviolent resistance is not well researched to date, quite a few experiments deal with punitive or aggressive behavior and offer various insights; moreover, two classic psychological experiments deal more directly with inducing people to become agents of repression. We might think that would be a difficult thing to do in an artificial laboratory experiment, but in both cases, researchers were remarkably effective. Indeed, these kinds of experiments are no longer done as their method poses severe ethical problems.

Milgram Experiments—Destructive Obedience to Authority

In 1963, Yale psychologist Stanley Milgram and his colleagues performed a set of experiments that purported to be about learning but actually tested participants' willingness to administer supposed electric shocks to a supposed learner in another room (Milgram 1974; Blass 2000). Participants were told that learners who failed simple tests had to be shocked at levels that started out low but increased in intensity with each wrong answer the learner submitted. Eventually, by design, there would be no correct answer, and a man in a lab coat would insist to participants that the experiment must continue, and that he would take responsibility for the completion of the tests, including the shocks that were to be administered. The researchers found that solid majorities of American participants, generally over two-thirds, progressed all the way to administering the highest level of shock, despite hearing noises of distress from the "learner" (who was in fact an actor). This set of studies launched one of the major findings of social psychology: even among people who bear no animosity to an immediate other—people who express that they are suffering great tension and who clearly state that they do not want to inflict pain on others—compliance with demands of authority is quite high. No threat or promise of rewards is necessary.

Why did this happen in the Milgram experiments? One reason is that the authority defined reality and what it meant. Another is that the participants had shifted all responsibility to the authority—the man in the lab coat explicitly stated that he was taking responsibility. So in spite of the fact that the participants were the ones administering what they were led to believe were increasingly severe shocks—much to their own dismay, as documented by video—they understood this as something the authority was doing, not something they were doing themselves. Therefore, it was the authority's responsibility rather than theirs. Finally, they had given their word that they would participate, so they understood nonparticipation as undermining the experiment and going against their word.

Similar experiments went on for years, by many different experimenters in different countries and using several different variations. They revealed little difference between compliance rates for nation, race, culture, class, gender, or how impressive the location of the experiment was. There was no change in the rate of compliance if the "learner" had a heart condition and thus would seem more vulnerable. However, there were some variables that triggered more participants to defect; that is, to refuse to seemingly administer higher levels of shocks:

1. The participants are shown that the "learner" has a contract to be released from the experiment on demand, and the experimenter is breaking the contract when insisting on continuing—*some drop, to 40 percent compliance.*
2. The experimenter calls orders in to participants by phone, not face-to-face—*dramatic drop, 20 percent compliance.*
3. Participants are free to choose the shock level—*very dramatic drop, only 1 in 40 went to maximum.*
4. A second experimenter argues with the first—*all participants stop by time of or soon after argument.*
5. A staged experiment is running at the same time in the same vicinity and in view, in which the participant rebels, thus offering a peer rebellion—*dramatic drop—1 in 10 compliance.*

All of these variations deal with perceptions of the legitimacy of the authority, and all can be applied to nonviolent movements. In real-life terms, the stolen election, or any other situation in which the ruler promised something and then does not deliver, fits the first situation of a contract being broken. The next two permutations, in which the authority is distant or allows participants some choice, can have an impact on the ordinary officer in a civil resistance situation where he or she is receiving commands from a distance. Of course, if they are in a death squad that operates with considerable autonomy, where both conditions apply, they may have been selected because they are among the 5–20 percent who comply in any event.

What about when two authorities argue with each other? If, say, the church or a large group of Buddhist monks or an out-of-country mullah argues with the government, then the government can lose its monopoly on legitimacy and the authority to compel compliance of the public without direct violence. In such cases, authorities may feel forced to order repression and violence, but then they may also lose the authority to compel their agents to repress challengers. In those cases, the population, police, and soldiers may take sides over which authority they prefer and find they prefer the nongovernmental one. In any event, when framing conflicts with significant movements of people, the nonviolent opposition is well-advised to find authoritative people whom police or soldiers respect. The real-world application would seem rather obvious: if one entity that is seen as an authority is a problem, then invite another entity with authority to counter the problem.

In the "peer rebellion" variation, noncompliance with the experimenter was increased by a role model of noncompliance. Police and soldiers in similar circumstances might be inclined to continue to do as they are told, but if they find themselves in a minority, the noncompliance from others in their group can have a significant impact on them as well.

The Stanford Prison Experiment

The Stanford Prison Experiment, conducted in 1971 by Phil Zimbardo, Craig Haney, and other colleagues, generated further well-accepted psychological principles that promise to shed light on the study of repression and its management. In this laboratory experiment, a simulated prison, designed to last two weeks, offered an arguably more realistic simulation of what agents of repression would be expected to do. In some ways, it was the opposite of the Milgram experiment. Instead of the experimenters encouraging more aggression, they tried to hold it in check. There was no deception. An institution—the jail and all of its personnel—rather than an individual, served as the critical source of authority.

However, the study had to be called off after only six days when the researchers came to understand that they had themselves become caught up in an abusive and destructive group dynamic. All participants were college students, screened to fall within normal psychological parameters and assigned randomly to prisoner or guard roles. Yet vast personality changes developed. Those playing the role of guards became cruel. Those playing prisoners became inordinately depressed. Even the experimenters got sucked into their roles as prison administrators. A consultant who had been a former prisoner found himself saying the same things while playing a parole officer that he had hated when he had been a prisoner on the receiving end of abuse in prison.[1]

The "terminator" of the experiment was a late entrant, an outsider. Christina Maslach was a trained psychologist herself, busy with other projects. She had not experienced the slow escalation from normal to abnormal behavior. Invited to observe after six days, she was appalled to see how inhumane the situation had become. The participants and experimenters themselves could not see this. After much argument, they came to understand she was right, and shut down the simulation (Blass 2000).

Maslach served on a small scale the function a nonviolent movement serves on a much larger scale: not only intervening in an unjust situation, but bringing insight to which the participants were blind. She had considerable influence as a fiancée of Zimbardo and a colleague to the other psychologists, advantages normally lacking in mass social movements. Of course, social movements take more time to develop extensive and similarly influential networks—a normal and expected difference between the laboratory and the real world. Though experiments are fairly artificial and oversimplified (not the same as the much more complicated reality), they can offer valuable insight.

What It Takes to Keep People Repressing

Though it may seem like a strange assertion given the prominence of repression throughout history, the human mind resists killing and committing violence. One early study that suggested this was conducted during World War II, when S. L. A. Marshall (1947) reported from postcombat interviews that only 15 to 20 percent of riflemen fired their weapons at an exposed enemy soldier. Firing increased greatly if a nearby leader demanded it (as would be expected from Milgram's findings on obedience). But when left to their own devices, the great majority appeared to avoid killing. Some have questioned Marshall's

1. A full account of the experiment is available at the Stanford Prison Experiment website (www.prisonexp.org).

results, but other studies with similar findings include French officers in the 1860s, Argentine firing rates in the Falkland War, the Napoleonic wars, American Civil War regiments, and numerous others (Grossman 1995; Grossman and Siddle 2008).

The same disinclination to kill extends to non-war situations as well: "Police hesitancy to fire even when life is in jeopardy was first formally reported outside of law enforcement circles in the early 1980s, when a study of police shootings in four major cities disclosed that officers in these departments shot in just a fraction of the cases that law and policy would allow" (Binder, Scharf, and Galvin 1982, 58).

Randall Collins (2008) shows from extensive photos and video recordings how this pattern applies to riots, bullying, and various forms of police repression: actual violence is committed by a small portion of officers. Tension, fear, and a low "competence" in actually doing harm to the target are common. To focus repression where authorities want it focused, those instructed to carry it out require training and the right conditions to overcome the natural human aversion to doing violence.

Conditioning and Desensitization

After World War II, the psychological means to overcome this resistance to kill was deliberately put into practice. Bull's-eye targets were replaced with realistic man-shaped targets that popped up on the shooting range and then fell when hit. Each hit was accompanied by an intricate awards system, in what behaviorist B. F. Skinner remarked was a perfect example of the operant conditioning he had used so well to train pigeons (Grossman 1995, 253).

This conditioning can influence behavior when people are frightened. For instance, fire drills condition terrified school children to respond properly during a fire. Such exercises do not merely provide information ahead of a catastrophe but condition children to behave a certain way when their thought processes are not at their best. With conditioning in flight simulators, frightened pilots can respond reflexively to emergency situations. The application of operant conditioning techniques did increase the rate of Americans firing their weapons in Korea and even more in Vietnam. Nevertheless, only a small portion fired frequently and only a small portion actually hit their targets (Grossman, 1995, 35).

Violent media as a whole—including movies and television shows with graphic violence—can also serve as a form of conditioning in a real-world setting called desensitization. Historically, the Roman gladiator games, the circus atmosphere at public executions, and similar popular violent entertainment could have served the same function. However, unlike realistic target practice or video games that develop shooting skills, in this case only the sight is being conditioned, not the action.

Fortunately, humans are not programmable robots. Conditioning is not some form of brainwashing that keeps people from thinking. It is only a form of training. Desensitization is easily countered by resensitization. Both conditioning and resensitization rely on a person finding the situation to be predictable. Therefore, novel and creative approaches can dissolve their influence rather quickly, if done with care. Soldiers and police are quite capable of deciding whether or not to use their training in a given situation—especially when the real-world situation does not present the kind of threat on which their training was based, and when there is no sense of imminent danger to themselves. Thus, nonviolent activists can strategically present agents of repression with circumstances that interrupt processes of conditioning and desensitization and thereby interrupt repression.

Group Solidarity

An external threat often increases group cohesion. Sometimes people remember wartime fondly as the time when petty quarrels ceased and people felt unified against the "enemy." This is a psychological experience that is often consciously utilized by commanders and rulers to bolster their power with the population as a whole and with their police and army in particular. (The 1997 film *Wag the Dog* presents a biting satire on this phenomenon.)

Police work together and army members often live together, so their sense of being a group that requires loyalty to one another develops as a matter of course. Add any sense of danger, and the loyalty to one another becomes intense. This group solidarity can interfere with nonviolent activists' attempts to reach the consciences of individual police or soldiers, since the value of loyalty to colleagues is also a matter of conscience for them. Yet there are occasions when this solidarity works in favor of the nonviolent rebellion: once even a small portion of individuals see a need to either defect to the side of the nonviolent rebellion or at least lay down arms so as not to repress the rebellion, then others in their group may feel the need to join them. Group solidarity can work in both directions.

What Are They Thinking?

The mental processes that allow or encourage police, soldiers, and death squads to engage in repressive violence need to be understood to make any effective outreach to them possible. In individual situations, of course, that involves listening to and persuading individuals, but there are some overarching group processes that deserve further examination.

Mechanisms of Moral Disengagement

Albert Bandura and his colleagues (1996) argue the most inhumane behavior comes about when principles of moral conduct are disengaged—people find ways to disconnect their actions from fundamental norms of conduct. Mechanisms to remove inhibitions have been extensively documented in historical atrocities and confirmed in laboratory studies of punitive behavior. The main psychological mechanisms identified by Bandura and others include:

- Change how you think about the act. For example, try to figure out how it is morally justified, use euphemisms, or compare it to worse conduct.
- Put the responsibility elsewhere, either by giving it to an authority or by giving it to the victims (commonly called scapegoating).
- Discount the effects of atrocious behavior by minimizing, ignoring, or distorting victims.
- Dehumanize the victims (Brennan 1995; Smith 2011).

One study tested the extent to which these mechanisms were used by capital punishment teams in the United States, compared with the support teams that provide solace to families involved, and compared to guards in the same prison who were not involved in carrying out executions at all. As would be expected, the execution staff had the highest level of justifying, disavowing personal responsibility, and dehumanizing (Osofsky, Bandura, and Zimbardo 2005).

The best and lengthiest study of agents of repression used extensive interviews with Brazilian police torturers and death squad participants, as discussed in the book *Violence Workers* (Huggins, Haritos-Fatouros, and Zimbardo 2002). Chapter 11 is devoted to illustrating how these mechanisms came up in the interviews carried out by the researchers. Interviewees explained that their acts were justified because of the Communist threat; they compared their own actions to those of other police by way of saying the others were bad and so they were not so bad by comparison; and they worded what they were doing in ways that made their actions sound less cruel. They blamed authorities for their orders, and they blamed their victims for being smug or not confessing. They understood their victims as less than human and indicated that they had no sense of how horrible a description of their actions would sound to others.

The authors compared yes-and-no answers from these Brazilian police about accepting responsibility for their actions or admitting their actions were wrong. There was only one case of someone both accepting responsibility and acknowledging the ethical problems with their work, simply admitting personal guilt. When individuals accepted personal responsibility but thought the act was not wrong, they engaged in justification, asserting that their cause was just. When they admitted the act was wrong but refused to accept personal responsibility, they blamed others, mainly their victims. Denial and shifting responsibility occurs when the act is not admitted as wrong nor is their personal responsibility for it.

How do nonviolent activists counter these processes of justification and denial? It depends on the situation, but if they look for signs of these kinds of reasoning, they can label them and try to counter them directly.

One method is to make an analogy to something that activists and agents of repression have in common. Rather than make direct accusations, which would more likely lead to defensiveness on the part of those accused, activists can offer an indirect story or situation. The moral of the story can be appreciated because it applies to somebody else, but this eases later applying it to one's own situation. This technique of offering a perspective outside the immediate situation has been used effectively in education in intense conflicts. For Israelis and Palestinians, for example, one technique that seemed to work better than others was to teach them not about their own conflict but about the conflict in Northern Ireland. Since they were outsiders to that conflict, they were able to learn about the dynamics of a similar conflict in a way that was not threatening and made sense to them. They could then apply what they learned to their own experience. They learned as outsiders first before learning directly (Salomon 2004).

Activists attempting to introduce new perspectives to agents of repression may cite authorities, institutions, or admired individuals to legitimize the new frames they introduce. In cases where the legitimacy of the regime is in serious question, there will generally be political or religious leaders, or even actors or sports figures, who are respected by the agents and can serve as persuaders, providing common connection between protesters and agents.

Fear

Bravado is common among people caught in an "us/them" mentality with "us" being understood as their own government and its supporters. But these people also often have fears that are important to consider. Agents of repression who are trained to not fear death or injury nevertheless fear the unknown, which may take various forms.

- The protesters are not only "them" to agents of repression but are also unknown. Only the course of time makes it possible for agents to predict how the protesters will behave.

- The authorities to whom agents of repression answer are another huge unknown. Even when agents are accustomed to dealing with those in a hierarchically superior position, they may be uncertain how those authorities will respond to the novel situation of the protests. Might they be angrier, and therefore more dangerous, than usual?
- The future is unknown. If the rebels win and a regime is replaced, will there be reconciliation, or a revenge spree? Will agents of repression be caught up in extreme punishment, or milder sanctions, such as being social outcasts or having difficulty finding employment? Once they have cast in their lot with one group (the current authorities) or the other (dissidents), they have a stake in the outcome of protest, and they could be very fearful for the consequences to their families.
- For those who take comfort in a well-established routine, including a job, salary, and basic services, the prospect of sweeping change can be a problem.

How protestors behave can undermine fear among agents of repression as patient yet firm interaction takes place. Protestors signaling the prospect of reconciliation with agents of repression may help alleviate some fears of the future. The interests of agents of repression (jobs, salary, and access to services) can be maintained to the extent that they do not perpetuate injustice, and sensitivity on this point by new leaders can help alleviate problems.

Finally, the agents of repression expect opponents to be monsters to be feared; they have been trained this way. Anything that instead establishes human interaction and undermines stereotypes can work against the normal fear reactions and thus diminish the likelihood or severity of any repression that is deployed.

Psychological Impact of Being an Agent of Repression

What is the psychological reaction these agents have to engaging in repression? Are acts of violence traumatizing to those who commit them? What insights will this give us as to how to persuade them to defect?

Perpetration-Induced Traumatic Stress

There is indeed quite a bit of evidence that people are traumatized not merely by being subjected to violence from others (which is known to be more traumatizing than suffering from hurricanes or car accidents) but also by inflicting violence on others. Not only is inflicting violence traumatic, but the evidence so far demonstrates that the trauma of violence is actually more severe for perpetrators than victims (MacNair 2002). Having more control in the situation does not protect against being traumatized by one's own acts of perpetration—in fact, that very feature may make it worse as the mind cannot shield itself from the horror by legitimately placing blame elsewhere.

The current term in psychology for post-trauma reactions is post-traumatic stress disorder (PTSD), a well-defined term in the diagnostic literature. I have coined the term perpetration-induced traumatic stress (PITS) for PTSD symptoms caused by being the person who caused the violence (MacNair 2002). This concept applies to a wide range of groups, starting with the combat veterans in whom it was first observed but also including people who carry out executions, police who shoot in the line of duty, and soldiers and police who carry out governmental orders for repression.

Symptoms of PTSD are divided into clusters.

1. Various ways of re-experiencing the trauma:
    - constant intrusive thoughts
    - repeating dreams about the event
    - flashbacks, which are rather like dreams when still awake
    - intense reactions to reminders of the trauma
2. Avoidance of reminders of the event
3. Negative thinking and moods:
    - feeling emotionally numb
    - feeling estranged and detached from other people
    - inability to remember key aspects of the event(s)
    - trouble concentrating
    - feeling a sense of foreshortened future

4. Arousal:
    - sleep disturbances
    - startle reactions
    - hypervigilance
    - irritability and outbursts of anger—aggressive, reckless, destructive and self-destructive behavior

Official definitions of PTSD can be found in the 2013 edition of the American Psychiatric Association's Diagnostic and Statistical Manual of Mental Disorders (DSM-5) and World Health Organization's 1992 International Statistical Classification of Diseases and Related Health Problems (ICD-10).[2] These two definitions of PTSD allow for the *idea* that committing violence is a kind of trauma that causes psychological problems with diagnosable symptoms; this allows for PITS to be unofficially defined as a form of post-trauma symptoms (MacNair 2002). The DSM-5, in contrast to previous versions, does address this point in a less-than-thorough way under the discussion accompanying the definition by adding to the list of causal factors: "for military personnel, being a perpetrator, witnessing atrocities, or killing the enemy." This remains a point that is not actually controversial but is also not often considered.

Both definitions also make clear that the phenomenon is cross-cultural. Though symptoms are naturally perceived and interpreted differently by different cultures, they are widespread enough that PTSD symptoms are understood to be a common human response to trauma and not some culture-bound construct.

Overconsumption of alcohol or other intoxicants—which can even include workaholism—is also a common post-trauma reaction among those who suffer from PITS. Feelings of guilt can be especially troubling

2. The DSM-5 criteria for PTSD are available on the US Department of Veterans Affairs website (www.ptsd.va.gov/professional/PTSD-overview/dsm5_criteria_ptsd.asp). The ICD-10 criteria are published on the World Health Organization's website (www.who.int/classifications/icd/en/GRNBOOK.pdf).

(especially when entirely justified, as opposed to the irrational survivor's guilt) and have commonly been reported by defectors.

While there are official clinical diagnoses, we are not only concerned with people who suffer from the full-blown disorder. Having symptoms is enough to warrant concern, and far more people have just one or two symptoms, which is nonetheless quite distressing.

Experiments and Case Studies

Craig Haney, one of the staff psychologists involved in the Stanford Prison Experiment, reports the kinds of nightmares that are a symptom of PTSD:

> As the prison atmosphere evolved and became thick and real, I sensed the growing hostility and distrust on all sides. On one of the nights that it was my turn to sleep overnight at the prison, I had a terribly realistic dream in which I was suddenly imprisoned by guards in an actual prison that Zimbardo, Banks, and I supposedly had created. Some of the prisoners in our study, the ones who in retrospect had impressed me as most in distress, were now decked out in elaborately militaristic guard uniforms. They were my most angry and abusive captors, and I had the unmistakable sense that there was to be no escape or release from this awful place. I awoke drenched in sweat and shaken from the experience. The dream required no psychoanalytic acumen to interpret and should have given me some pause about what we were doing. But it didn't. I pressed on without reflection. After all, we had a prison to run and too many day-to-day crises and decisions to allow myself the luxury of pondering the ultimate wisdom of this noble endeavor that had already started to go wrong. (Haney 2000, 226–27)

Haney's experience offers some insight into why people continue to engage in violent behavior even as they begin to suffer acute symptoms. This also suggests that the absence of such symptoms cannot be assumed merely because a person continues in the activity.

In a 1960s psychiatric case study, Frantz Fanon (1961) describes the real-life experience of a European police inspector who tortured

Algerian rebels for information. He had lost his appetite, with sleep frequently disturbed by nightmares. He had sought psychiatric help for what he called "fits of madness," which seems to align with the symptom of explosive outbursts:

> "Can you give me an explanation for this, doctor: as soon as someone goes against me I want to hit him. Even outside my job. I feel I want to settle the fellows who get in my way, even for nothing at all. Look here, for example, suppose I go to the kiosk to buy the papers. There's a lot of people. Of course you have to wait. I hold out my hand (the chap who keeps the kiosk is a pal of mine) to take my papers. Someone in the line gives me a challenging look and says 'Wait your turn.' Well, I feel I want to beat him up and I say to myself, 'If I had you for a few hours my fine fellow you wouldn't look so clever afterwards'" (267).

The psychiatrist's case report indicates that these outbursts were not limited to thoughts but led to domestic abuse:

> The patient dislikes noise. At home he wants to hit everybody all the time. In fact, he does hit his children, even the baby of twenty months, with unaccustomed savagery. But what really frightened him was one evening when his wife had criticized him particularly for hitting his children too much. (She had even said to him. "My word, anyone'd think you were going mad.") He threw himself upon her, beat her, and tied her to a chair, saying to himself "I'll teach her once and for all that I'm master in this house." Fortunately his children began roaring and crying. He then realized the full gravity of his behavior, untied his wife and the next day decided to consult a doctor, "a nerve specialist." (267–68)

The police inspector told the doctors that he had not been like this before, rarely punishing his children or fighting with his wife. This had only started "since the troubles." The man could not get sick leave, and he did not want to be declared as having psychological problems, so he wanted treatment while he continued to work. The psychiatrist comments on this:

> The weaknesses of such a procedure may easily be imagined. This man knew perfectly well that his disorders were directly caused by the kind of activity that went on inside the rooms where interrogations were carried out, even though he tried to throw the responsibility totally upon "present troubles." As he could not see his way to stopping torturing people (that made nonsense [*sic*] to him for in that case he would have to resign) he asked me without beating about the bush to help him to go on torturing Algerian patriots without any prickings of conscience, without any behavior problems, and with complete equanimity. (269)

It is normal for people to try to avoid becoming or remaining victims of trauma. Would it not follow that people with acute symptoms resulting from their own actions would stop the actions to avoid the trauma? Yet we find otherwise; the psychological dynamics leading to the actions remain strong.

There is another problem: besides those who manage to overcome ethical barriers, a few people actually get a rush out of acts of violence. They experience a state of euphoria. These come from brain opioids released by the stress of committing violence. If bottled and artificial, these would be addictive and similar to cocaine (Southwick, Yehuda, and Morgan 1995). This is where the idea of being "bloodthirsty" comes from. As with cocaine, the feeling of exhilaration is followed by withdrawal symptoms, and PTSD symptoms can worsen. These are only a small portion of cases, but they may be associated with particularly brutal instances of violence.

PITS and Repression Management

Can we apply psychological knowledge about agents of repression being traumatized by their own actions to any practical applications that encourage them to defect, or at least withdraw from repression against civilians? There have been no studies published on this specific topic at the time of writing and very little by way of experience. We only have studies of techniques that have historically been successfully used directly on agents of repression to positively influence their behavior (Binnendijk and Marovic 2006; Cascio and Luthans 2013). However, we can put forward several questions that may serve to guide further research on the topic:

1. *How often do security personnel who actually commit violence against protesters defect, as opposed to those who witness violence but do not actively do it themselves?* It is common that a large portion of people are only witnesses of the violence done by other individuals. But are there a substantial number of people who commit violence among the defectors? This should be established first before moving on to further research into whether circumstances can be established by nonviolent activists that would encourage those suffering from PITS to defect.

2. *Would suffering from PITS symptoms make individuals more likely to defect, or less likely?* We know that PITS symptoms may cause further violence, thus fueling cycles of violence. The symptoms of angry outbursts and of a feeling of detachment and estrangement from other people lend themselves to further acts of violence, so that engaging in violence continues to happen, even though it traumatizes the person doing it (Silva et al. 2001). We have little information on the opposite tack: bolting from the violence. Does escape lessen symptoms, or provide any kind of therapeutic benefit?

It could be that those who suffer from PITS symptoms are less likely to defect because they are suffering symptoms that lead them into further violence instead. Conversely, post-trauma symptoms could create a drive for relief that leads people to the options of defecting or otherwise refusing orders. Or perhaps both paths are more likely, and which one is taken will depend upon the individual and the circumstances they encounter, including those in confrontations with protestors.

Might the potential for defection also be influenced by an intervention that could help enable agents of repression to escape cycles of perpetration? This could, for example, involve providing knowledge that such symptoms are normal, that committing further violence exacerbates them, and that refusing to commit further violence might provide some relief. If so, activists could craft such an intervention appropriate to their own culture and circumstances.

3. *Would anticipating suffering from PITS (consciously or not) make individuals more or less likely to defect, and can this be used to encourage defections?* This is more problematic to ascertain as we do not know what forms such anticipation might take. Might agents of repression fear the onset of PITS symptoms, or is the anticipation more likely to manifest as feelings of guilt? Understanding the universality of post-trauma symptoms as situational and not individual has itself been shown to have therapeutic aspects as people are relieved to understand that it is the situation that is causing their problems and not that they are themselves "crazy" (Lipke 2000; Yalom 1995). So what would anticipation do? What would happen with efforts in advance to educate? Might there be education campaigns to help agents of repression understand PITS and recognize symptoms in colleagues?

4. *What would be the effect if protesters who had personal interaction with agents of repression mentioned the symptoms of intrusive thoughts and dreams or other appropriate symptoms? How often would this lead to insight that might help the agent make progress toward understanding his or her condition and defecting in order to avoid PITS? Would knowledge of possible symptoms at least help protesters better understand what is going on and inform their strategic and tactical attempts at repression management?* Those involved in nonviolent civil resistance need to understand PTSD symptoms before they can design and develop appropriate actions. Tailoring actions may be difficult if agents have not become symptomatic. If one-third of them become symptomatic, that is a huge portion, and the problem is widely prevalent—but that still leaves two-thirds who do not have the problems. Any initial attempts to address individuals' symptoms would probably be ill-suited and ineffective. Asking questions rather than making assertions is likely to be more productive. Cross-cultural variations in symptoms and the circumstances that allow for their discussion would also need to be taken into account.

Since people normally react to PITS symptoms as unusual or offensive, might it be more helpful if activists understand that these are actually symptoms of normal people thrust into extraordinary situations? To better empathize with agents of repression and develop creative strategies, nonviolent activists should become familiar with

PITS symptoms, such as unexpected outbursts of irritability, jumpiness (hypervigilance), trouble concentrating, or emotional numbness.

5. *If agents were to be aware that the symptoms are actually common and normal, can this lead to interaction among agents to confirm this among themselves? If so, what impact would this have on the reliability of agents to carry out repression?* This question has to be approached carefully, because agents could suffer ridicule by other agents, either because the others do not have the symptoms or have them only mildly, or because the others have them and do not want to admit it. Symptomatic individuals can be branded as crazy or cowardly. In most cultures, mental problems carry stigma. Hiding symptoms from others is therefore quite common, and people may studiously ignore symptoms rather than admit them even to themselves. Are there times and places where group solidarity and a hope for healing can overcome stigma? Those with authority over agents of repression or people with potential authority, such as local or foreign psychologists, may be best placed to educate potential PITS sufferers. Activists would do well to identify the most effective spokespersons for any campaigns to interrupt repression by educating agents of repression about the dangers of PITS.

6. *Do those suffering from PITS find defection to be a good therapy?* Refusing to take part in violent repression would likely help diminish intrusive imagery such as unwanted thoughts, nightmares, and flashbacks. It may be that defection would only replace such intrusions with a different reality. This would be a healthy form of self-medication. People have used alcohol or intoxicating drugs to self-medicate, a practice that obviously causes worse problems and is unlikely to work well as a permanent solution. Being a workaholic has also been used this way, a method far more amenable to healthy outcomes, but frenzied work is often an effort to push away feelings of trauma that return with intensity later in retirement, when work is no longer available to push them away.

One of the techniques for dealing with intrusive dreams is to consciously write scripts for alternative, healthier endings. This is called "imagery rehearsal therapy," and indications are that it not only helps with the dreams but spreads out to alleviate other symptoms as well

(Moore and Krakow 2010). It would stand to reason that the alternative scripts would work even better if they were not merely imagined but actual reality.

So what would be most promising from the viewpoint of the nonviolent movement may also be most promising from a therapeutic perspective. The nonviolent movement wants agents to at least refrain from following violent orders from the repressive regime, and ideally to become more active in helping the nonviolent opposition. If a case can be made that the individuals being given the orders are also not only better off but in actual therapeutic need of this, then perhaps there are institutions (e.g., local psychologists, religious bodies) who can use this knowledge to create an intervention that benefits everybody involved.

7. *If agents of repression find defection to be good therapy, is there a way of using this knowledge to encourage defections?* This is a new idea that will take time to develop. Studies on actual defectors have not been conducted, but information can be gathered from people who have left any form of violent institution to understand their experiences of defection.

For example, insights can be gleaned from former executioners who turn into death penalty abolitionists. Fred Allen, who was part of the tie-down team in about 120 executions, described in an interview why he had stopped three years earlier:

> I was just working in the shop, then all of a sudden something just triggered in me and I started shaking and I walked back into the house, and my wife asked, "What's the matter?" and I said, "I don't feel good," and tears, uncontrollable tears, was coming out of my eyes. . . . "I just thought about that execution that I did two days ago, and everybody else's that I was involved with." And what it was, was something triggered within and it just—everybody, all of these executions, all of a sudden all sprung forward. (National Public Radio 2000)

Allen spoke later in this interview about his experience of continuing intrusive imagery:

> Just like taking slides in a film projector and having a button and just pushing a button and just watching over and over, him, him, him. I don't know if it's a mental breakdown, I don't know if—it will probably be classified more as a traumatic stress, similar to what the individuals in war had, you know, and they'd come back from the war and it might be three months, it might be two years, it might be five years, all of a sudden they relive it again, and all that has to come out. You see, I can barely even talk because I'm thinking more and more of it, you know. There was just so many of them.

Several former execution staff people have written about and actively campaigned against the death penalty. This suggests that, at least for some people, the initial acts were indeed traumatic and active opposition to the actions that traumatized them is plausibly therapeutic. Wardens who have written full autobiographical books opposing the death penalty include Donald Cabana (1996) and Jerry Givens (2012). Warden Alan Ault (2011) oversaw five executions, and in one of many interviews reports: "The men and women who assist in executions are not psychopaths or sadists. They do their best to perform the impossible and inhumane job with which the state has charged them. Those of us who have participated in executions often suffer something very much like posttraumatic stress. Many turn to alcohol and drugs. For me, those nights that weren't sleepless were plagued by nightmares." As early as the 1800s, James Berry served as a hangman for over a hundred people, but spent his later years actively campaigning against the death penalty; he kept a diary showing that his post-trauma symptoms were extensive (Atholl 1956).

Was writing and talking about opposition to the death penalty therapeutic? Probably; expressing is commonly understood as helpful therapy for trauma. In this case, that expression provides a service by perhaps helping others avoid the traumatizing activity. This provides the further therapeutic benefit of helping to undo the sense of helplessness, a common exacerbating feature of feeling traumatized. Former agents of state violence, such as Ault and Berry, may also serve as important interlocutors with former colleagues, offering critiques of state violence, modeling defection, raising awareness about the psychological dangers of violence and repression, and introducing sufferers to therapeutic options.

Except for James Berry, these are all US cases where the behavior that executions were intended to repress is premeditated murder. Most people regard such behavior as worthy of repression, including those who oppose executions as the proper response. Those being executed are not liable to receive the same kind of sympathy that nonviolent activists can generate. Thus, the knowledge that defections from death penalty practice do come about with people who report trauma symptoms portends well for the hope of strategically encouraging such defections.

The cases relayed above showed that people who obeyed orders and were traumatized by their own actions can turn out to campaign against the orders. There was no intervention that caused this to occur, other than critiques by death penalty opponents and their willingness to welcome and cooperate with whistleblowers. It may be that more defections among execution staff could have come about with a more developed intervention, just as it is possible that interventions with this knowledge may encourage defections among agents of repression.

Conclusion

There are several ways that repression can backfire. A country's elite or international groups can offer condemnation and thus embarrass those who carried out the repression. An ally can be aghast and withdraw. Most particularly, repression can get people excited and focused and angry, and make the movement it was supposed to repress actually grow.

However, repression can also affect those individuals expected to carry it out. If it leads to massive defections or to collective inaction—a decision to stop engaging in the repressive tactics—then the backfire goes to the very heart of any institution's ability to carry out further repression as its power disappears.

Erica Chenoweth and Maria J. Stephan (2011) found defections associated with the size of nonviolent campaigns. More protesters, more defectors. More protesters contribute to a sense or calculation that the campaign will succeed and that it is time for agents of repression to jump ship. More protesters also generate more chances for interaction between agents of repression and the protesters themselves, allowing more opportunities to undermine fear of one another and socially redefine the situation.

The Milgram electroshock experiments demonstrated that authorities often define the situation so as to bring about destructive obedience to authority. However, the experiments also revealed the potential for rebellion to authority. One major condition that could prompt rebellion is that a contract that the authority made is broken (say, a stolen election, or not paying agents of repression). Another major condition is that there are authorities who argue with each other, so if one is a problem, activists can try bringing in another to counter the first (say, the government and the main religious institution).

Another strategy that psychology experiments affirm is the importance of outside insight and influence. In some cases, outsiders are able to see what is not obvious to insiders, as happened with Christina Maslach, who initiated the termination of the Stanford Prison Experiment. Teaching the agents and those in their circles about the dynamics of repression through reference to an outside conflict with which they have nothing to do can allow them to learn in a way that does not arouse defenses. Then they are in a better position to apply what they have learned to their own situation.

Agents of repression have been conditioned and desensitized, but novel and creative approaches crafted by people who are aware of this can break through this conditioning. There tends to be high group solidarity among the agents, and while this often works as a front against protesters, it can also serve as an aid when dealt with carefully. Agents often have fears, especially of their superiors and of what happens to them in the aftermath of conflict, all of which can be addressed during nonviolent civil resistance campaigns. However, agents will often be more impressed by words from authorities they respect than by the most articulate protester.

Finally, there is the pioneering area of dealing with PITS, post-trauma symptoms from committing acts of violence. It would be a more satisfying conclusion to report on what interventions have been done so far and give advice on techniques that might be adapted to different cultures. However, we do not yet have studies, because first we need to understand the concepts that these studies might test. As the field of nonviolent action progresses, we should be able to study what does and does not work, and then offer more practical advice.

Nonviolent activists have attempted to cause defections by being friendly, being understanding, and making it clear to potential defectors that being among the protesters is a safe place. How much more can we encourage defections if we are educated and mindful of the psychological dynamics that can lead to them? As Mohandas Gandhi ([1940] 2005, 80) said, "We are constantly being astonished these days at the amazing discoveries in the field of violence. But I maintain that far more undreamt of and seemingly impossible discoveries will be made in the field of nonviolence." In general, the study of psychology is a treasure trove of concepts and experiments that can be explored for such discoveries. In particular, knowing how violent acts are traumatizing to those who commit them, and crafting interventions accordingly, is one of those discoveries that more experience can give us.

References

American Psychiatric Association. 2013. *Diagnostic and Statistical Manual of Mental Disorders*, 5th ed. Washington, DC: American Psychiatric Association.

Atholl, J. 1956. *The Reluctant Hangman: The Story of James Berry, Executioner 1884–1892*. London: John Long Limited.

Ault, Alan. 2011. "I Ordered Death in Georgia: The State's Former D.O.C. Commissioner on 'Rehearsed Murder.'" *The Daily Beast*, Sep. 25. https://prisonwatchnetwork.org/category/alan-ault/.

Bandura, A., Barbanelli, C., Caprara, G. V., and Pastorelli, C. 1996. "Mechanisms of Moral Disengagement in the Exercise of Moral Agency." *Journal of Personality and Social Psychology* 71: 364–74.

Binder, A., P. Scharf, and R. Galvin. 1982. *Use of Deadly Force by Police Officers: Final Report*. Washington, DC: National Institute of Justice.

Binnendijk, Anika Locke, and Ivan Marovic. 2006. "Power and Persuasion: Nonviolent Strategies to Influence State Security Forces in Serbia 2000 and Ukraine 2004." *Communist and Post-Communist Studies* 39: 411–29. https://tavaana.org/sites/default/files/power_and_persuasion_-_pdf_-_english.pdf.

Blass, T. 2000. *Obedience to Authority: Current Perspectives on the Milgram Paradigm*. Mahwah, NJ: Lawrence Erlbaum Associates.

Brennan, W. 1995. *Dehumanizing the Vulnerable: When Word Games Take Lives*. Chicago: Loyola Univ. Press.

Cabana, Donald A. 1996. *Death at Midnight: The Confession of an Executioner*. Boston: Northeastern Univ. Press.

Cascio, Wayne F., and Fred Luthans. 2013. "Reflections on the Metamorphosis at Robben Island: The Role of Institutional Work and Positive Psychology Capital." *Journal of Management Inquiry*, Feb. 5. Sage Journals Online.

Chenoweth, Erica, and Maria J. Stephan. 2011. *Why Civil Resistance Works: The Strategic Logic of Nonviolent Conflict*. New York: Columbia Univ. Press.

Collins, Randall. 2008. *Violence: A Micro-sociological Theory*. Princeton, NJ: Princeton Univ. Press.

Fanon, Frantz. 1961. *The Wretched of the Earth*. New York: Grove Press, Inc.

Gandhi, Mohandas. [1940] 2005. *All Men Are Brothers: Autobiographical Reflections*. Edited by K. Kripalani. New York: Continuum.

Givens, Jerry. 2012. *Another Day Is Not Promised*. Bloomington, IN: Westblow Press.

Grossman, Dave. 1995. *On Killing: The Psychological Cost of Learning to Kill in War and Society*. Boston: Little, Brown and Company.

Grossman, Dave, and Bruce Siddle. 2008. "Psychological Effects of Combat." In *Encyclopedia of Violence, Peace and Conflict*, 2d ed., edited by Lester R. Kurtz, 1796–1805. Amsterdam: Elsevier.

Haney, C. 2000. "Reflections on the Stanford Prison Experiment: Genesis, Transformations, Consequences." In *Obedience to Authority: Current Perspectives on the Milgram Paradigm*, edited by Thomas Blass, 193–237. Mahwah, NJ: Lawrence Erlbaum Associates.

Huggins, Martha K., Mika Haritos-Fatouros, and Philip G. Zimbardo. 2002. *Violence Workers: Police Torturers and Murderers Reconstruct Brazilian Atrocities*. Berkeley: Univ. of California Press.

Johnstad, P. G. 2012. "When the Time Is Right: Regime Legitimacy as a Predictor of Nonviolent Protest Outcome." *Peace and Change* 37: 516–43.

Lipke, H. 2000. *EMDR and Psychotherapy Integration*. Boca Raton, FL: CRC Press.

MacNair, Rachel M. 2002. *Perpetration-Induced Traumatic Stress: The Psychological Consequences of Killing*. Westport, CT: Praeger.

Marshall, S. L. A. 1947. *Men against Fire*. New York: Morrow.

Milgram, Stanley. 1974. *Obedience to Authority: An Experimental View*. New York: Harper and Row.

Moore, Bret A., and Barry Krakow. 2010. "Imagery Rehearsal Therapy: An Emerging Treatment for Posttraumatic Nightmares in Veterans." *Psychological Trauma: Theory, Research, Practice, and Policy*, 23: 232–38.

National Public Radio. 2000. "Witness to an Execution, An Extraordinary Glimpse into the Chambers of a Texas Death House." *All Things Considered*, Oct. 12.

Osofsky, Michael J., Albert Bandura, and Philip G. Zimbardo. 2005. "The Role of Moral Disengagement in the Execution Process." *Law and Human Behavior* 294: 371–93.

Salomon, G. 2004. "Does Peace Education Make a Difference in the Context of an Intractable Conflict?" *Peace and Conflict: A Journal of Peace Psychology* 103: 257–74.

Silva, J. A., D. V. Derecho, G. B. Leong, R. Weinstock, and M. M. Ferrari. 2001. "A Classification of Psychological Factors Leading to Violent Behavior in Posttraumatic Stress Disorder." *Journal of Forensic Sciences* 46: 309–16.

Smith, D. L. 2011. *Less than Human: Why We Demean, Enslave, and Exterminate Others*. New York: St. Martin's Press.

Southwick, S. M., R. Yehuda, and C. A. Morgan. 1995. "Clinical Studies of Neurotransmitter Alterations in Post-Traumatic Stress Disorder." In *Neurobiological and Clinical Consequences of Stress*, edited by M. J. Friedman, D. S. Charney, A. Y. Deutch, 335–50. Philadelphia: Lippincott-Raven.

World Health Organization. 1992. *International Statistical Classification of Diseases and Related Health Problems*, 10th rev. Geneva, Switzerland.

Yalom, I. 1995. *The Theory and Practice of Group Psychotherapy*. New York: Basic Books.

5

Backfire Online

Studying Reactions to the Repression of Internet Activism

Jessica L. Beyer and Jennifer Earl

In January 2011, Egypt exploded in protest. Inspired by similar events in Tunisia and propelled by a list of grievances, including unemployment and harsh treatment by authorities, thousands of Egyptian men and women took to the streets demanding reform. While the grievances were timeless, one of the central mechanisms facilitating the protests was not. The Egyptians protesting used digital media—in particular, social networking websites such as Facebook—to criticize the regime, organize collective action, and connect to other protesters. A central rallying point was a Facebook page in memory of Khaled Said, a blogger the Egyptian police beat to death for exposing corruption in their ranks.

In a survey of Egyptian protesters' media use in February 2011, Tufekci and Wilson (2012, 370) found that about 28 percent of protesters became aware of the protest using Facebook. They also found that protesters who used online sources for general information were more likely to have attended the protests on the first day—with early participants in the demonstrations using social networking sites such as Facebook, email, and phones for information (371–73). As Tufekci and Wilson point out, in repressive contexts, small protests are extremely

We would like to thank Heidi Reynolds-Stenson for her research assistance.

dangerous to participants. Thus, the hard work of online activists in the time leading up to the first protest in January 2011 was key to empowering people who had never protested previously—two-thirds of those surveyed (376).

In response to the integral role of the Internet in facilitating the protests, the Mubarak regime attempted to "turn off" the Internet in Egypt on January 28, 2011. This effort managed to wipe out most Egyptian Internet traffic, but when the Internet went dark, more people spilled out into the streets (Howard and Hussain 2011, 39). Although the Mubarak regime could halt digital traffic, it could not stop people's curiosity (which, in the blackout, could only be satisfied by physically going to protest spots) or willingness to continue putting themselves at risk for change. In the end, the Internet blackout cost the Egyptian economy at least $90 million (Olson 2011) and helped to push forward the protests that ended Mubarak's reign.

As this example illustrates, repression and backfire are not just phenomena that affect offline protest. While scholars are most familiar with thinking about the repression of traditional, offline movements, we argue that repression also occurs with some frequency in reaction to Internet activism. Sometimes, that repression takes place online—as, for example, with the censorship or monitoring of specific websites—but repression may also bleed offline, for instance, occurring when online protesters are arrested.

We lay the foundation for a robust study of repression and its consequences online, particularly backfire, by examining several topics in turn. First, we examine what protest can look like online. Because Internet activism means so many different things to different people, it is important to understand the range of activities authorities might seek to repress. Second, we describe the different forms online repression might take. Some forms of repression, such as the arrests discussed above, will be familiar to students of repression. But other forms of repression, such as shutting down websites, are unique to the online environment. Throughout this discussion, we examine cases where repression has been thwarted, as we begin to introduce the dynamics of online backfire. Third, we move squarely to unpacking the effects of repression by examining the backfire and deterrent effects of repression. We delineate between a large number of actors—from individuals to groups and wider publics—to describe how scholars can identify both backfire and deterrent effects of repression of Internet activism at different levels and/or on different kinds of actors.[1] We close with a consideration of three lines of inquiry that could further research on the paradox of repression, and the study of repressive consequences more generally, both online and offline. Our goal across these four topics is to lay a solid theoretical foundation for future research on backfire and attempts to repress Internet activism.

Distinguishing between Different Types of Internet Activism

Just as there are myriad ways to support social movements and protest offline, there are also a large number of ways to support movements, and even to engage in protest, while online, whether that involves accessing and distributing forbidden information on the Falun Gong in China, participating in a distributed denial of service (DDoS) attack[2] to protest a corporate decision, or collaborating with others through online chats and posting boards to organize coordinated offline protest rallies. While this level of variation is a boon for social movements—offering people many avenues through which to engage and support movements—the diversity of forms of Internet activism serve as a challenge to scholars. In particular, because the covering term "Internet activism" can refer to so many widely divergent forms of action, it can be hard to understand the growing welter of findings about online activism (Earl and Kimport 2011).

1. In discussing backfire, we use the broad definition endorsed by Chenoweth (chapter 2), which sees backfire as an outcome of repression that authorities (whether regime or private) would not desire.

2. A DDoS attack occurs when a group attempts to make a web resource inaccessible to valid users by flooding it with so many requests that it cannot handle the traffic and subsequently shuts down or crashes. Some online activists argue that DDoS attacks are the online equivalent of a sit-in.

To organize our discussion, we borrow a typology of Internet activism introduced by Earl, Kimport, Prieto, Rush, and Reynoso (2010) that identifies four different broad types of Internet activism. First, the Internet can be used to support movements through brochure-ware, a type of Internet activism that sees information provision as critical to supporting movements and uses the Internet primarily to distribute information (Earl et al. 2010). This distribution may include simple implementations, such as static webpages, or complex implementations, which involve very dynamic and media-rich websites. For instance, digital rights activists have disseminated information about decrypting DVDs, particularly for operating systems like Linux where DVD decryption software was not initially licensed (Eschenfelder, Howard, and Desai 2005; Eschenfelder and Desai 2004; Postigo 2012). The lack of licensed decryption made DVD drives in Linux machines relatively useless until digital activists stepped in. Likewise, supporters of the Falun Gong in China have tried to distribute information about the forbidden group online, where it is usually censored by Chinese authorities (Faris and Villeneuve 2008).

Second, the Internet can be used to recruit for and support offline protest events (as our opening example illustrated), which Earl and Kimport (2011) refer to as e-mobilization. Implementations may be as simple as advertising for an upcoming event on an online calendar, or may involve providing potential participants downloadable signs, access to rides, roomshare boards, and other coordinating tools. Anonymous's emergence as a political actor in early 2008 included using the Internet for e-mobilization. As Beyer describes, in late January 2008, the online collective Anonymous moved from engaging solely in online actions—such as DDoS attacks against Church of Scientology websites and faxing reams of black paper to church offices—to organizing offline protests (Beyer 2014a). The first offline protests took place outside Scientology buildings around the world on February 10, 2008, at 11 a.m. local time.

To organize these offline protests, people used a wide range of online tools. Some discussed the action using posting boards and Internet Relay Chat (IRC), others used YouTube to disseminate information about the protest itself and the laws governing protest in different locations, and local subsets of Anonymous created their own posting board systems to communicate about each specific protest (Beyer 2014a; Coleman 2015). Online sources instructed potential protesters on how to behave and what to say if questioned by law enforcement, the media, passersby, or Scientology members. Participants used online forums to distribute flyers for the protest, and, in various online locations, veteran activists offered advice for how to prepare to protest—such as suggesting that protesters wear comfortable shoes and bring something to hide their faces from Church of Scientology officials.

Following this extensive online coordination, protests occurred in 108 cities across seventeen countries on February 10. Between five thousand and eight thousand individuals participated in what was the first in a series of offline protests organized online by Anonymous members (Beyer 2014a). Over time, Anonymous protests have continued, including smaller scale, offline actions. In November 2013, Anonymous held the "Million Mask March," which occurred in more than four hundred cities around the world (Cameron 2013).

Third, the Internet can be used to actually organize online protest campaigns or movements. For instance, Earl and Schussman (2003; Schussman and Earl 2004) studied the online strategic voting movement that developed in the closing days of the 2000 presidential election, which featured a notoriously tight race between George W. Bush and Al Gore. Both candidates faced third-party challenges—Pat Buchanan threatened to pull right-leaning supporters away from Bush, and many worried that Ralph Nader would pull left-leaning supporters away from Gore. Strategic voting offered a way to work around this dilemma, and, for some, it also offered a way to secure in-practice voting reforms that had been long sought, such as instant runoff voting. Websites were created that allowed individuals to "trade" votes with one another across state lines. For instance, it was common for a left-leaning voter in a highly contested state to agree to vote for Gore if a left-leaning voter in a fairly uncontested state would agree to vote for Nader. It is clear that the movement to identify and match these like-minded, but unconnected, individuals could not have developed as quickly, or had as far a reach, without the benefit of the web. Likewise, Gurak (1999,

1997; Gurak and Logie 2003) studied a number of campaigns against corporate and government targets that all played out entirely online and were organized entirely through websites and blogs. More recently, the anti–Stop Online Piracy Act (SOPA) campaign entailed a great deal of virtual coordination. Also, all of Anonymous's actions, Internet-based and offline, are organized entirely online (Beyer 2014a).

Finally, it is possible for individuals to engage in activism while online; that is, the actual form of participation takes place over the Internet. Conventional versions of online participation involve online petition signing and/or email campaigns. However, more controversial Internet-enabled forms of participation, such as DDoS attacks (Vegh 2003), have also been used. As we have already indicated, this has been a favorite tactic of Anonymous. One of the most well-known examples of an Anonymous DDoS attack is the 2010 mobilization against Visa, MasterCard, and PayPal on behalf of WikiLeaks, a whistleblowing website (Cohen 2010). Anonymous rallied to support WikiLeaks in 2010 after these corporations succumbed to US governmental pressure and cut ties with the website, removing critical infrastructure and severely crippling its ability to raise money or stay online (Beyer 2014b; Coleman 2015; Earl and Beyer 2014).

It is important to distinguish between these different types of Internet activism for several reasons. First, these distinctions remind scholars that "Internet activism" is not a unitary concept and that different dynamics may be at work in each different type of online protest. Second, they give readers a map for understanding the diversity of examples that are regularly reported in the media. Finally, and most importantly, these distinctions help us to understand what kinds of repression might be directed at each form of Internet activism. We turn to this topic next.

Repressing "Internet Activism"

We identify several basic kinds of repression that public and private authorities might engage in online (although our list is meant to be illustrative, not exhaustive). First, *public authorities might try to limit access to particular types of information or particular online locations.* For instance, in response to the strategic voting movement, several state-level secretaries of state and elections officials decided that strategic voting sites were engaged in illegal brokering of votes and, thus, sent cease and desist letters to have the websites removed. The letters threatened webmasters with criminal prosecution, often warning of separate counts for each vote matched through the website. As Earl and Schussman (2004) found, these threats were enough to convince several webmasters to remove their websites or eliminate aspects of their sites that directly matched voters. Howard (2010) discusses the many ways that authoritarian governments censor online content, such as the case of Iran, where the government more aggressively blocks Farsi language websites than English language websites, and the contrasting case of Oman, where the government focuses on blocking international content over Omani content.

Governments have also worked to block digital rights websites. For instance, in 2006 the US government reportedly threatened the Swedish government with sanctions if it did not close down The Pirate Bay, a popular filesharing website created and run by information activists. Bush Administration representatives told a Swedish trade delegation in Washington, DC, that the sanctions would be implemented along with a World Trade Organization complaint against Sweden for failure to protect intellectual property (Roper 2006).

Diplomatic cables released by WikiLeaks reveal that the US government's preoccupation with The Pirate Bay included worries about how to thwart the growing digital rights movement in Sweden and manage what information was available to the public and supporters. As one of these documents states, "the Government of Sweden struggles, with good intentions, against a very negative media climate and against a vocal youth movement" (Embassy Stockholm 2009a). These documents also indicate that, over time, the US government continued to make closing The Pirate Bay a component in its dealings with the Swedish government.[3] In the same diplomatic cable, the author stated:

3. This can be found in WikiLeaks Document 09STOCKHOLM276_a, which discusses Sweden's potential place on the US government's watch list due to piracy,

> Press coverage was largely, and still is, unfavorable to the positions taken by rights-holders and the U.S. government. The Pirate Bay raid was portrayed as the Government of Sweden caving to U.S. government pressure. The delicate situation made it difficult, if not counter-productive, for the Embassy to play a public role on IPR issues. Behind the scenes, the Embassy has worked well with all stakeholders. (Embassy Stockholm 2009a)

The US government's efforts resulted in some temporary downtime for The Pirate Bay website, although it was limited. As we discuss below, repressors' efforts to remove online content are often contested and may even result in backfire when digital activists work to make the censored content even more widely available.

Second, *private actors might also try to limit information access or access to particular Internet locations* (Earl 2003, 2004). A good example of this kind of activity comes from the Church of Scientology's attempts to limit access to anti-Scientology rhetoric online. As Peckham (1998) reports, the movement against Scientology often used the release of sacred Scientology texts and analyses of those texts as a tactic to indict Scientology. The Church of Scientology reacted through an extensive legal campaign arguing that the Church's copyrights were being violated. Whatever the merits of any given case, a well-funded church with extensive legal resources was facing off against critics with far fewer resources. Peckham argued that the church used this as a way to siphon off resources from critics and to limit access to anti-Scientology material online.

The motion picture industry also has a long history of using litigation to stop behaviors that it felt threatened its intellectual property, even when those same behaviors were seen as movement tactics by digital rights activists. For example, Postigo (2012) discusses the

and discusses The Pirate Bay, in particular (Embassy Stockholm 2009b). WikiLeaks Document 09STOCKHOLM141_a outlines the Swedish government's progress in ending intellectual property violations and mentions The Pirate Bay and the Pirate Party (Embassy Stockholm 2009a).

entertainment industry's response in the late 1990s to efforts by digital rights activists to distribute software—known as DeCSS—that enabled Linux operating systems to play DVDs. As mentioned above, the Linux development community distributed DeCSS widely, including efforts by digital rights activists who believed that the code should be openly accessible. However, the entertainment industry viewed these actions as a violation of its intellectual property rights and, in response, filed two cases, one in California and one in New York, against individuals or collectivities posting or linking to DeCSS online (Postigo 2012, 88). As we discuss below, these private attempts to censor material are often met with attempts to widely distribute suppressed content.

Third, *state authorities might use the Internet as a tool for surveillance.* For example, in some Arab states, authorities have allegedly monitored social networking sites and posts to learn more about a movement and its members (Howard 2010). In fact, the ability of authorities to use the Internet for surveillance and repression, as evidenced in the Arab world, is one of the primary indictments that Internet activism critic Morozov (2011) has made. Likewise, Yang (2011) reports that the Chinese state uses a range of approaches for policing interactive online spaces, including relying on site owners' monitoring of content. If site owners do not monitor their spaces to the satisfaction of Chinese authorities, the state sends officials to have "informal" conversations with website owners to request that they do a better job of policing content (Yang 2011). Here again, as we will discuss more below, there are ways for activists to fight back. For instance, awareness of surveillance in China has caused online participants to develop sophisticated visual tactics, such as image-based puns, for avoiding the eyes of the state hired censors and for evading mechanized surveillance tactics, such as keyword filters (Wiener 2011).

Finally, *state authorities are likely to employ the same arsenal of repressive tools they have used to target leaders of offline movements against leaders and participants in online movements.* Authorities might arrest actors involved in, or thought to be organizing, online protests. While this seems like an activity that would only occur in nondemocratic nations, two people have been arrested for their Twitter use during the G20 protests in Pittsburgh (Citizen Media Law Project 2010; Moynihan 2009). Police argued that the individuals had compromised police by tweeting about police activity. A raid on one of the accused's apartment followed the arrests.

Similar events have unfolded in the United Kingdom. Following the August 2011 riots in England, individuals were held accountable for anything that they had posted online that was thought to have furthered the offline unrest. Two young men were sentenced to four years for their posts on Facebook about the riots, although neither Facebook post resulted in any offline behavior, and neither man physically participated in the riots (Bowcott, Siddique and Sparrow 2011). The seemingly disproportionate harshness of the sentences was likely attributable to the fact that magistrates received a memo from senior justice clerks telling them to ignore sentencing guidelines when dealing with the rioters (Ford Rojas, Whitehead, and Kirkup 2011; Travis, Ball and Bawdon 2011). Indeed, the imprisonment rate for those arrested during the riots was 43 percent—a significant increase from similar arrests in 2010, when the imprisonment rate was 12 percent—and sentences were two or three times longer than past sentences for similar crimes (Travis, Ball, and Bawdon 2011).

The harsh sentencing is similar to the prison time Anonymous members have received for participating in actions such as DDoS attacks. In 2009, after being found guilty for his involvement in the 2008 DDoS attacks against Church of Scientology websites, Dmitriy Guzner was sentenced to pay over $37,000 in restitution and to serve a 366-day federal prison term and two years of probation (Associated Press 2009). One response to this kind of repression in more authoritarian countries has been to try to publicize government action in hopes of gaining international attention and creating international pressure.

"Crossing" Internet Activism Types with Repressive Activities

Thus far, we have treated different forms of Internet activism and different types of repression as independent. In Table 5.1, we further this examination by "crossing" these two dimensions. The table outlines what these different forms of repression look like when directed at each

TABLE 5.1 Examples of Repression across Different Types of Internet Activism

	Brochure-ware	*Online Facilitation of Offline Protest*	*Online Organizing*	*Online Participation*
Public authorities limit online access	Chinese authorities attempted to limit information about Falun Gong online.	Egyptian authorities "turned off" the Internet during the 2011 Arab Spring.	Secretaries of state used their power to try to force website operators to remove strategic voting sites (Earl and Schussman 2004).	Authorities worked to stop the reproduction and distribution of DeCSS code online.
Private authorities limit online access	Companies such as Amazon limited the online presence of WikiLeaks on behalf of the US government.	Twitter spoke to the British government about limiting Twitter use during periods of social unrest following the 2011 British riots.	The Church of Scientology works to limit anti-Scientology materials online and reduce the online resources of critics (Peckham 1998).	Twitter has a history of banning Anonymous accounts. In addition, Facebook has taken down protest-related sites, which reduced participation (Earl 2012).
Public authorities engage in surveillance	Surveillance systems are used to watch for information requests and to monitor activists.	The Chinese government has one of the most sophisticated Internet surveillance systems in the world, which it uses to target dissent online and punish activists. The state reacts particularly harshly to speech that proposes offline meetings or protest.	The Chinese government allows certain types of criticism in online speech, but there are limits to what is acceptable. Extensive mechanized controls and human-powered surveillance mean that speech organizing protest of any kind is treated harshly.	After arresting Sabu in June 2011, the FBI used him as an informant to gather information then used in the arrests of others.

TABLE 5.1 Examples of Repression across Different Types of Internet Activism *(continued)*

	Brochure-ware	*Online Facilitation of Offline Protest*	*Online Organizing*	*Online Participation*
Public authorities target leaders or participants for offline repression (e.g., arrests)	Governments around the world have arrested individuals for simply posting online.	The Chinese government arrests individuals for using text that is considered to be facilitating offline protest.	The Chinese government arrests and/or visits individuals who are engaging in online discussion that it feels is dangerous.	Anonymous members involved in DDoS attacks have been arrested.

Source: Jessica L. Beyer and Jennifer Earl

of the four different types of Internet activism we outlined in the first section of the chapter. In each case, we provide illustrative examples.

Where brochure-ware is concerned (see first column of Table 5.1), examples of all four styles of repression exist. Chinese attempts to prevent access to information about the Falun Gong, or Arab states' efforts to limit access to specific types of information, represent our first repressive form applied to brochure-ware. The role of Visa, MasterCard, and other companies in limiting the online presence of WikiLeaks on behalf of US government interests represents an example of private action to limit information access (Beyer 2014b; Earl and Beyer 2014). The use of surveillance systems to monitor for requests for censored information and to monitor activists illustrates the application of the third type of repressive response to brochure-ware (Deibert, Palfrey, Rohozinski, and Zittrain 2008, 2010). Finally, the arrest of individuals for simply posting online, as we have noted occurs in both democratic and authoritarian nations, represents the use of traditional forms of repression to control brochure-ware/information access.

In response to attempts to repress online activists distributing brochure-ware, activists may take advantage of the distributed nature of the Internet to publicize the effects of the crackdown, making repression visible. For example, as mentioned, the Khaled Said memorial Facebook page became a central touchstone for ordinary Egyptians when Said's brother posted a photo showing his savagely beaten face (Howard and Hussain 2011, 38). The image was circulated among thousands of people using cell phones, email, and websites, and ultimately inspired many people to participate in protests. Other types of online information distribution can also be hard to stop. For instance, the use of mirror websites (i.e., content copied and hosted on a variety of sites) can be particularly effective in evading efforts to stop brochure-ware, as we will discuss below.

All four styles of repression can also be found in examining the online facilitation of offline action, also known as e-mobilization (Earl and Kimport 2011), as outlined in the second column of Table 5.1. As discussed at the start of this chapter, Egyptian authorities, who were worried that Facebook and other online tools were contributing to growing mobilizations, limited online access in late January 2011 by "turning off" the Internet. However, the move backfired, resulting in far greater protest participation.

At times, private companies can be complicit in attempts to limit online tools that facilitate offline action. Following the British riots in 2011, Twitter met with the British government to discuss strategies for limiting use of the platform in future instances of social unrest. The Chinese government and other authoritarian regimes regularly engage in surveillance by monitoring online speech about offline protest. The Chinese government even uses text that is considered to facilitate offline protest as the justification for arrest and persecution of activists and others, thereby applying traditional means of repression against those that directly support offline protest using digital tools (Yang 2011).

In response to efforts to quell e-mobilization, activists may use popular social networking websites and other websites that have broad audiences. In doing so, activists both hide among the masses of nonactivists, but also increase the possibility that repression of online content will help convince others to participate in protest. For example, Zuckerman (2008) has put forward the "Cute Cat Theory," which argues that when governments attempt to stop online activism by banning social websites, nonactivists will be radicalized because their government's censorship prevents them from engaging in innocuous pleasures, such as looking at cute cats online.

Individuals and groups attempting to use online tools to organize dissent are also frequently targeted with each of these four kinds of repression (see third column of Table 5.1). Earl and Schussman (2004) found that various secretaries of state put considerable pressure on website owners of strategic voting movement websites to remove their sites. This is an example of authorities trying to limit access to organizing tools online. In relation to private authorities working to limit online organizing, as stated previously, Peckham (1998) found that the Church of Scientology worked hard to reduce the online resources of critics. The Chinese government also engages in surveillance of online discussion in an attempt to identify online organizing and organizers that it feels are dangerous; it, at times, also takes a more aggressive posture toward these organizers, including arrests or holding informal warning visits.

To facilitate online organizing in the face of repression, people may attempt to use clever and easily used tactics to avoid state repression that the general public may also adopt. For example, Chinese Internet users will speak in terms of the "river crab"—a word that sounds very much like the word "harmony" when said out loud. Bloggers whose posts have been censored will often state that the posts have been "harmonized" (Wines 2009). Thus, the river crab becomes one of many ways to speak about state action in such a way that evades state censors (Fisher 2012). In another example, Porzucki (2012) relates a conversation she had with an interview subject who mentioned seeing a reference to an "eight times eight incident" online. The words "Tiananmen Square" and the date of the incident, 6/4, are both censored online—but eight multiplied by eight equals 64. Using evasive language enables Chinese citizens to criticize the government and even organize protests under the eyes of the state.

In another example, in 2011, the Chinese government arrested famed Chinese artist and government critic Ai Weiwei and charged him with tax evasion. After a harsh eighty-one-day detention, he was slapped with a huge fine that the government claimed was what he owed in taxes. In response, people organizing on Chinese microblogging services, such as Sina Weibo, began transferring funds directly into his bank account, while others mailed him money through the postal service or threw money over the walls of his garden. The action was not sufficient to cause a state crackdown, but it was large-scale enough to show widespread support for Weiwei (Ramzy 2011).

Finally, participants who use the Internet to participate in protest while online have also been targeted for different types of repression (see last column of Table 5.1). In the previously mentioned case of DeCSS code reproduction and distribution, public authorities attempted to limit online access to the code and prevent its distribution without much success.[4] In the case of private authorities limiting online access, both Twitter and Facebook have frustrated activists through account banning and/or removal of protest related pages, sometimes without prompting from authorities (Earl 2012).

Activists have an array of tools available to counter efforts to stop online participation in protest. They may use tools that are more difficult for law enforcement to track and find, such as Internet Relay Chat. Further, activists may use tools that require low sunk costs to set up, such as Twitter accounts or very simple websites, which can be resurrected without much trouble if the account or website is banned or blocked. In 2010, as Anonymous engaged in DDoS attacks against corporate entities such as MasterCard on behalf of WikiLeaks, it used Twitter to announce DDoS targets. These Twitter accounts were frequently banned, but as soon as one central informational node was shut down, new accounts opened to continue disseminating information.

4. Postigo (2012) argues that, for digital rights activists, distributing suppressed code such as DeCSS is itself a movement tactic. Because information access is a core movement concern, directly providing access to suppressed code moves an action from being merely an information provision to an actual tactic in the digital rights movement. This is not dissimilar to other kinds of classic nonviolent interventions, such as claiming and using a shared resource such as water.

The bans themselves encouraged many people to create accounts and begin sharing content, creating informational resilience in the face of the crackdown.

Still focusing on the last column of Table 5.1, governments of all types have a long history of using surveillance as a way to catch individuals engaging in subversive activities. For example, in March 2012 it was revealed that longtime Anonymous participant and LulzSec member Sabu had become an FBI informant after his secret arrest in June 2011. As an informant, he had been reporting on Anonymous, LulzSec, and others to authorities who then used the information to arrest people (Brodkin 2012). Governments also use classic repressive techniques, such as arrests of online protest participants. An example of this is the arrest and trials of Anonymous members involved in DDoS attacks.

The use of surveillance is meant to quell activism both by making it difficult for activists to organize without opening themselves up to repression and by making people too fearful to engage in forbidden online activity. Often, such surveillance is not secret. For example, requiring users to enter identifying information before accessing the Internet in Internet cafes is intended to make people aware that their every click is monitored. In Syria, prior to the civil war, Internet café owners had been required to log any comments people posted online since 2007 (Steavenson 2011). Thus, activists who wish to use online resources to disseminate information, organize online or offline protests, or look for forbidden information may choose to anonymize themselves online using tools such as Tor, Virtual Private Networks, and pseudonyms. Zuckerman (2008) points out that surveillance can cause average users to educate themselves about how to remain anonymous online, which is presumably the opposite effect the state is hoping to have.

As is evident from this discussion, there are a wide variety of kinds of Internet activism, a wide variety of ways that authorities try to limit that activism, and a variety of reactions to that repression. In the next section, we focus on how repression might lead to backfire or serve as a deterrent force.

Backfire and Deterrence

One of the most hotly debated issues in research on repression involves the effects of repression (Davenport 2007), and numerous reviews of the scholarship show that there are a wide variety of hypotheses regarding repression's effects. Even more confusingly, there is empirical evidence supporting divergent hypotheses (Earl and Soule 2010; Earl 2011). Out of all the potential effects, the effect that authorities are presumably hoping for involves deterrence; by raising the costs of participation, authorities hope that protest will become less desirable (Opp and Roehl 1990). But it is possible that repression backfires—creating the paradox of repression that is the subject of this volume. As Chenoweth (chapter 2) argues, backfire can be defined as any unanticipated consequences of repression that authorities do not desire. Research has been unable to create a unified account of when repression is likely to lead to backfire versus deterrence (or some other outcome).

We argue that one of the reasons research has been so conflicted is that too little attention has been paid to differences in how repression may affect different kinds of actors, ranging from individuals to larger publics. Thus, we try to advance research on repression generally, and research on the repression of Internet activism specifically, by tracing how backfire and deterrence would operate at different levels when Internet activism is repressed: its effects on individuals, activist networks, and movements.[5]

Effects on Individuals

Many of the examples already cited in this chapter involve repression that is targeted at individuals and, therefore, is likely to have individual-level effects. In criminology, punishments that are meant to dissuade specific individuals (i.e., protesters in this case) from engaging

5. To reduce complexity, we do not cross these levels of effect with the types of Internet activism and repression discussed in Table 5.1. However, we hope that future scholarship will undertake this complication.

in an activity are said to provide *specific* deterrence. When specific deterrence is effective, online organizers or participants will limit or entirely stop their protest engagements.

Conversely, individuals may be radicalized by repression (Hirsch 1990). Online organizers or participants might find repression to be offensive, they might develop additional grievances as a result of repression, or they may simply become more committed to their cause after considering whether the cause was worth their sacrifice. For instance, in 2009, four men—three of whom were information activists—were tried and convicted for their involvement running the popular filesharing website The Pirate Bay. The Pirate Bay's administrators framed their involvement in filesharing in political terms—government repression was the result of an overreaching United States, particularly regarding copyright and intellectual property, and the entertainment industry's attacks were symptomatic of overly restrictive intellectual property laws and corporate profit overriding all other considerations (Beyer 2011). In the aftermath of the trial and after exhausting all appeals, one of the three individuals, Peter Sunde, faced an eight-month prison sentence and a fine in the millions (Essers 2013). While this might be enough to dissuade many, Sunde remained committed to political reform and was the Finnish Pirate Party's candidate in the 2014 European Parliament election. In a blog post, Sunde (2013) stated, "I am doing what I can to help solve the problems we have today, as well as the ones we will have in the future. That's why I've decided to participate in the election for the European parliament 2014."

The development of additional grievances and recommitment to a cause can be seen in other contexts as well. For instance, in 2006 Alaa Abd El-Fattah, an Egyptian political activist and a blogger, was arrested along with other bloggers and activists. He was released after over a month in jail and returned to his political activities. El-Fattah was subsequently rearrested for protesting in October 2011 but was not dissuaded from activism. El-Fattah's case could be seen as representative of many political bloggers (Toumi 2013).

Sometimes, however, repression, or the threat of repression, can serve to dissuade individuals who are not subject to repressive actions.

Generalized deterrence, as discussed below, is the deterrent effect of observing or being aware of punishment but not being subject to punishment; it is primarily relevant to bystanders. For example, in April 2009 on the day a new antipiracy law went into effect in Sweden, a number of book publishers applied to the courts to make Internet service providers reveal large-scale filesharers' identities. On the same day, Internet traffic also dropped by 33 percent (BBC 2009); by November 2009 it had returned to pre-April levels (Enigmax 2009). While filesharers often state that they do not believe that what they are doing is wrong, and there is some support for a change in copyright law (Beyer 2014a), the threat of individual legal consequences appeared to be sufficient to cause behavioral change.

Effects on Networks

Repression might also impact networks of activists and the relationships among activists (Starr et al. 2008). For instance, traditional repressive tactics, such as infiltrating groups and then encouraging dissension or distrust, have been used to undermine relationships between activists for some time (Cunningham 2004). Repression directed at Internet activism can have these same impacts, although it can also have the opposite effect.

For instance, while the intent of repression can be to undermine activist networks, repression can strengthen or create network connections among protesters. Beyer (2014b) has argued that there is some indication that online activists (such as Anonymous groups), activists championing transparency (such as those tied to WikiLeaks), and activists pushing for copyright reform (such as the Pirate Parties or The Pirate Bay) are together a nascent freedom of information social movement. These groups do not act in a coordinated manner nor are they officially tied to each other; however, they use common rhetoric about intellectual property law reform, the evils of censorship, and the Internet's potential to transform the world.

This movement toward coordination of activist networks around freedom of information appears to be somewhat inspired by state repression. For example, WikiLeaks volunteers were involved in writing the Icelandic Modern Media Initiative in the aftermath of the 2008 economic collapse, former WikiLeaks volunteers Birgitta Jónsdóttir and Smári McCarthy served as candidates for the Pirate Party in Iceland's 2013 parliamentary election (with Jónsdóttir winning a seat), and the Swedish Pirate Party hosted both WikiLeaks and the Pirate Bay websites in response to state attempts to remove them from the Internet. Whether this "freedom of information" movement reaches its potential or not, its appearance indicates that interaction between people in online spaces and across online activist groups is creating a single network of activists working toward a common goal in a way that, so far, is uncoordinated (Beyer 2014b).

However, when the state turns its full attention to breaking activist networks, the impact felt by online activists can be very similar to the impact felt by offline activists. An Iranian journalist and activist reported to the *Guardian* in May 2013, four years after Iran's so-called Green Revolution, that the sum total of the government's repression has led to a fractured community (Anonymous 2013). He stated that he did not protest in 2009 because he did not believe the street protests would have an impact if the regime was not engaged in a dialogue. Under conditions of anonymity he spoke to the interviewer about the people he knows who have had to flee Iran saying:

> The self-exile of many of my journalist friends . . . I think that was the worst blow. I lost many of my friends, my emotional and professional supports. . . . How long will it take to develop such friendships in my life again? All contacts with friends who have left Iran have been severed, because of my caution and their prudence. I have no contact with anyone on the other side. No one. And you certainly know our situation inside [Iran].

The activists interviewed in the article continue to work for their cause, but all discussed the negative effects of years of state oppression on the movement itself.

At a more informal level, the Iranian blogosphere also suffered from increased state crackdowns. A German media source reported that Arash Abadpour, an Iranian blogger and activist, said that the state's crackdown in the run up to the elections not only had an effect on what people were willing to publish, making them less critical of the government, but also impacted dramatically the number of people willing to read their blogs (Kiani 2012). While this was not necessarily explicitly a weakening of the network, the decrease in those willing to engage in online activity meant that there was an impact on the connections between activists.

It is important to note, though, that although online and offline activist networks may feel similar effects of repression, the ability of online activist networks to draw on the affordances of information and communication technologies may make them more resilient in the face of state repression. The cross-national nature of the Internet means that activists in wired countries can use the Internet to find allies in other contexts, building an international activist network. This is particularly the case when crackdowns on Internet-related activism are part of a censorship campaign. Online there are ready-made freedom of information activist networks that provide support to activists in oppressive contexts, including groups such as Anonymous, WikiLeaks, and Telecomix. For example, WikiLeaks makes leaked government documents available to the world and refuses to give up its sources; the hacktivist collective Anonymous provides "tool kits" and other support to educate people about how to remain anonymous online and will attack government websites on behalf of struggling activists; and the activist group Telecomix offers real-time consulting for activists wanting to learn how to evade state authorities and use digital technology to the fullest. Activists who are able to make their plight known to such groups, and who are able to frame their grievances in such a way as to harmonize with international activist concerns about information freedom, can draw on a broader Internet-savvy activist network.

Effects on Social Movement Organizations

Social movement organizations (SMOs) can be impacted by repression in at least two ways. First, sometimes experiences of repression catalyze SMOs, leading to stronger or more emboldened groups. An illustrative example of this type of process is the political mobilization that has occurred around The Pirate Bay, which has been fostered by groups such as Anonymous and the international Pirate Parties. One of the reasons for The Pirate Bay's fame is its resilience in the face of a concerted effort to remove it from the Internet. While numerous prominent filesharing sites have disappeared due to legal pressure, The Pirate Bay has not only remained online but has continued to frame its online presence in political terms. For example, on March 3, 2013, the official Pirate Bay blog satirically announced that the site would be hosted in North Korea.[6] The post stated that:

> The Pirate Bay has been hunted in many countries around the world. Not for illegal activities but being persecuted for beliefs of freedom of information. . . . This is truly an ironic situation. We have been fighting for a free world, and our opponents are mostly huge corporations from the United States of America, a place where freedom and freedom of speech is said to be held high. At the same time, companies from that country is [*sic*] chasing a competitor from other countries, bribing police and lawmakers, threatening political parties and physically hunting people from our crew. And to our help comes a government famous in our part of the world for locking people up for their thoughts and forbidding access to information.

The Pirate Bay's leadership has continually framed its actions in political terms and, as such, has served as a focal point for individuals interested in copyright reform. Instead of being cowed by state and industry responses to The Pirate Bay, people have become more politically active as illustrated by the success of the Pirate Party, particularly in Sweden and Germany, where it has managed to win seats in various elections (Beyer 2014a).

In contrast, when a large number of members are repressed as individuals, this can have deterrent impacts on the organization, as

6. This was later revealed to be a political joke meant to highlight what the activists running the website view as the hypocrisy of the US government.

social movement organizations absorb many of the costs associated with repression. For example, Barkan (1984) noted the deleterious effect of high bail amounts and attorneys' fees on civil rights SMOs based on mass arrests. Conceptually, one would expect that the same thing could be true with organizations and online activism. However, we were unable to identify example cases of this kind of effect. Instead, we tended to find cases where individuals shouldered a burden instead of a formal SMO.

Given work challenging the dominance of SMOs as organizing vehicles online (Earl and Kimport 2011; Earl 2013), we suspect that our failure to find illustrative examples of this kind of effect was more attributable to the changing organizational infrastructure of online protest, versus a declining interest in repression by authorities. For example, while there were millions of individuals exchanging content through The Pirate Bay website and there were many activists and volunteers involved with running The Pirate Bay, the Swedish government made Svartholm, Sunde, Neij, and Lundström legally responsible for the website by putting them on trial. These four individuals have subsequently paid the very costly legal consequences for the entirety of the filesharing and activist community surrounding The Pirate Bay—something they chose, asking supporters to refrain from donating any money to help their legal struggles. Arguably, The Pirate Bay's actions and the response of the public illustrate that even when individuals shoulder the brunt of state repression, this can lead to the strengthening of an organization whose identity is broader than that of individual leaders.

In addition to enduring the aggregate effects of repression of its individual members, SMOs qua organizations are sometimes targeted for repression. For instance, specific SMOs have historically been banned in some countries. Repression targeted at groups can embolden them or escalate their tactics (Zwerman, Steinhoff, and della Porta 2000; Zwerman and Steinhoff 2005). Anonymous has a history responding to government action offensively. In early 2012, Anonymous participants recorded a conversation between the FBI and the Scotland Yard regarding their investigation into Anonymous. They then released the conference call online (Zetter 2012). The release was part of a series of releases for what Anonymous named "FuckFBIFriday" or #FFF (RT.com 2012), exemplifying Anonymous's challenge to authority figures.[7] This action followed the US government arrests of individuals who participated in pro-WikiLeaks DDoS attacks on corporate websites.

Likewise, in late 2010 following WikiLeaks's release of a trove of US diplomatic cables, the US government began a systematic effort to drive WikiLeaks off the Internet. The effort began with a sustained DDoS attack on WikiLeaks that was followed by US government pressure on an array of corporations to stop providing infrastructural support for the website (Ernesto 2010; O'Connor 2010). WikiLeaks remained online, largely due to the efforts of WikiLeaks volunteers and a broader group of assorted activists, many of whom were associated with Pirate Party International.

Effects on Movements

When individuals or groups are targeted for repression, this can have effects on an entire movement. Movement scholars have tended to fear that repression, particularly using legalistic tactics such as arrests, tends to reduce the legitimacy of a social movement (Barkan 1984; Earl 2005). This may be true online too. For instance, the music and motion picture industries have worked hard to portray the digital rights, or "copyleft," movement as promoting tools that allow stealing (Postigo 2012), as opposed to supporting information and technology freedom.

Of course, sometimes repression actually raises awareness about movements or serves to increase the movement's legitimacy. In leaked US diplomatic cables, authors speak about the dangers of increasing the legitimacy of the movement through crackdowns on The Pirate Bay, particularly crackdowns perceived to originate from the US

7. This action was undertaken by Antisec, a group that is affiliated with Anonymous but was much smaller and made up of more technically savvy individuals.

government. One cable states, "We want to highlight the risk that negative media attention on the filesharing issue gives the Pirate Party a boost in the EU Parliamentary elections in June 2009" (Embassy Stockholm 2009a). Indeed, whenever The Pirate Bay was in the news in Sweden because of its legal woes, the membership of the Swedish Pirate Party grew in response (Beyer 2014a).

Effects on Bystanders

Whereas specific deterrence is designed to discourage the subject of repression from being involved in protest again, generalized deterrence is built around what repression is observed or rumored to be by bystanders. One could think of generalized deterrence as a deterrence multiplier—a smaller amount of repressive resources directed at a few subjects can potentially discourage a much wider pool of potential protesters from participating.

Online, individualized and extremely punitive punishment of actors engaging in forbidden behavior creates an environment in which many are deterred from action. Scholars who study authoritarian contexts acknowledge that repressive tactics surrounding forbidden speech and behavior are an effective aspect of social control (e.g., Wedeen 1999). If a government can create a context in which individuals who defy censorship are punished it may be able to limit dissent online. For example, MacKinnon (2012) argues that in China online speech could be characterized as "authoritarian deliberation." She asserts that while some public debate and activism are occurring online, ultimately the state sets strict limits on permitted political speech, which thwarts democratization efforts. *The Economist* (2013) also calls the state of the Internet in China "adaptive authoritarianism" and reports that "dissidents in China say that freedom is knowing how big your cage is." The incentives for bystanders to self-regulate their speech are high. Freedom House (2013) reports innumerable arrests and other punishment in China related to online speech and has ranked it as "Not Free" with significant numbers of bloggers and other information technology users arrested. For example, individuals involved in websites that reported on Uighur issues were sentenced to prison terms that ranged from fifteen years to life in 2009 following the ethnic violence in Xinjiang (Freedom House 2013). It is difficult to assess whether nondissent in a context such as China is due to generalized deterrence but it is intuitive to assume that harsh punishment of activists makes an impression on bystanders.

However, there is some indication that the potential for technologically savvy actors to remain anonymous online gives activists an additional set of tools for challenges to state power and may increase the possibility of drawing bystanders into protest, even in the face of state repression. For example, Howard and Hussain (2013) argue that the Internet has created an alternative public sphere in nondemocratic countries, allowing a space for civil society to flourish outside of state control. As mentioned, Yang (2011) asserts that in China, the Internet has become a space for activists to challenge Chinese state power, playing a cat-and-mouse game with state authorities and censors. When used effectively, these tools can make activists difficult to catch.

Additionally, tied to the new political spaces the Internet makes available, online activism can be used to hurt the image of an omnipotent authoritarian state, opening pathways for ordinary citizens to challenge state power in small ways and diminish state legitimacy (Beyer 2013). Authoritarian states project an image of complete power that is combined with repressive policies meant to stifle dissent of any kind (e.g., Wedeen 1999; Yurchak 2005). This projection of state power is manufactured not only through the use of coercion and violence but also through the imagery of power. Activists can challenge this image through online collective action, including hacktivist campaigns that deface government websites. Further, they can help to give ordinary citizens an understanding that their beliefs about the government are shared by others. For instance, Howard and Hussain's (2011) discussion of the Arab Spring highlights digital media as key in creating McAdam's "cognitive liberation," which occurs when political protesters can see their collective strength. Alternately, Tufekci (2011) has argued that digital media in the Arab Spring surmounted a situation of "pluralistic ignorance" in which everyone believed the government was illegitimate but thought no one else did.

In fact, bystanders are not always deterred; sometimes they are actually pulled into a situation in reaction to repression they observe (Earl and Beyer 2014). In China, activists take significant risks to continue using the Internet to disseminate information (*The Economist* 2013) as they do in authoritarian contexts around the world. Moreover, activists can be very creative in their attempts to evade censors. For instance, in 2010 when WikiLeaks was under sustained DDoS attacks and was looking for a stable home, activists began mirroring the site in an effort to keep it online. As the concerted effort to remove WikiLeaks continued, this simultaneous effort meant hundreds of mirrored sites appeared, ensuring that the content on WikiLeaks also remained accessible (Somaiya 2010). Simultaneously, as previously mentioned, Anonymous, which was not affiliated with WikiLeaks, mobilized in response to the repressive tactics used against WikiLeaks, engaging in aggressive DDoS attacks against actors believed to be involved in the anti-WikiLeaks efforts (Beyer 2014b; Earl and Beyer 2014).

The Next Frontier

In this chapter, we have (1) provided a description of online activism, repression, and backfire, and (2) introduced an infrastructure for future research on online repression and its effects (particularly backfire) by noting important distinctions among different types of Internet activism, showing how a core set of repressive tactics might be applied across these different types of Internet activism, and tracing out the effects of online repression across a range of levels, from individuals to the general public. This scaffolding sets up future scholarship to undertake three lines of inquiry that would substantially advance our collective understanding of backfire and repression online.

Distinguishing Impact Based on Type of Internet Activism and Repression

First, it is important that future research take two important steps to build on the analytical infrastructure developed in this chapter: (1) identify other repressive tactics that might be added to Table 5.1; and (2) use a structure like Table 5.1 to map likely impacts across different levels of actors. In other words, this next research step involves making Table 5.1 three-dimensional by adding an axis for the level of affected actor. For instance, what are the impacts of online surveillance of brochure-ware-style online activism on individuals, networks, SMOs, movements, and the public as bystanders to repression? When is backfire likely to occur at each of these levels? How do impacts on individuals, networks, SMOs, movements, and the public as bystanders differ when one considers the impacts of online surveillance of offline protesters who use the Internet to publicize their events? Likewise, how do impacts on each level of actor change when one considers governmental attempts to limit access to forms of protest participation online such as online petitioning? Is backfire more likely in some of these settings than others?

There is not yet enough research on instances of online repression to build out such a three-dimensional view in a thorough and illustrative way. But developing sufficient research on the topic to understand such a three-dimensional space is an important goal because it would significantly advance our collective understanding of online activism and repression.

Understanding How Effects from Different Levels Aggregate

As we mentioned above, one of the reasons that research on the consequences of repression has been so mixed is that repression can have impacts across a number of different levels. This insight suggests two critical trajectories for future research on the consequences of online repression. First, researchers need to reconsider whether commonalities in research findings emerge when studies examining the same level of impact are compared. That is, once Table 5.1 is expanded into a three-dimensional space and is populated with sufficient research, researchers will need to examine questions such as whether there are clear trends toward backfire when looking only at impacts on one level of actor (i.e., individuals, networks, etc.).

Second, researchers need to take a much more difficult step: we need to collectively consider how impacts at different levels may happen simultaneously, thus complicating what the overall net consequences of repression may be. For instance, US government and private repression against WikiLeaks may have deterred some current supporters of WikiLeaks, but it had a backfire effect for many online bystanders (Earl and Beyer 2014). These online bystanders, organized through Anonymous, then took substantial action to support WikiLeaks even though Anonymous was not acting under the direction of WikiLeaks. The net effect was backfire, but that net effect was built from two underlying and opposing effects at different levels: one effect was an individual-level deterrence effect, but that effect was outweighed by a larger backfire bystander effect. It is possible that the positive backfire from repression would be enhanced if activists were to include outreach to bystanders in their strategic planning for actions that will likely evoke repression, or when managing repression after it has taken place. Activists should work to frame potential reactions to repression in ways that harmonize with other activists' goals and philosophies.

Understanding competing or amplifying effects across levels may also help scholars to make sense of the many inconsistencies in research findings on backfire. Divergent findings may be due to differences in how specific effects across actor levels aggregate. The study of how these factors aggregate is a vital frontier for research on repression generally, regardless of whether there is an online component.

Understanding the Determinants of the Impacts of Repression

Finally, we argue that researchers need to clarify the kinds of determinants that are likely to shape the impacts of repression. Most models of repressive consequences are somewhat simplistic—they assume that if repression is applied, it will have a specific outcome. But, these approaches do not contextualize the impact of repression as depending on other factors. Based on existing research on repression, we suggest several factors that should be taken into account when trying to unpack the consequences of repression. First, researchers clearly need to be distinguishing between the kind or type of repression. Earl (2003) showed that the type of repression is important to understanding the predictors of repression; it would make sense that the type of repression should also impact its consequences. Research by a number of scholars supports this claim (e.g., Barkan 1984; Koopmans 1997).

Second, it is important to consider the amount of repression applied. While this seems obvious, it is nonetheless the case that a large number of studies examine repression empirically as a dichotomous variable—repression occurred or it did not (e.g., Koopmans 1993). Even when repression is not analyzed through presence or absence, researchers often fail to parse comparable findings based on whether or not common levels of repression were observed.

Third, it is likely that the backgrounds of actors or organizations significantly affect how actors react to repression. For instance, Linden and Klandermans (2006) showed that when activists were recruited into activism ideologically and held an expectation that they would be repressed for their political activities, repression did not lead to deterrence. However, when participants were recruited into activism through network connections and did not hold preexisting expectations of repression, they were more likely to be deterred and exit the movement. Beyond this, the literature thus far has done very little to link background to likelihoods of backfire or deterrence. Further, research has largely failed to consider whether SMO or movement histories—or even an authoritarian context, which creates a shared public history of repression—affects the likelihood of backfire or deterrence.

Fourth, much as McCarthy and Zald (1977) argued that resources were important to explaining which grievances must emerge to have movements form around them, it is likely that the resources available to actors affect how they respond to and view repression. For instance, movements with deep technological resources and expertise might be quite able to handle online surveillance, meaning that such repressive efforts would be unlikely to deter participation and may even lead to backfire. Conversely, movements with very few technological resources might find themselves reliant on easily monitored platforms and unable to circumvent repression.

Fifth, scholarship has already shown that the effects of repression may vary by the time frame that is being examined (Moore 1998;

Rasler 1996). It is important that scholars try to understand *why* time seems to matter so we can make better predictions about when and how timing will affect outcomes. Until we understand why time matters, we will be unable to understand what relevant time frames for alternating effects are and we will be unable to generate useful expectations about how consequences will fluctuate over time.

Sixth, scholars have been slow to consider how characteristics of the repressor, such as the legitimacy of the repressive agent and the resources available to repressors, affect backfire or deterrence. One might imagine that backfire might be more likely when repressive agents are widely seen as illegitimate, which appears to be what happened in Egypt (Castells 2012). But, deterrence may be more likely when the state is seen as having vast resources for repression that are deployed to compensate for questionable legitimacy, as is the case in China.

Seventh, research has established that repression might lead protesters to change tactics (Lichbach 1987; Moore 1998), but scholars have not considered whether the tactics that protesters were using when repressed affect how they react to repression. For instance, the repression of individuals engaged in peaceful civil disobedience might have different impacts on individuals, networks, SMOs, movements, and the public as bystanders when compared to the repression of individuals engaged in violence or property damage. Online, there may be differences in how the repression of online tactics such as online petitions impacts actors versus the repression of DDoS attacks or other forms of hacktivism.

Repression researchers may be able to readily identify other potential determinants that were not included in this list. The overall point would remain unchanged: part of unraveling the puzzle of when repression leads to backfire versus deterrence likely involves complicating the connections between repression and outcomes, the context in which repression occurs, and the kinds of actions against which it occurs. This will be important to scholars studying both online and offline activism.

Conclusion

As the use of digital technology in the Arab Spring illustrates, online activism has become an increasingly important part of social movements and activism. However, online activism is not just important as an extension and facilitator of offline activism. Action taken only online has also become important on its own terms, as Anonymous protests and Chinese activists' sophisticated engagement with government censors indicate. As online and online-facilitated activism increases, it is crucial to understand the ways in which this type of activism and the activists behind it interact with the state and other entities interested in silencing them. To this end, we have attempted to lay a foundation for studying the ways in which online activists are repressed and how individuals and organizations respond to this repression.

Understandably, past work on repression has focused on repression of offline movements, and so, in this chapter we have focused on the ways online activism occurs and the interaction between different types of "Internet activism" and repressive tactics. We examined different forms of online protest, including that which is only online and does not cross into the offline world (such as DDoS attacks) as well as online activism that does cross into offline activities (such as disseminating information online and planning offline protest). We also discussed four different types of repression used against Internet activism and described how these could be applied to the four different types of Internet activism that we discussed (see Table 5.1). We differentiated between backfire and deterrence across multiple levels of analysis, being careful to consider individuals and groups and public and private actors.

We argue that our analysis makes several important contributions. First, we have moved beyond general vagaries of discussing online repression to concretize exactly how repression might operate online, particularly in reaction to different kinds of "Internet activism." The specificity we have introduced through Table 5.1 should spur research in the field and allow scholarship to develop a robust research agenda around each of these types of repressive activity. Doing so may also open new doors. For instance, although beyond the scope of this chapter, it is also possible that different formats for protest may be associated with different forms of, or incidence rates of, repression. Online censorship as a form of repression may be more likely to be associated with Internet activism focused on information provision, whereas potentially illegal forms of online participation, such as participation in DDoS attacks, might be more often associated with arrests. Without the level of specificity delivered by Table 5.1, it would difficult for researchers to generate such hypotheses, let alone test them.

Second, by distinguishing between different levels of direct effects, we are hoping to contribute to research on both online and offline repression. Distinguishing between these different levels of direct effects is critical for a variety reasons. Each kind of effect is likely to have a different mechanism (e.g., individuals react to repression through different dynamics than organizations). Each kind of effect may also happen independently of other effects. This introduces the important possibility that multiple direct effects may result from a single repressive incident. While at times these effects may all be in the same direction and therefore amplify one another (e.g., all deterrent effects), at other times it may be that the direct effects are countervailing and what observers witness as the "outcome" of repression is actually the net effect of multiple, competing direct effects (Earl and Beyer 2014). Being aware of this difference between direct and complex effects is critical.

Finally, we have tried to catalog the range of reasons that the direct effects of repression may vary, including discussing such factors as intensity and timing. We hope that by cataloging these potential variables, we push scholarship toward critically considering these factors, particularly when comparing research findings on repression. We suspect that more robust findings about the effects of repression would be achievable if direct effects with similar attributes were more systematically compared. While beyond the scope of this chapter to complete such a comparison, we have provided a foundation that would make it possible.

In closing, the task of understanding the paradox of repression in Internet activism will only grow more pressing as time goes on and will preoccupy an increasing number of scholars. It is our hope that this type of delineation of types of activism, types of repression, and types of responses to repression in combination with a careful look at their interaction will help to further the study of repression online as the rate and ferocity of online activism continues to develop around us.

References

Anonymous. 2013. "Green Movement Activists Live in Fear as Iran's Presidential Election Nears." *Guardian*, May 17. http://www.guardian.co.uk/world/2013/may/17/green-movement-activists-iran-repression.

Associated Press. 2009. "Dmitriy Guzner: Teen Sentenced in Scientology Cyber Attack." *Huffington Post*, Nov. 18. Accessed Jan. 21, 2017. https://web.archive.org/web/20130529030809/http://www.huffingtonpost.com/2009/11/18/dmitriy-guzner-teen-sente_n_362713.html.

Barkan, Steven E. 1984. "Legal Control of the Southern Civil Rights Movement." *American Sociological Review* 49 (4): 552–65.

BBC. 2009. "Piracy Law Cuts Internet Traffic." *BBC News*, Apr. 2. Accessed Nov. 15, 2012. http://news.bbc.co.uk/2/hi/7978853.stm.

Beyer, Jessica L. 2011. "Youth and the Generation of Political Consciousness Online." PhD dissertation, Department of Political Science, University of Washington, ProQuest/UMI.

———. 2013. "Come for the Revolution, Stay for the Lulz: Anonymous and Authoritarian Regimes." In *State Power 2.0: Authoritarian Entrenchment and Civic Engagement Worldwide*, edited by P. N. Howard and M. M. Hussain, 153–62. Burlington, VT: Ashgate.

———. 2014a. *Expect Us: Online Communities and Political Mobilization*. New York: Oxford Univ. Press.

———. 2014b. "The Emergence of a Freedom of Information Movement: Anonymous, WikiLeaks, the Pirate Party, and Iceland." *Journal of Computer-Mediated Communication* 19 (2): 141–54. doi:10.1111/jcc4.12050.

Bowcott, Owen, Haroon Siddique, and Andrew Sparrow. 2011. "Facebook Cases Trigger Criticism of 'Disproportionate' Riot Sentences."

Guardian, Aug. 17. Accessed Nov. 15, 2012. http://www.guardian.co.uk/uk/2011/aug/17/facebook-cases-criticism-riot-sentences.

Brodkin, Jon. 2012. "All the Latest on the Unmasking of LulzSec Leader 'Sabu' Arrests." *Ars Technica*, Mar. 6. Accessed Nov. 15, 2012. http://arstechnica.com/tech-policy/2012/03/all-the-latest-on-the-unmasking-of-lulzsec-leader-sabu-arrests/.

Cameron, Dell. 2013. "In Trademark Masks, Anonymous Makes Its Presence Felt Worldwide." *Daily Dot*, Nov. 5. Accessed Nov. 15, 2012. http://www.dailydot.com/news/anonymous-million-mask-march-photos/.

Castells, Manuel. 2012. *Networks of Outrage and Hope: Social Movements in the Internet Age*. Malden, MA: Polity Press.

Citizen Media Law Project. 2010. "United States v. Madison." Jan. 10. Accessed Mar. 13, 2018. https://web.archive.org/web/20120317071256/http://www.citmedialaw.org/threats/united-states-v-madison.

Cohen, N. 2010. "Web Attackers Find a Cause in WikiLeaks." *New York Times*, Dec. 9. http://www.nytimes.com/2010/12/10/world/10wiki.html.

Coleman, G. 2015. *Hacker, Hoaxer, Whistleblower, Spy: The Many Faces of Anonymous*. New York: Verso Books.

Cunningham, David. 2004. *There's Something Happening Here: The New Left, the Klan, and FBI Counterintelligence*. Berkeley: Univ. of California Press.

Davenport, Christian. 2007. "State Repression and Political Order." *Annual Review of Political Science* 10: 1–23.

Deibert, Ronald J., John G. Palfrey, Rafal Rohozinski, and Jonathan Zittrain, eds. 2008. *Access Denied: The Practice and Policy of Global Internet Filtering*. Boston: MIT.

Deibert, Ronald J., John G. Palfrey, Rafal Rohozinski, and Jonathan Zittrain. 2010. *Access Controlled: The Shaping of Power, Rights, and Rule in Cyberspace*. Cambridge: MIT Press.

Earl, Jennifer. 2003. "Tanks, Tear Gas and Taxes: Toward a Theory of Movement Repression." *Sociological Theory* 21 (1): 44–68.

———. 2004. "Controlling Protest: New Directions for Research on the Social Control of Protest." *Research in Social Movements, Conflicts, and Change* 25: 55–83.

———. 2005. "You Can Beat the Rap, But You Can't Beat the Ride." *Research in Social Movements, Conflict, and Change* 26: 101–39.

———. 2011. "Political Repression: Iron Fists, Velvet Gloves, and Diffuse Control." *Annual Review of Sociology* 37: 261–84.

———. 2012. "Private Protest? Public and Private Engagement Online." *Information, Communication and Society* 15 (4): 591–608.

———. 2013. "Spreading the Word or Shaping the Conversation: 'Prosumption' in Protest Websites." *Research in Social Movements, Conflicts, and Change* 36: 3–38.

Earl, Jennifer, and Jessica Beyer. 2014. "The Dynamics of Backlash Online: Anonymous and the Battle for WikiLeaks." *Research in Social Movements, Conflicts and Change* 37: 207–33.

Earl, Jennifer, and Katrina Kimport. 2011. *Digitally Enabled Social Change: Activism in the Internet Age*. Cambridge, MA: MIT Press.

Earl, Jennifer, Katrina Kimport, Greg Prieto, Carly Rush, and Kimberly Reynoso. 2010. "Changing the World One Webpage at a Time: Conceptualizing and Explaining 'Internet Activism." *Mobilization* 15 (4): 425–46.

Earl, Jennifer, and Alan Schussman. 2003. "The New Site of Activism: On-Line Organizations, Movement Entrepreneurs, and the Changing Location of Social Movement Decision-Making." *Research in Social Movements, Conflicts, and Change* 24: 155–87.

———. 2004. "Cease and Desist: Repression, Strategic Voting and the 2000 Presidential Election." *Mobilization* 9 (2): 181–202.

Earl, Jennifer, and Sarah A. Soule. 2010. "The Impacts of Repression: The Effect of Police Presence and Action on Subsequent Protest Rates." *Research in Social Movements, Conflicts, and Change* 30: 75–113.

Economist, The. 2013. "China's Internet: A Giant Cage," Apr. 6. Accessed Jan. 15, 2018. http://www.economist.com/news/special-report/21574628-internet-was-expected-help-democratise-china-instead-it-has-enabled.

Embassy Stockholm. 2009a. "Special 301 for Sweden: Post Recommendation." WikiLeaks Cable: 09STOCKHOLM141_a. Mar. 2. https://wikileaks.org/plusd/cables/09STOCKHOLM141_a.html.

———. 2009b. "Special 301 for Sweden: Results Discussed with GOS." WikiLeaks Cable: 09STOCKHOLM276_a. May 5. https://wikileaks.org/plusd/cables/09STOCKHOLM276_a.html.

Enigmax. 2009. "Swedish Internet Traffic Recovers after Initial IPRED Scare." *Torrent Freak*, Nov. 13. Accessed Nov. 15, 2012. http://torrentfreak.com/swedish-internet-traffic-recovers-after-initial-ipred-scare-091113/.

Ernesto. 2010. "Troubled WikiLeaks Moves to Pirate Party Domain." *Torrent Freak*, Dec. 3. Accessed Nov. 15, 2012. http://torrentfreak.com/troubled-wikileaks-moves-to-pirate-party-domain-101203/.

Eschenfelder, Kristin R., and Anuj C. Desai. 2004. "Software as Protest: The Unexpected Resiliency of U.S.-Based DeCSS Posting and Linking." *The Information Society* 20 (2): 101–16.

Eschenfelder, Kristen R., Robert Glenn Howard, and Anuj C. Desai. 2005. "Who Posts DeCSS and Why? A Content Analysis of Web Sites Posting DVD Circumvention Software." *Journal for the American Society for Information Science and Technology* 56 (13): 1405–18.

Essers, Loek. 2013. "Pirate Bay Co-Founder Peter Sunde to Run for EU Parliament." *PC World*, May 15. Accessed Jan. 15, 2018. http://www.pcworld.com/article/2038780/pirate-bay-cofounder-peter-sunde-to-run-for-eu-parliament.html.

Faris, Robert, and Nart Villeneuve. 2008. "Measuring Global Internet Filtering." In *Access Denied: The Practice and Policy of Global Internet Filtering*, edited by R. J. Deibert, J. G. Palfrey, R. Rohozinski, and J. Zittrain, 6–27. Cambridge: MIT Press.

Fisher, Max. 2012. "Explaining Ai Weiwei's 'Grass Mud Horse' Obsession." *Washington Post*, Oct. 24. Accessed Nov. 25, 2013. http://www.washingtonpost.com/blogs/worldviews/wp/2012/10/24/explaining-ai-weiweis-grass-mud-horse-obsession/.

Ford Rojas, John-Paul, Tom Whitehead and James Kirkup. 2011. "UK Riots: Magistrates Told 'Ignore the Rule Book' and Lock up Looters." *Telegraph*, Aug 15. Accessed Nov. 15, 2012. http://www.telegraph.co.uk/news/uknews/crime/8703370/UK-riots-magistrates-told-ignore-the-rule-book-and-lock-up-looters.html.

Freedom House. 2013. "China." *Freedom on the Net 2013*. Washington, DC: Freedom House. Accessed Jan. 15, 2018. https://freedomhouse.org/report/freedom-net/2013/china.

Gurak, Laura J. 1997. *Persuasion and Privacy in Cyberspace: The Online Protests over Lotus Marketplace and the Clipper Chip*. New Haven: Yale Univ. Press.

———. 1999. "The Promise and the Peril of Social Action in Cyberspace." In *Communities in Cyberspace*, edited by M. A. Smith and P. Kollock, 243–63. London: Routledge.

Gurak, Laura J., and John Logie. 2003. "Internet Protests, from Text to Web." In *Cyberactivism: Online Activism and Theory and Practice*, edited by M. McCaughey and M. D. Ayers, 25–46. New York: Routledge.

Hirsch, Eric L. 1990. "Sacrifice for the Cause: Group Processes, Recruitment, and Commitment in a Student Social Movement." *American Sociological Review* 55 (2): 243–54.

Howard, Philip. 2010. *The Digital Origins of Dictatorship and Democracy: Information Technology and Political Islam*. New York: Oxford Univ. Press.

Howard, Philip, and Muzammil Hussain. 2011. "The Upheavals in Egypt and Tunisia: The Role of Digital Media." *Journal of Democracy* 22 (3): 35–48.

———. 2013. *Democracy's Fourth Wave?: Digital Media and the Arab Spring*. New York: Oxford Univ. Press.

Kiani, Yalda. 2012. "Iran Clamps Down on Internet Activists." *Deutsche Welle*, Mar. 3. Accessed Nov. 15, 2012. http://www.dw.de/iran-clamps-down-on-internet-activists/a-15775255.

Koopmans, Ruud. 1993. "The Dynamics of Protest Waves: West Germany, 1965 to 1989." *American Sociological Review* 58: 637–58.

———. 1997. "The Dynamics of Repression and Mobilization: The German Extreme Right in the 1990s." *Mobilization* 2 (2): 149–65.

Lichbach, Mark Irving. 1987. "Deterrence or Escalation? The Puzzle of Aggregate Studies of Repression and Dissent." *Journal of Conflict Resolution* 31 (2): 266–97.

Linden, Annette, and Bert Klandermans. 2006. "Stigmatization and Repression of Extreme Right Activism in the Netherlands." *Mobilization* 11 (2): 213–28.

MacKinnon, Rebecca. 2012. *Consent of the Networked: The Worldwide Struggle for Internet Freedom*. New York: Basic Books.

McCarthy, John D., and Mayer N. Zald. 1977. "Resource Mobilization and Social Movements: A Partial Theory." *American Journal of Sociology* 82: 1212–41.

Moore, Will E. 1998. "Repression and Dissent: Substitution, Context, and Timing." *American Journal of Police Science* 42 (3): 851–73.

Morozov, Evgeny. 2011. *The Net Delusion: The Dark Side of Internet Freedom*. New York: Public Affairs.

Moynihan, Colin. 2009. "Arrest Puts Focus on Protesters' Texting" *New York Times*, Oct. 4, A19. http://www.nytimes.com/2009/10/05/nyregion/05txt.html.

O'Connor, Anahad. 2010. "Amazon Removes WikiLeaks from Servers." *New York Times*, Dec. 2, sec. World. https://www.nytimes.com/2010/12/02/world/02amazon.html.

Olson, Parmy. 2011. "Egypt's Internet Blackout Cost More than OECD Estimates." *Forbes*, Feb. 3. http://www.forbes.com/sites/parmyolson/2011/02/03/how-much-did-five-days-of-no-internet-cost-egypt/.

Opp, Karl-Deiter, and Wolfgang Roehl. 1990. "Repression, Micromobilization, and Political Protest." *Social Forces* 69 (2): 521–47.

Peckham, Michael H. 1998. "New Dimensions of Social Movement/Countermovement Interaction: The Case of Scientology and Its Internet Critics." *Canadian Journal of Sociology* 23 (4): 317–47.

Pirate Bay, The. 2013. "Press Release, New Provider for TPB," Mar. 23. Accessed Nov. 25, 2013. https://web.archive.org/web/20131125083151/http://thepiratebay.sx/blog/229.

Porzucki, Nina. 2012. "How Technology Is Changing Chinese, One Pun at a Time." *Public Radio International*, July 11. Accessed Nov. 25, 2013. http://www.pri.org/stories/2012-07-11/how-technology-changing-chinese-one-pun-time.

Postigo, Hector. 2012. *The Digital Rights Movement*. Boston: MIT Press.

Ramzy, Austin. 2011. "To Help Dissident Artist Ai Weiwei Pay Tax Bill, His Supporters Try Microlending." *Time World*, Nov 7. Accessed Nov. 25, 2013. http://world.time.com/2011/11/07/thousands-pitch-in-to-pay-dissident-artist-ai-weiweis-tax-bill/.

Rasler, Karen. 1996. "Concessions, Repression, and Political Protest in the Iranian Revolution." *American Sociological Review* 61 (1): 132–52.

Roper, Louis. 2006. "US Government behind Pirate Bay Raid." *The Local*, Jun. 2. Accessed Nov. 15, 2012. http://www.thelocal.se/3969/20060602/.

RT.com. 2012. "Anonymous Reveals Haditha Massacre Emails," Jan 3. Accessed Nov. 15, 2012. http://rt.com/usa/anonymous-time-wuterich-attorneys-463/.

Schussman, Alan, and Jennifer Earl. 2004. "From Barricades to Firewalls? Strategic Voting and Social Movement Leadership in the Internet Age." *Sociological Inquiry* 74 (4): 439–63.

Somaiya, Ravi. 2010. "Hundreds of WikiLeaks Mirror Sites Appear." *New York Times*, Dec. 5. Accessed Nov. 15, 2012. http://www.nytimes.com/2010/12/06/world/europe/06wiki.html.

Starr, Amory, Luis A. Fernandez, Randall Amster, Lesley J. Wood, and Manuel J. Caro. 2008. "The Impacts of State Surveillance on Political Assembly and Association: A Socio-Legal Analysis." *Qualitative Sociology* 31 (3): 251–70.

Steavenson, Wendell. 2011. "Letter from Damascus: Roads to Freedom." *The New Yorker*, Aug. 29. http://www.newyorker.com/reporting/2011/08/29/110829fa_fact_steavenson.

Sunde, Peter. 2013. "EUP 2014." *Copy Me Happy*, Mar. 14. Accessed Jan. 15, 2018. http://blog.brokep.com/2013/05/14/eup-2014/.

Toumi, Habib. 2013. "Bahrain Court Releases Al Wefaq Leader Khalil Marzouq." *Gulf News*, Oct. 24. Accessed Nov. 25, 2013. http://gulfnews.com/news/gulf/bahrain/bahrain-court-releases-al-wefaq-leader-khalil-marzouq-1.1246798.

Travis, Alan, James Ball, and Fiona Bawdon. 2011. "English City Riots Involved 'Hardcore' of Repeat Offenders, First Analysis Shows." *Guardian*, Sep. 15. http://www.guardian.co.uk/uk/2011/sep/15/english-riots-hardcore-repeat-offenders.

Tufekci, Zeynep. 2011. "New Media and the People-Powered Uprisings." *MIT Technology Review*, Aug. 30. Accessed Nov. 25, 2013. http://www.technologyreview.com/view/425280/new-media-and-the-people-powered-uprisings/.

Tufekci, Zeynep, and Christopher Wilson. 2012. "Social Media and the Decision to Participate in Political Protest: Observations from Tahrir Square." *Journal of Communication* 62: 363–79.

Vegh, Sandor. 2003. "Classifying Forms of Online Activism: The Case of Cyberprotests against the World Bank." In *Cyberactivism: Online Activism and Theory and Practice*, edited by M. McCaughey and M. D. Ayers, 71–95. New York: Routledge.

Wedeen, Lisa. 1999. *Ambiguities of Domination: Politics, Rhetoric, and Symbols in Contemporary Syria*. Chicago, IL: Univ. of Chicago Press.

Wiener, Seth. 2011. "Grass-Mud Horses to Victory: The Phonological Constraints of Subversive Puns." Paper presented at the North American Conference on Chinese Linguistics, Eugene, Oregon. http://naccl.osu.edu/sites/naccl.osu.edu/files/NACCL-23_1_11.pdf.

Wines, Michael. 2009. "A Dirty Pun Tweaks China's Online Censors." *New York Times*, Mar. 12. Accessed Nov. 25, 2013. http://www.nytimes.com/2009/03/12/world/asia/12beast.html.

Yang, Guobin. 2011. *The Power of the Internet in China: Citizen Activism Online*. New York: Columbia Univ. Press.

Yurchak, Alexei. 2005. *Everything Was Forever, Until It Was No More: The Last Soviet Generation*. Princeton, NJ: Princeton University Press.

Zetter, Kim. 2012. "Anonymous Eavesdrops on FBI Anti-Anonymous Strategy Meeting." *Threat Level: Wired*. Feb. 3. Accessed Nov. 15, 2012. http://www.wired.com/threatlevel/2012/02/anonymous-scotland-yard/.

Zuckerman, Ethan. 2008. "The Cute Cat Theory Talk at Etech." *My Heart's in Accra*, Mar. 8. http://www.ethanzuckerman.com/blog/2008/03/08/the-cute-cat-theory-talk-at-etech/.

Zwerman, Gilda, and Patricia Steinhoff. 2005. "When Activists Ask for Trouble: State-Dissident Interactions and the New Left Cycle of Resistance in the United States and Japan." In *Repression and Mobilization*, edited by C. Davenport, H. Johnston and C. Mueller, 85–107. Minneapolis: Univ. of Minnesota Press.

Zwerman, Gilda, Patricia G. Steinhoff, and Donatella della Porta. 2000. "Disappearing Social Movements: Clandestinity in the Cycle of New Left Protest in the U.S., Japan, Germany and Italy." *Mobilization* 5 (1): 85–104.

6

Overcoming Fear to Overcome Repression

JENNI WILLIAMS

Suffering under the brutal dictatorship of the Robert Mugabe regime in Zimbabwe, a group of women rose up courageously as "mothers of the nation" to challenge his elite rule and build grassroots democratic change in their communities. Women of Zimbabwe Arise (WOZA) mobilized a campaign of "tough love," using the traditional role and moral authority of mother to scold the repressive and corrupt leaders of the country and call for a new kind of society where equality and social justice prevail. This joining of love, power, and justice echoes the vision and experience of Rev. Martin Luther King Jr. (1967, King, Carson, and Shepard 2001), who declared, "Power without love is reckless and abusive, and love without power is sentimental and anemic. Power at its best is love implementing the demands of justice, and justice at its best is power correcting everything that stands against love."

The idea of tough love emerged and added value to the role of motherhood we embraced. Tough love is the disciplining love a "mother" uses for a "child" who has gone astray or is disrespecting the family. Robert Mugabe and members of the ruling Zimbabwe African National Union-Patriotic Front (ZANU-PF) Party are first and foremost children of Zimbabwe, who are disrespecting the "family"—the nation. For us as women, our issues were not about political rule but about the everyday issues that affect us and our families. Finding our kitchens empty and the cat using the stove to warm itself, we moved from the kitchen to the streets. We found we had a talent for organizing and put nonviolent direct action behind our collective voice to loudly demand dramatic changes for Zimbabwe and to call for Zimbabweans to choose love and unity over hatred and violence.

Forging a culture of resistance among courageous women, WOZA helped women to overcome their fear of the repressive forces governing the country. Following the words of Gandhi, we looked upon time spent in police custody as a trip to our fields to plant seeds for a good harvest. So, we turned arrests into a celebration of successful resistance. We regarded our time under arrest as a chance to "workshop" or educate the police officers about human rights and to correct those in positions of power who harassed us. We called on them to stop their childlike behavior and abuse of power. Because we were able to play our motherly role so well and with such love, we were able to make our persecutors respect us and appreciate the issues that drove us into the streets in protest. With demonstrations of love—even for arresting police officers—WOZA women provided the nation with a new way to hold policymakers accountable. The high-visibility protest with women speaking truth to power shocked the nation out of its complacency. This form of tough love also challenged a deeply polarized political environment, opening up a new space in the center white line on the "highway" of Zimbabwean political life: women standing their ground on their issues demanding attention as the politicians and citizens drove by to the left and to the right.

Tough love was a litmus test to prove that the power of love can overcome the love of power.

Political and Social Contexts in Zimbabwe

WOZA was founded in 2002 at a time when a raft of unjust laws were put in place in Zimbabwe, entrenching dictatorship and closing down space for any form of resistance. With the media now restricted, the Public Order Security Act then limited the association and assembly of citizens. WOZA was established to create a collective voice for women to speak out on their everyday issues. WOZA wanted to empower them with knowledge and nonviolent direct action skills and thereby provide a platform for them to demand social justice. WOZA knew that this mandate would also challenge the authoritarian rule of Robert Mugabe and that this empowerment would build a new foundation for democratic change.

Robert Mugabe's rule emerged from a protracted violent struggle for independence in Zimbabwe in which he played a minor role. Mugabe's initial overtures of tolerance and forgiveness were quickly overturned by elite pacts and patronage systems to keep the military in check and to maintain the loyalty of a partisan civil service that held the nation hostage with liberation rhetoric and false appeals for social justice. A one-party state was being set in place, and the dictatorship was entrenching itself.

During colonial times, the white political system governed Zimbabwe. At independence in 1980, a black ruling elite supplanted this system. This entrenched dictatorship is still in place thirty-seven years later in the form of the ZANU-PF Party, which has politicized all arms of the state, the economy, and even the citizens. ZANU-PF has captured democracy, and all citizens are supposed to give their loyalty unquestioningly. Zimbabwe's economy continues to bounce along the rock bottom, with over 90 percent formal unemployment widening the gap between the rich and the poor. The crisis of governance has destroyed the education and health systems of the nation, once the pride of Africa, preoccupying citizens with daily survival and leaving little time to mobilize citizen power. Those who find life intolerable have left the country as economic or political migrants, further tearing apart the social fabric of an otherwise peace-loving and always smiling nation.

The Public Order Security Act established in 2002 barred meetings of more than three people and required notification of the police regarding any meetings. Meanwhile, the word "notification" was in practice changed into "approval" for any meeting by the police. The Protection of Privacy Act curtailed access to information, so all the various spaces in which people could formerly express themselves or speak out were effectively closing. The ruling party simultaneously co-opted television and radio stations and major daily newspapers to ensure distribution of party propaganda.

The nation was thus silenced and rendered unable to organize due to indiscriminate arrests of opposition and other activists by the police and intelligence forces, and life became intolerable for women and their families. Gender discriminatory norms limited their mobility, and poverty constrained their ability to run for the borders and other greener pastures as men could do.

Enacting Tough Love

When women gathered and started to discuss the formation of WOZA, the silence had become too loud to bear, and the culture of fear that prevailed shot right through to our bones—we had to put our fear aside and act. As women sat and talked, we viewed ourselves as "the mothers of the nation," still a key phrase in our movement today. We said we had to do something within the role God had ordained for us. We had to be visible to Zimbabweans and show citizens a new way to speak out about ordinary people's everyday needs.

WOZA members wanted to address simple issues of their everyday lives but with far-reaching impact that would touch all Zimbabweans, even the police officers whom we knew would be sent to beat and arrest us: the cost of bread and staple diet of maize meal; the rapidly deteriorating state of the education for our children; prevailing joblessness; and poor service delivery in the health sector. We were deeply concerned about the continuing violence permeating all parts of society, including the increasing domestic violence against women. One of our first protests was over the high cost and general unavailability of sanitary pads for women, a vital but basic monthly need but a major source of female dignity.

We also said we would not speak without acting. If we were going to hold the moral high ground—if we were going to do something effective—we also needed to appropriate a very visible space showing love and highlighting our issues in our own language. So, our version of nonviolent strategy is firmly grounded in our gender and our mothering role, so ordained. More than fifteen years later, we are still in the streets showing love, speaking about our issues and how they affect us and our families.

Because the number of participants is important for peaceful protest (see Erica Chenoweth, chapter 2 in this volume), we decided to build a mass movement and invented a democratic structure that could mobilize numbers through a shared leadership model. We wanted to make sure we remained grounded in our constituency. We also wanted to make sure that we could stand on the center white line on the "highway" of Zimbabwean political life, opening a space for these issues and drawing the attention of fellow citizens who had grown accustomed to our highly polarized society. In Zimbabwe, you are either ZANU-PF or you are opposition, and we felt that this segmenting of society could be healed with the spirit of love that we wanted to build and sustain. We chose to stand on issues, not on formal political platforms, and this was the hardest part of our mandate, but we have succeeded in remaining in our own independent space. The Zimbabwean and global human rights networks have also agreed that socioeconomic rights are as important as civil and political rights, and the new Zimbabwean constitution now has an expanded bill of rights to include these.

Challenging Patriarchy and Repression

Beyond the realm of politics, it is important to note that patriarchy rules in Africa. When we decided to form WOZA, we realized that the time had come for women to be out front and visible demanding policy change in society. We wanted to show that we are good at mobilizing around issues and organizing within communities on their issues. Just as we organize our families, we can organize in public life. An integral part of the tough love approach is the use of nonviolent tactics and strategies of peaceful protest that deliver visibility, amplify important messages, and motivate us to invent new ways of organizing and communicating. Within our femininity we also found creativity and use this in formulating our protest theatrics.

We, as women, are breaking stereotypes and breaking patriarchy as well as the space it commands. We are proud to say that organizing is a skill women naturally command; we quickly commit to a course of action and stay the course to deliver the message. The belief that women must be quietly confined to the kitchen is slowing fading away. We act out our right to make demands, and we expect the police to respect our right to peaceful protest.

Many people assumed our strategy was too risky and that we would not be able to build and sustain our movement. We were breaking those stereotypes too. Women are collectively challenging power and unjust laws and rule in a way that builds democracy and empowers individual people to feel that they are whole citizens—we call this the work of EVEolution, not revolution.

Africa is a continent of contradictions—women can be indiscriminately beaten in their homes, but the same society looks down on a man beating a woman in public. So, we addressed the issue of repression in our first strategy session and debated what the typical African male anti-riot police officer would do upon seeing us in the street. Would other men look on and encourage them to beat us? Our answer came in the form of baton stick injuries. The Mugabe regime has demonstrated its willingness to use open repression against those who challenge its legitimacy. Mugabe has boasted that he has "degrees in violence" and has declared, "If I am a Hitler, let me be a Hitler tenfold."

Along with the beatings came arbitrary arrests and detentions in police cells and also in prison. And then, paradoxically, the beatings, arrests, and detentions became a badge of honor. I remember this period well, and joined in the singing of a religious hymn with lyrics modified from "will your name be called when you reach heaven?" to "will the police call your name as one of those arrested for defending your rights?"

When one is in custody, every day all detainees are lined up and their names are called. We would face horrid harassment and insults during these parades, and very soon we responded with pride, heads held high. When our names were called we each walked forward saying "human rights defender" while staring the police officers straight in the face. It is quite a feat to be proud when you are barefoot and stinking, having been kept in inhumane conditions, sleeping on hard concrete floors in lice-infested police cells.

The police saw that their repression was backfiring, that the core activist base was becoming radicalized and that our movement was expanding and had now won the moral high ground. Police officers were surprised when bystanders shouted at them for beating peaceful mothers of the nation. When hundreds were arrested, crowded into trucks, or frog marched to police stations, bystanders expressed their concerns verbally by telling off the police officers. The police officers were forced to develop new strategies for dealing with us. They adopted tactics, such as conducting random stops and searches, to attempt to prevent the protests from starting or from reaching their planned target point. They set up police cordons around cities to block women from entering the city, directly accusing any woman of being a "WOZA woman." Police officers thought that if they stopped every woman, they could confiscate any banners and handwritten placards and thus prevent the protest from taking place. This tactic prompted us to restrategize as well—we conducted simultaneous multiple protests using different routes to get to the targeted location and deliver our demands. This new tactic stretched police resources, rendering them unable to stop all protest groups.

On Valentine's Day 2014, our traditional day of protest, more than 150 anti-riot police occupied Bulawayo's central business district at 8:00 a.m. in anticipation of an 11:00 a.m. protest. Police were deployed in groups of four on main street corners. They expected us to be intimidated and fail to enter the city. We not only came to our starting points but ignored the police and mobilized such high numbers that, as we started the protests, the police officers began studying the polish on their shoes in fear while we marched away and reached the government complex peacefully singing. On this occasion, the police were forced to return to their barracks in embarrassment.

The state went a step further to try to demobilize our tough love. They used persecution by prosecution. Requiring a person to appear constantly in court on charges constitutes a form of harassment. At one time, I was personally appearing in court on four different charges, with appearance dates synchronized around or in anticipation of known protest dates, such as Valentine's Day or International Woman's Day on March 8. The state even concocted criminal charges against the leadership in hopes of criminalizing the movement—this too failed.

Despite the efforts of the police, WOZA adopted a high risk mandate during the height of repression. Some might have said what we planned was impossible, impractical, dangerous, or foolish, but that would have underestimated the lived reality of Zimbabweans in 2002. We had to do something courageous, something expected of us as the mothers of the nation, and we did it. But to do it well, we had to be able to shove fear aside and put something else in its place.

Overcoming Culture of Fear and Building a Culture of Resistance

It was important that we break the culture of fear that prevailed in Zimbabwe, and we found that repression often backfired on Mugabe's regime, especially once people were empowered and fear was replaced with a culture of resistance. An incident in July 2003 illustrates the shift from isolation to solidarity that we experienced. We held a wonderful protest, marching along with placards, singing our songs with our messages, and calling for the repeal of the Public Order Security Act.

As we dispersed, we entered a large bus terminal; as I walked through the terminal, a police officer tapped me on the shoulder and said to me, "Jennifer, you are arrested."

As I turned to him, I said "Ok, well, what for?"

He replied, "You were leading the protest."

I said, "Ok, let's go." He started to walk with me, and fellow WOZA members turned to walk with me as well.

The officer pointed to the others and said, "No, no, no, no. You are not under arrest. Go away."

My comrades asked, "Why not?" and he said, "We are only arresting Jennifer. She was leading the protest."

They replied, "No, we were *all* leading the protest."

As we marched back through the bus terminal with this police officer, the news quickly spread that I was being arrested. By the time we got to the police Land Rover, it was already full of members who had turned themselves in. There was no room for me in the vehicle, but in high spirits my fellow protesters created room, and I was squeezed in. As the vehicle drove to the nearby police station, other members walked or ran there and marched into the police station, arresting themselves as well. By accepting and even courting arrest, we had taken away the regime's major weapon of repression, turning it instead into a source of empowerment for the movement and individual participants.

What happened to make people so committed and confident about what we were defending together, what our protests were all about? In the culture of fear that prevailed under the Public Order Security Act, most people did not want to be arrested. Our resistance and the solidarity arrests came as quite a shock for the police, and we have maintained and built on that momentum by building a leadership structure that empowers the movement. We also draw energy from exposing injustice, because our members feel they own the issues and that they can be defended through thick and thin.

Ironically, during the war for liberation (1964–1979), Mugabe and other nationalists had also been arrested under the public order acts and had promised to repeal these repressive laws. But now, here they were, the so-called liberators, arresting women and charging them under the very same repressive law they had faced when challenging colonialism. The hypocrisy of their use of repression was only highlighted in contrast with our peaceful marches and singing. However, to capitalize on the power of this framing of Mugabe's authoritarian and patriarchal rule, we had to build a movement that empowered Zimbabweans to overcome fear and take risks. We had to prove that the power of love could conquer the love of power.

Leadership

The way in which we constructed our style of leadership has been a key in mobilizing people within a culture of fear. We agreed that any elected leader of WOZA must be prepared to lead in all the necessary spaces, including peaceful protest. In most situations in Zimbabwe, political leaders would send other people to do the hard work of protest, making them take the risk of being beaten. They would not risk getting their bottoms beaten. However, WOZA leaders must be prepared to be in the front of peaceful demonstrations. If there are to be beatings, leaders must be among the first to suffer as well. Consequently, people were able to feel, "If that is the way a leader in WOZA behaves, then I will never be alone and beaten by myself."

It would be wrong to give the impression that responsibility always falls on the same leaders. Shared leadership is also important. It is true that, in the first few years, I had to be the one to start the demonstration and call out the first slogans in the center of the street. As with the July 2003 protest, police identified me as the one who started the protest and perceived me to be the "organizer." Also, because WOZA never formally notifies police of a protest, the police target the one who starts the protest. WOZA actions begin with gathering members together at a central business district point. Then, somebody has got to be brave enough to walk into the street and start the demonstration and open up the banner. So, in the initial phases, I often took on that role. However, I was later able to embolden other people to initiate the demonstration, and now everyone wants a chance to start the demonstration or hold the banners at the front of the march. Leadership by example became shared leadership.

The police began to target leaders, hoping to break the growing culture of resistance they had established, and in hopes that people would run away because the leaders were no longer there. Soon, however, there were too many leaders and too many brave faces to remember due to our movement structure. Authorities then tried taking photos of the protests to identify the leaders, but ordinary members increasingly wanted a chance to start the protests. Consequently, the police officers could not keep track of the growing number of faces and names. This also translated into police officers refusing to allow large numbers to be arrested, as the handwritten, tedious paperwork required to process members into detention (along with photographs and fingerprints) meant late-night shifts without overtime pay. By overcoming fear and building collective leadership, we were able to face and effectively manage or blunt repression.

Empowerment

The building of a culture of resistance involves a redefinition of repression and of how the system secures obedience. When we challenge dictatorship and patriarchy, we may risk being beaten, but in receiving that beating without retaliating we score a victory for the oppressed. From our perspective, repression is not only a victory for the cause but also an indication that the issue being addressed has currency and credibility. I have been in custody many times with other members, and we are all battered and blue, but we are elated! How can we be so elated and yet also be in such pain? Because in our minds we had planned and implemented a successful campaign, kept nonviolent discipline, and neutralized repression. A power holder can only use their power over you if you let them, but by simply flicking the switch and taking our power back, we reverse the roles and disempower the authorities. We also decided not to be the victims of repression but to be the victors, celebrating each victory, which helps shake away fear. This process is empowering and boosts personal confidence, building strength of character and leadership capacity. Interestingly, despite the amount of trauma we have suffered, these experiences are stored not in the negative part of our brains but in the positive side.

Civic Education

WOZA members used to have a one-track mind that was always focused on peaceful protest, but we learned that building a culture of resistance requires more than effective protest; it takes building a movement and creating a daily culture of activism—daily vigilance. And so we started to build a movement around the culture of resistance. Not many people realize that 98 percent of our work is conducted quietly through trainings at the community level. We began to conduct very concise, specific civic education campaigns. To build daily activism and vigilance, we translated Gene Sharp's (2005) 198 methods into all the local languages, built independent activist capacity to plan a protest, and conducted workshops on how to overcome fear. Ultimately, we stress that the 198 methods approach is something people can use to plan and organize around their own local issues by themselves.

Building and then expanding the culture of protest helped to maintain the sustainability of the movement by inculcating members with the habit of noting repression but then immediately trying to manage the repression while exposing it as an injustice. Suddenly, the police could not target only certain leaders. There were people doing things in the community seemingly all by themselves and unconnected to the main organization of WOZA, yet operating under the banner of WOZA. Additionally, WOZA found that this decentralized culture of resistance would also strengthen the likelihood that repression would backfire. Police at more suburban police stations live within those communities, are more familiar with bad governance, and quietly support WOZA. These police who live outside the center of official power are less susceptible to patronage and corruption, so they can more easily be pulled over to support people power.

Repression Management

Repression is a common experience in our movement, and we work intentionally to prepare ourselves, to build solidarity, to build effective strategy, and to gain advantage despite repression and sometimes even because of repression. We may organize a protest and walk away battered and bruised, and we acknowledge that we have put ourselves in that circumstance. We put ourselves there, and we were injured, but we created a dilemma for the security apparatus. The dilemma presented by our protest could be described this way: "Leave us to our peaceful protest on our issues, which is also your personal lived reality, Mr. Policeman," or "Beat us and arrest us for our peaceful protest and only you look bad to ordinary citizens for using violence against peaceful women, mothers of the nation. Beating us is also an acknowledgement that our issues carry weight." We may be injured, but by the repression the regime's leaders have made themselves look bad.

Who won and who lost? We have to be careful about how we define victory: If I am beaten, one could say I was successful at commanding my space with moral authority, which forced them to do something that undermines their moral authority. I do not want to be killed, obviously, but we must take some responsibility for the role we play as activists when we put ourselves out there and challenge authoritarian rule with the tough love of a mother.

On Valentine's Day each year, we hold a signature protest. In 2013, police arrested twenty of our members, mostly young males. In response to this arrest and discrimination, 180 of us marched politely and quietly into the courtyard of the police station in downtown Bulawayo. It fell to a senior police officer to address us. He had been at the scene of the protest and had refused to give the order for arrest. He addressed us in his courtyard saying, "We don't know how you people got to be here, but anyway, please will you leave?" So, it appeared that instead of being arrested, we were being un-arrested, if there is such a thing. However, we refused to leave because they were keeping the male members in custody, and we demanded that all of us should be released. We proceeded to conduct a sit-in to make sure that we were all released. They had to deploy the anti-riot police to come into the police station and un-arrest us! The police officers started to walk among us hitting their baton sticks against their hands making ready to beat us as we sat there in disbelief at the change of tactic. After a brief consultation, we asked those seated to stand up calmly and walk out of the police station, making the point that we were able to maintain discipline and determine the course of action, just as we had done by entering the courtyard in the first place.

We have come to redefine and take advantage of repression while at the same time building a spirit of resistance and collective solidarity. It is a hard fact to understand, but collective action and unity of purpose is more easily mobilized than the blind loyalty of a police constable ordered to beat a woman demanding more affordable food. A democratic movement structure working on issues of concern to the members themselves is much more likely to elicit buy-in than orders flowing along a militaristic chain of command.

Managing Fear

We must also address fear, which is an underestimated issue. Conducting workshops and refresher workshops on overcoming fear is a vital activity. Due to the courage displayed by top leadership, ordinary WOZA members could have been demotivated in the face of repression—telling themselves that they are not as brave as others. I do not believe fear can be completely overcome, as there are physically occurring symptoms that manifest. But by making fear something even the top leadership experienced, we made ordinary members capable of managing fear.

A man once came to me in a supermarket and said, "I am glad you are not wearing a mini skirt, or your balls would be showing." This was an awkward compliment, but it drove home to me that people think I am a superwoman (or man in this case), when really I am still fearful for my life. It is just that I am more fearful of doing nothing. If you do not recognize that you are afraid, you will not take the next step to overcome fear.

There are ways to overcome fear, and many can be facilitated. For example, we conduct workshops covering what to do if you are under arrest and what your rights are during detention. We then insist on detailed planning before we conduct a protest. Planning introduces predictability and helps to dispel fear of the unknown. In the planning session, we go through the details of the issue about which we are demonstrating. We develop a collective understanding of the facts and how they affect us and our families. We then decide on which policy maker we need to target during the protest, what demands we will make, how the protest will start, and the route to be taken. We also decide the song that will be sung to communicate the message. All this detail helps members "see" the protest and immerse themselves within it. This immersion process helps prepare protesters to confront all possible outcomes and eventually helps them to overcome fear.

We use singing and dancing a lot. In the first few years of our resistance, I was bothered that many people were dancing during the protests, especially the very young. I would say, "Hey, come on, let's be serious, this is a serious issue." However, I began to realize that when people begin exercising their freedom on their own terms, they become hooked on their freedom and the empowerment of that space they have created and enjoyed together. It becomes a catalyst for the person's own self-identity. It builds their personal confidence and makes them feel, "I can do this. I can lead others doing this." It gives them their full citizenship, and this is a joyful achievement. For that moment, there is no hunger, no repression, only the joy and the need to dance. Once they have collectively abandoned fear for freedom, they are able to locate themselves as full citizens.

We must respect and nurture the transformation of our members. There is a level of responsibility before, during, and after peaceful protest, especially under repression. We must have support and security structures in place. We plan for the worst case scenario and prepare to take people to the doctor or at least offer some care for their injuries. Providing practical care and encouraging members in their quest to overcome or at least manage their own fears is a crucial step in keeping people mobilized.

Police, Fear, and Repression

In order to understand repression and how to manage it, we must also understand what motivates those who threaten and even attack us. Over many years of activism, I have become very familiar with police procedures and strategy, as well as the behavior and thinking of police officers. In my experience, rank-and-file police officers operate by habit, training, and sometimes perceived orders or loyalties. They automatically want to repress because an authoritarian system is in place. Police officers at low levels in the command structure do not make decisions; junior police officers are trained to follow orders without thinking. There is little benefit in questioning the baton-stick holder's cost-benefit analysis regarding beating this person or arresting that person. They do not think, and it is not their role to think. Sadly, some officers seem particularly prone to repression and have internalized it during their training. We often see the same police officers perpetrating abuse over and over, perhaps because of an addiction to trauma, much as Rachel MacNair describes in chapter 4.

I will never forget how once, when I was arrested and taken for fingerprinting, the police officer who was holding my hand and fingerprinting me said, "These are the hands of someone who is telling the truth." He was still fingerprinting me out of habit even as he was declaring his belief that my actions were just. I was still charged, and I was sent to prison for three weeks.

Strategic decisions do take place at a higher level of command, where officers must decide "What order should I give? How do I give the order?" or "How do I make sure no one sees that it is me giving the order?" Consequently, when we are in the street, we know that very few senior police officers want to be on the ground and seen doing the dirty work. We engage that level of our arresting police officers by demanding their names and details so that we can prepare for our legal cases of police harassment. We also mention that we will place a press statement on the Internet mentioning their harassment. This has proven to be a good strategy for police at this level. The higher level police officer has to be dealt with on a legal basis by lawyers and occasionally cited in constitutional court challenges.

We should also understand that the regime and its agents of repression are influenced by fear. In my experience, some of the police officers—if you watch them closely—have severe fear. I am not sure if it is fear of me, my colleagues, or what the chain of command will do to them. I know that our actions can create fearful dilemmas for them. They fear we will build a critical mass and then wonder what will be done with that critical mass. How will they fare as change unfolds? Interestingly, declining fear among activists increases fear on the other side. As that fear is increased, there is a tendency for agents of repression to employ more violence. Nevertheless, as ranking officers decide whether to employ the baton stick, they must also think about how they will maneuver through the reporting process that follows. They may fear for their own consciences and their futures, the kind of future the protestors are offering them. Will it feature retaliation or inclusiveness?

Repression Management through Tough Love

Our tough love approach is one of the integral ways in which we have reduced repression or made it more likely to backfire on the police. We call the police to accountability while also signaling the kind of inclusiveness that only mothers could represent. We show love in our peaceful protest by holding our hands up in the shape of the letter L. Our commitment to love takes the sting out of some of the baton sticks. It is tough on the police to have such a loving protest converge upon their position. It is tough to have the whole of WOZA come loudly singing, carrying placards, and making pavement speeches. But it is done under the banner of disciplining love. To ensure that love rules, we observe strict nonviolent discipline during marches. We also insist that members sign a code of conduct observing nonviolence in their lives.

In every city block, or at the traffic lights, someone goes to the front of the protest group and chants a slogan asking protest participants to sit down and observe nonviolent discipline. This is an important message to all, including the police: "We are marching for the love of Zimbabwe, which means that we care about you. We are not a threat to you, but the love that motivates us is powerful and makes us committed to fighting for our rights and yours, too." The observance of discipline is so pronounced in the movement that many times the police officers have to engage us to quiet the protest. They will come to one of us and say, "Please, can you keep people quiet now?" and so then we will be *empowered by the police* request. We then chant the slogan and sit the protest down. So the police now have to actually ask for our help to facilitate them addressing the protest participants. Nonviolent discipline helps us maintain moral authority—the high ground—and shows that we are prepared to continue our nonviolent direct action until our issue is addressed. It is tough love. It is love, but we recognize it is tough to be on the receiving end because it means you will have done something wrong needing discipline.

The power to respond to repression relies on the ability of a dispersed network of activists to shift tactics. An activist movement can more easily change tactics than its monolithic adversary. Whereas the state uses authoritarian force and hard and fast command structures, our planning allows us to respond to the potential for violent repression by becoming more flexible and nimble than the police. Officers deployed to specific street corners have no latitude to change position without a highly militarized and bureaucratic chain of command, and low ranking officers are often too scared to make suggestions to their bosses. Dispersed networks of activists can more quickly shift tactics to cope with or blunt repression and implement a successful protest action. This ability to shift gears often stretches police resources or leaves them looking silly, standing on street corners in helmets with shields and batons sticks in the hot sun.

When police occupied all our starting points in the central business district of Bulawayo on February 14, 2014, we knew that we could not pull off ten smaller protests so we shifted and combined starting points so there would be higher numbers at three places and that our numbers might work in our favor to get the police to back off. The higher ranking police officers, seeing that we had higher numbers and the upper hand, tried to drive a huge truck into the road and threatened to run us over, honking loudly. Once again, we had to draw on courage and ignore this threat; we got the protest group to pack in close together and march away from the truck before it ran us over. This ability to restrategize (and a huge dose of courage) made for a successful protest.

Repression management can involve elaborate proactive measures. For example, to ensure that police engage in more cost-benefit analysis before arresting someone, we have taken successful proactive legal actions against the police that remind them such repression can have predictable costs. In 2010, three colleagues and I sued the police commissioner for keeping us in filthy conditions in Harare police cells for seven days, making some of us remove our underwear. The Constitutional Court has ruled for a structural modification of police cells and that women cannot be forced to remove underwear or shoes. This kind of sanction of police requires lawyers who have an activist orientation and are brave enough to take on such cases. Through this legal challenge, WOZA has established an increased level of respect for rights for millions of citizens and possibly changed arrest procedures and practice in Zimbabwe.

Conclusion

The experience of Women of Zimbabwe Arise provides a number of insights about repression and its management, notably the advantage of culturally resonant themes in a movement's message, the ability to shift from a culture of fear to a culture of resistance, the importance of innovative leadership structures, and the value of being creative in relating to police.

The basic impression management strategy of WOZA activists involved refashioning the traditional role of women in Zimbabwean society, which provided unique opportunities for action. Transforming the stereotypical motherhood role into one of political activism created a dilemma for government authorities, especially the police who were the government agents interacting with WOZA participants on a regular basis.

Part of a mother's role is providing tough love, a critical perspective, and direct confrontation over unacceptable behavior in order to benefit the child and the family. It is the mother's job to correct, guide, and shape the behavior of family members who are damaging the social fabric of the family. WOZA expanded that domestic role into the public sphere, where authorities, who were usually accustomed to obeying their mothers, found themselves confronted and corrected in the streets for engaging in their official duties. This clash of roles made it difficult for them to use their limited repertoire of repressive acts successfully against the women of WOZA. Indeed, arresting officers were publically shamed when they attempted to use incarceration as a way to suppress the movement, and we essentially arrested ourselves, piling into police vehicles to be taken to jail and thus grabbing even the authority to arrest away from the police. By responding to the authorities with love rather than fear—and expressing it with our iconic symbol of a hand sign making an L for love, we were able to manage repression more successfully.

Showing the love sign while also practicing tough love was a successful action in transforming the culture of fear into a culture of resistance, empowering Zimbabweans to confront the regime and participate as citizens demanding democratic reform. This transformation of the emotions of fear is something like the transformation of fear into excitement that George Lakey discusses in chapter 11 of this volume. It begins with an acknowledgement that one is afraid—but then thinking about the options, such as what would happen if one does nothing—and then finding outlets. WOZA activists sometimes used singing and dancing, for example, as a way of expressing freedom in the face of repression, and these expressions of exuberance empowered us to carry on despite the danger.

A third strategy for repression management was a creative leadership structure that enabled the movement to continue even when our most visible leaders were jailed. A dispersed leadership network was more flexible than the rigid authoritarianism of the security forces, so while we could adapt tactically to whatever situation we faced, they were constantly stuck with the same narrow set of options.

This approach is related to a final central strategy for managing repression, an ability to understand the agents of repression and be creative in relating to them. The police were themselves responding with fear, and our tough love tactics could often disarm them, creating dilemmas for them and reducing their ability to repress the movement. Whereas the police establishment has a limited repertoire of tactics, the activist movement's possibilities are almost unlimited, bounded only by norms against violence.

In short, even the authoritarian regime of Robert Mugabe in Zimbabwe, with all of its resources—weapons, state power, and security forces—has not repressed the movement. They could make our lives difficult and manage to postpone the inevitable collapse of the dictatorship, but they could never defeat us. Anyway, it was never about Mugabe and his ruling elite—it was not about a revolution. It was a story about EVEolution—women taking the lead and showing Zimbabweans that the power of love can conquer the love of power.

References

King, Martin Luther, Jr. 1967. "'Where Do We Go From Here?' Delivered at the 11th Annual SCLC Convention | The Martin Luther King, Jr., Research and Education Institute." Accessed Oct. 17, 2017. https://kinginstitute.stanford.edu/king-papers/documents/where-do-we-go-here-delivered-11th-annual-sclc-convention.

King, Martin Luther, Clayborne Carson, and Kris Shepard, eds. 2001. *A Call to Conscience: The Landmark Speeches of Dr. Martin Luther King, Jr.* New York: IPM (Intellectual Properties Management), in association with Warner Books.

Sharp, Gene. 2005. *Waging Nonviolent Struggle: 20th Century Practice and 21st Century Potential.* Boston: Porter Sargent.

7

Culture and Repression Management

Lee A. Smithey and Lester R. Kurtz

The paradox of repression is often more a cultural phenomenon than a political one, and its occurrence more a consequence of cultural processes than straightforward political confrontation. As Doron Shultziner notes in chapter 3, repressive events often become transformational, radically shifting the political climate and upending long-held attitudes, beliefs, and even social structures and institutions. They are what Victor Turner (1967) calls "liminal moments" in which the world is turned upside down. They open up space for more permanent transformations.

This chapter focuses on the culture of repression and its management—that is, the more symbolic aspects of repression and its backfire, seen more as a dance between a power and its dissidents, a regime and its insurgents, as they contest the frames used to make meaning of events and social arrangements, of justice and injustice. We will examine the two sides of this framing struggle: first (in this chapter) by focusing on efforts of change activists to choreograph actions in order to enhance the backfire effect of repression, and then (in chapter 8) by examining the growing efforts of elites to be more strategic about how they use repression in order to mitigate the effects of its potentially backfiring.

Repression Management and Preemptive Choreography

In this volume, we address the management of repression by social movements trying to bring about change in a system. It is perhaps more apropos to refer to this strategic practice as the "arts" of facing repression, since "management" conjures up notions of clean, efficient processes and predictable causes and effects. Hardly anything could be farther from the truth in the give and take of political contention. However, we follow James Jasper's (2010) lead in subscribing to the idea that tactical choices are important. In the harried flow of conflict, strategic decisions are made in a whirl of incomplete information, past experience, cultural taste, biographical experience, and reciprocal anticipation. Nevertheless, there remains the possibility of "virtuosity," and chains of choices that can influence the trajectory of a conflict in desired directions. "Artfulness is crucial here, for people make choices, and those choices matter" (Jasper 2010, 320). Tactical choices within social movement organizations (SMOs) that anticipate and attempt to mitigate or transform repression to their own advantage command our attention in this chapter, and we turn to the theoretical models of framing and cultural pragmatics, both of which trace their lineage back to Goffman's (1959, 1974) work on dramaturgy and frames (cf. Vinthagen 2015).

Repression can jolt one's sense of identity and sharpen the sense of belonging or not belonging to one of the parties of a conflict—a movement participant, a member of the establishment seeking to mitigate or destroy the movement, and so forth. An uninvolved bystander may then decide either to avoid assiduously any connection or appearance of connection to the movement, or, alternatively, to become involved because of a perceived resonance between their identity and the frame proffered by movement participants. Repression gets people's attention and precipitates a choice regarding a movement campaign. Similarly, a member of the elite perpetrating oppression may find their identity shifting if they become sufficiently repulsed by the brutality of the repression. This is, of course, exactly the kind of frame shift that movement leaders will try to facilitate. It is worth noting that most authorities—even the most authoritarian among them—recognize that there are limits to repression based on their understanding of public opinion and the popular legitimacy on which their authority rests. They tend to reserve repression as a measure of last resort to avoid triggering the very social psychological effects that we are addressing in this chapter.

One primary task of nonviolent actionists, we argue, is to set the stage, so to speak, on which repression takes place. Erving Goffman's (1974) dramaturgical approach to interpreting social interaction sheds light on the process by which movement actors attempt to manage the repression they almost inevitably face as they confront and try to change unjust systems. Just as Goffman observes that individuals and groups engage in impression management through a variety of dramaturgical tactics, so too we see SMO actors engaging in repression management.

Cultural Pragmatics and Performance Theory

In his work on cultural pragmatics, Alexander (2004, 540) re-energizes the field of performance studies and argues that in increasingly complex differentiated societies, public performance of rituals is increasingly problematic as symbolic action becomes professionalized and disconnected from communal life, leading to "the appearance of greater artifice and planning. Performative action becomes more achieved and less automatic." Alexander focuses his attention on what is necessary for actors to align various aspects of performance so that they connect with audiences in convincing and authentic ways. If actors can achieve this fusion of elements, the performance becomes ritual-like in that the audience, through psychological identification with the authors, cathect to the meaning intended by the performers. Successful performances fuse actors with audiences against background representations through means of symbolic production. Alexander also notes that the public sphere has become increasingly available to a broader range of political actors. As Shakespeare has said, "All the world's a stage." This applies equally to SMOs, and Alexander cites one of the most prominent nonviolent actions in US history, the Boston Tea Party, as an example of the way in which a collective action dramatized colonists' resistance to British rule. Such successful performances enact scripts that draw on collective background representations, "the universe of basic narratives and codes and the cookbook of rhetorical configurations from which every performance draws" (Alexander 2004, 550). Successful scripts coordinate narratives and codes to condense meaning into symbols and narratives that are agonistic, pitting good against evil.

The choice of symbols used in action is critical to its overall effect, as it is central to the communicative capacity of the event. It is also important to remember that each action is situated in a web of meaning that is connected to all other possible interpretations of the event, including all possible reactions by the regime. George Lakey (1973) describes a campaign against chemical warfare in the United States in 1970. Campaigners wanted to plant pine trees on the grounds of the Edgewood arsenal, a chemical weapons facility in Maryland. After repeated confrontations and arrests, the arsenal eventually accepted the tree. Lakey asserts, "The point is that if rival symbols were to be juggled, the tree had them licked before they started. In symbol language, when the tree said life, all Edgewood could say back was death, no matter how daintily it picked its phrases" (107). Lakey calls this creative and careful use of choreography "propaganda of the deed."

So far, the application of performance theory to social movements has revolved around issues of mobilization, essentially extending framing theory to the dramatic potential in collective action. Eyerman (2006) argues that movements progress by "fusing individuals into collectives and collectives into focused and directed social forces. This is accomplished through social conventions like public demonstrations and their constitutive ritual practices" (207). We, of course, agree that protests and demonstrations can become "ritual-like," building solidarity and calling people to further action (Alexander 2004). However, we also believe there is a great deal of analysis to be done regarding the tactical choices that SMOs make. Eyerman (2006, 203) ventures into this territory citing Gandhi's choice of traditional clothing to challenge Western images of masculinity and to disarm opponents. Gandhi was a master of making dramatic strategic choices that were symbolically rich (see Kurtz 2008; Johansen and Martin 2008). His preference for traditional clothing was significant not only in relation to potential Western allies and opponents but also because it symbolized in dramatic ways for a mass movement of Indians the injustice of British economic policy regarding the cotton trade in India. He turned religious practices like fasting, praying, and going on pilgrimage into protest tactics, and secular activities like spinning into symbolic acts that were simultaneously political and sacred. The low-risk tactic of spinning one's own clothes became the predominant symbol of participation in the Indian freedom movement, and Gandhi regarded it as a kind of spiritual meditation practice as well as a mode of resistance. Even though everyone knew what the tactic meant, and the Congress Party handed out free spinning wheels, it was impossible for the authorities to arrest people for spinning their own clothes.

We want to build on work that reveals the cultural underpinnings of social movement, and in this chapter we restrict ourselves to examining ways in which certain symbolically rich tactics can draw on widely recognized narratives that dramatize a problem (e.g., religious, ethical, or cultural) to mobilize public opinion, particularly in situations of repression. In other words, these tactics are tailored for the possibility of repression, either preventing it or helping to ensure that repressive events are interpreted in ways that favor the movement.

Eyerman (2006, 210) asserts that "social movements move even those who view them from afar, but whom they move and in which direction is not something easy to control or predict. The world that is watching is multifaceted, and the media which mediates the message adds its own refraction. Movements move, but in differing directions." Indeed, as W. I. Thomas and Dorothy Swaine Thomas said, if people "define a situation as real, it is real in its consequences" (1928, 572); it is mutually constructed out of the dialectical dance between authorities and dissidents (Lyng and Kurtz 1985). As Brian Martin (2007, 189–90) asserts in his book *Justice Ignited: The Dynamics of Backfire*, regimes can be highly adept at framing and "agenda management," especially since they usually have unequaled access to the media. He details common methods, such as covering up acts of repression, stigmatizing activist groups, seeming to concede with small gestures or meaningless inquiries, and bribing or intimidating critics.

We agree the challenge is difficult, but it is not impossible, even against formidable elites; nor is it so unpredictable as to preclude a field of study that focuses on the strategy and execution under duress of effective symbolic action, or repression management. What we are proposing is that much of repression management is in fact the preemptive management of the *perception* of repression. In this section, we explore the dimensions along which movement activists attempt to manage repression by identifying four ways in which choreography and strategic tactical choices can contribute to repression management.

1. Activists can set the stage by framing their cause in popular ways and encouraging the development of ethnic, nationalist, or other collective identities. Thus, when the movement is attacked, bystanding publics who have adopted the overarching nationalist or ethnic identity are more likely to feel as if the attack were directed at them as well.
2. Careful choreography of tactics can contribute to diagnostic framing in which the action itself labels or reveals injustice. Repression only makes the frame resonate even more strongly.
3. Preexisting collective identities can be activated by choreographing events that symbolically or ritualistically express deeply held, sometimes sacred, identities, raising the likelihood that repression against fellow followers will generate moral outrage.
4. Tactics can be designed to encourage ethical dilemmas by framing confrontation in ways that force agents of the regime to reconcile repression, on the one hand, with their own ethical systems, on the other. When repression occurs, it is more easily interpreted as violating shared ethical norms and can precipitate divisions within the ranks of the regime or encourage sympathy for the movement among bystanders who subscribe to the same ethical system.

Before going any further, we must emphasize that the first rule in successful repression management is to *remain nonviolent*. This in itself is a fundamental choreographic decision. Nonviolent discipline is crucial for helping to ensure that any violent repression is understood to have been instigated by the regime and should be defined as illegitimate or disproportionate. Sharp (2005) has pointed out that state regimes often welcome the use of violent tactics by SMOs because it allows them to more easily justify their own use of violence. They have been known to deploy *agents provocateurs* to provoke violence by protesters. Indeed, the very fact that repression needs to be justified signals the presence of countervailing norms calling for limits to the use of violence. Working to ensure that those norms prevail is at the heart of repression management. Beyond nonviolent discipline, however, there are other ways to enhance the likelihood that public opinion will shift in favor of social movements or, more precisely, shift away from the regime.

Setting the Stage: Framing Collective Identity

Even in apparently asymmetrical conflicts, what Vaclav Havel calls the "power of the powerless" can be evoked through effective repression management that causes the broader public—and sometimes even adversaries in a conflict—to reframe and redefine themselves and the situation. Framing has been brilliantly developed by what could have at one time been called the Texas School of movement scholarship, which was initiated by David Snow, Burke Rochford, Steven Worden, and Robert Benford (1986, 21), drawing on Goffman's social theory for the study of social movements. Their framing perspective emphasizes what Goffman calls the "'schemata of interpretation' that enable individuals 'to locate, perceive, identify, and label' occurrences within their life space and the world at large" (464). As Benford and Snow (2000, 214) put it, "Frames help to render events or occurrences meaningful and thereby function to organize experience and guide action." The ability of movement actionists to be successful in having their frame accepted by their potential audience is profoundly related to "frame resonance"; that is, the degree to which their preferred frame appeals to others in that it is credible, salient, and generally produces a positive response in the intended audience (Benford and Snow 2000, 218).

Effective framing involves an adept handling and reshaping of the flow of history in a desired direction. Sørensen and Vinthagen (2012,

449–51) emphasize the impact of borrowing powerful symbols, such as national flags, religious icons, and even images from popular culture. This exemplifies one of the most important cultural dynamics of contention: symbols, rituals, or other familiar practices may be appropriated for insurgent ends. The "worthiness or legitimacy" (Sørensen and Vinthagen 2012, 451) associated with the symbols can be transferred to movements and their claims (Smithey and Young 2010). During the Iraq War, one often saw bumper stickers, banners, and flags in the United States proclaiming "Peace is Patriotic" in an attempt by antiwar activists to "harness hegemony" (Woehrle, Coy, and Maney 2008, 34–35). As Tarrow (1988, 118) puts it, "The lesson of the civil rights movement is that the symbols of revolt are not drawn like musty costumes from a cultural closet and arrayed before the public. Nor are new meanings unrolled out of whole cloth. The costumes of revolt are woven from a blend of inherited and invented fibers into collective action frames in confrontation with opponents and elites."

Sørensen and Vinthagen (2012) go even further and argue that fundamental cultural principles or "'old' culture" can be appropriated or simply highlighted to elevate the status of nonviolent activists. Jenni Williams describes in chapter 6 how the Women of Zimbabwe Arise (WOZA) movement borrowed motherhood and Valentines tropes from their traditional culture to challenge the Zimbabwean regime. WOZA activists claimed authority as mothers to scold the president and regime elites for their misbehavior and held major annual demonstrations on Valentine's Day to demonstrate their love for their country and its people.

The consequences of repression for movement mobilization may be profoundly affected by how nonviolent actions and repression are framed and whose frames dominate cultural discourse both within the movement and in the larger society. A movement is more likely to benefit rather than just suffer from repression if it can manage the frames through which the repression is interpreted (Woehrle, Coy, and Maney 2008). The rich literature on the relationship between identity and cultural meaning in new social movements has also yielded much new understanding about social movement mobilization, but this literature has seldom focused on the actual acts of participation—the tactics and methods of movement actors.

In an exception, Kern (2009) draws on Alexander's cultural pragmatics, claiming that the Minjung movement in South Korea following World War II cultivated a broad, populist Korean identity, including a Buddhist messianic vision against which to contrast the state's attempts to consolidate its legitimacy through a cultural "One-People Principle" program. Through the deployment of traditional practices and rituals, such as dances, music, and recitation, intellectuals and artists encouraged mobilization by establishing a frame that not only drew distinctions between the state and the people but drew powerfully on myths and collective memory, thus successfully fusing South Koreans' national identity with the democracy movement's agenda. Activists promoted a framing of Korean history in which the Minjung repeatedly challenged repression, a narrative that, through the inclusion of traditional practices, was reenacted in each protest. "In this way, protest events removed the boundary between the present and the (mythic) past; every tear gas grenade that exploded and every arrest of activists strengthened the faith of the (mostly) students and stimulated further confrontations" (Kern 2009, 311). By successfully reviving a widely known agonistic narrative, democracy activists managed to influence the interpretation of contemporary confrontations with the state. Because the stage had been set in the minds of South Koreans, state repression was more likely to be interpreted according to the movement's framing and lead to mobilization.

In some cases, the preservation and appropriation of histories of repression can prepare activists and publics to interpret contemporary repression as yet another affront and indignity. Activists in Hungary made significant use of historical processions and funerals during resistance to Soviet rule in the late 1980s. On March 15, 1989, one hundred thousand Hungarians participated in a Revolution Day march that passed six locations connected with the democratic Hungarian revolution of 1848, linking the contemporary movement with a widely shared nationalist history. Three months later, another powerfully symbolic event was held to commemorate the death of Imre Nagy, a

Hungarian communist prime minister, who had supported another revolution in 1956 against the Stalinist People's Republic of Hungary. Soviet forces brutally repressed the 1956 revolution, but the resulting indignation remained suffused in popular memory and was revived when Hungarian demonstrators commemorating Nagy's death were violently dispersed by police in 1988. In 1989, the Communist Party had agreed to the reinterment of Nagy's and other revolutionaries' remains in hopes of appropriating the legacy of the revolution, but instead the funeral became a critical opportunity for contemporary opposition. Commemorations in Hungary not only tapped into powerful and almost sacred nationalist narratives to rally participation but also came to inscribe memories of repression and thus sustained indignation over decades, reminding us that the paradox of repression is not limited to discrete events but can accumulate over time, creating a rhythm of resistance (Kern 2009; Smithey and Kurtz 1999).

Diagnostic Framing

Benford and Snow (2000, 614) identify three core tasks in the framing process: the diagnostic, the prognostic, and the motivational, all of which SMO actors use to manage impressions. As they put it, movement adherents negotiate a shared understanding of some problematic condition or situation they define as in need of change, make attributions regarding who or what is to blame, articulate an alternative set of arrangements, and urge others to act in concert to affect change.

A major aspect of the diagnostic process is the establishment of what William Gamson (1995) calls "injustice frames" that define movement participants as victims. Injustice frames are thus a mode of interpretation that often precedes "collective noncompliance, protest, and or rebellion" (Benford and Snow 2000, 614). Strategic actions can be choreographed to present a diagnosis of a social problem and undermine a regime's authority. If authorities react to the framing with repressive measures, they only serve to strengthen the diagnosis. Lakey (1973, 103) refers to such actions as "dilemma demonstrations": "The best kind of action is one which puts the opponent in a dilemma: whichever response he makes helps the movement. If he allows the demonstration to proceed, the movement gains that opportunity to educate the people. If he represses the demonstration, the people are awakened further to the underlying nature of the regime." Thus, the repression itself amplifies and dramatizes victimization in a way that movement participants cannot do by themselves, and ends up ironically as a collaborative effort between the regime and its dissidents.

Diagnosis involves identifying not only aspects of the system that need change but also the linkage between the repression change agents have suffered, on the one hand, and the inherent problems and injustice of the system itself, on the other. The violence of the repression a regime inflicts on a movement is framed as symptomatic of what is wrong with the system in the first place. When Major Dyer ordered his soldiers to fire on unarmed Indian demonstrators demanding Indian independence (demonstrators who were unable to escape the courtyard in which they were meeting), it was not, according to Gandhi, a fluke instance of one officer run amok but characteristic of the very nature of the colonial system, which was held in place by brutal violence and the people's acceptance of it.

More to the point here, certain tactics can dramatize an issue and bring others into the arena. When Dr. Martin Luther King Jr. appeared on NBC's *Meet the Press* in 1960, he was asked by his host if it would not have been more effective simply to boycott white businesses that did not serve "Negro" customers rather than creating the kind of confrontation emerging from lunch counter sit-ins.

> I think, Mr. Spivak, sometimes it is necessary to dramatize an issue because many people are not aware of what is happening, and I think the sit-ins serve to dramatize the indignities and the injustices which Negro people are facing all over the nation, and I think another reason why they are necessary and they are vitally important at this point is the fact that they give an eternal refutation to the idea that the Negro is satisfied with segregation. If you didn't have the sit-ins, you wouldn't have this dramatic and not only this dramatic but this mass demonstration of the dissatisfaction of the Negro with the whole system of segregation (King 2005, 434).

The sit-in strategy was designed to draw attention not only to the lunch counters but also to "injustices which negro people are facing all over the nation." When locals attacked activists in department stores, King's indictment of segregation across the South only resonated more strongly.

Demonstrators entered the lunchrooms in Nashville anticipating that they would be beaten and arrested—it was part of the strategic plan developed by Rev. James Lawson, a United Methodist clergyman who had returned from three years in India studying Gandhi's freedom movement and was sent by Dr. King to work on desegregation campaigns in the American South. The protestors of Jim Crow laws thus choreographed their actions in advance to take repression into account. They were trained to endure violent attacks from bystanders and arrest by law enforcement officials. In workshops prior to the sit-ins, Lawson had them role play various scenarios involving verbal and even physical abuse, thinking carefully about how to respond in a disciplined, nonviolent manner so as to ensure that their frame prevailed (Isaac et al. 2012). By carefully choreographing (including wardrobe), rehearsing, and playing out the lunch counter sit-ins, civil rights activists revealed their diagnosis of Jim Crow practices, ensuring that the beatings and arrests that followed would further support their injustice frame.

Raising the Cultural Stakes: Representing Deeply Held Identities

Tactics that tap into discourses of national identity, religious commitment, or other affinity can also create a strategic dilemma for repressive regimes. Sørensen and Vinthagen (2012) discuss the paradigmatic way in which the Khudai Khidmatgar, a nonviolent army of Islamic Pathans led by Abdul Ghaffar Khan in the British-controlled North-West Frontier Province drew on Islam and the code of Pukhtunwali to mobilize and discipline nonviolent action. The greater jihad or inner "struggle" through which Muslims pursue devotion and justice can be joined with the lesser jihad of external struggle against enemies in a call to nonviolent action. Pukhtunwali sacralized freedom, and thus acts of repression by British authorities (such as otherwise humiliating strip searches and beatings) could be reinterpreted as opportunities to demonstrate freedom and resistance through disciplined nonviolent resistance. Within their particular cultural context, Khudai Kidmatgars evoked the paradox of repression as the viciousness of British subjugation contrasted starkly with the actions of these nonviolent warriors, violating Pukhtunwali and compelling more Pathans to join the movement.

When authorities are seen as attacking or disrespecting widely shared symbols, they may mobilize people in defense of shared collective identities. Thus, tactics that symbolically invoke events or principles that are deeply embedded in collective memory and identity can take on an almost sacred quality and present a dilemma to authorities who want to repress a movement but would do so at the risk of offending a much larger population.

More than 500,000 people attended the funeral of the student Jan Palach in Czechoslovakia in 1969. Palach martyred himself through self-immolation during the Soviet invasion of Czechoslovakia. Twenty years later, civic organizations planned events to commemorate his death, essentially reenacting the repression of an earlier time and, in a sense, harvesting the indignation of the earlier event for contemporary mobilization. Repression of the commemoration in 1989 only compounded the insult of 1969 and helped to activate the paradox of repression. Eda Kriseová (1993, 235) explained how the two events became linked in the movement's favor: "The proud authorities would not allow people to honor the memory of a dead man, and by this they had done more to revive his memory than Havel could if he had spoken, and perhaps more than a new human torch could have done, if one had been lit. Face to face with truncheons, people felt even closer to Jan Palach, who had intended his death to be a warning against this kind of violence. As if by a miracle, the years all merged together."

This case could also fall into our first category of preparing collective identities, but here we want to focus on how discrete events can tap into preexisting core identities and raise the stakes of repression. In another example, Timothy Garton Ash (1993, 80) has said that repression during the 1989 commemoration of the death of Jan Opletal, who was killed by Nazis, was "the spark that set Czechoslovakia alight" (quoted in Smithey and Kurtz 1999, 100–101).

Besides these examples of historical significance, simply holding certain *types* of events that are widely considered sacred and have a deep emotional connection among the public can improve the chances that repression provokes indignation and mass mobilization. Funerals and commemorations, such as Imre Nagy's, Jan Palach's, and Jan Opletal's, condense meaning (e.g., national pride and, often, religious beliefs) into a specific point in time and space. Similarly, candlelight vigils and "prayers for peace" at the Church of St. Nicholas in Leipzig evoked sacred moments of spiritual reflection among the predominantly Christian German population during the Peaceful Revolution that overthrew the Communist regime in East Germany.

Nonviolent strategy can appropriate cultural values associated with individuals' statuses in much the same way as certain types of events. In some cases, the value of religious authority has been leveraged. In June 1968, 130 Brazilian priests organized by Archbishop Dom Helder Camara formed a chain and placed themselves between police and protesting students (Lakey 1973, 115). In a similar example, during the 1986 EDSA Revolution (*Epifanio de los Santos Avenue*) in the Philippines, two military factions of the Filipino army engaged in a standoff in Manila after one of the factions mutinied and planned to overthrow the Marcos government. Archbishop Sin urged the population to support the mutiny, and hundreds of thousands of people gathered to intervene in the standoff while trained activists, along with nuns and priests, worked to maintain nonviolent discipline and deter the military factions from engaging one another (Johansen and Martin 2008; Schock 2005, 78). In both of these vastly Roman Catholic countries, clergy played important roles in managing protesters and raising the stakes of repression by authorities. (Even representations of iconic and popular figures such as Santa Claus, clowns, and cartoon characters can present a challenge to authorities! [Johansen and Martin 2008].)

Leveraging Shared Cultural Resources and Encouraging Ethical Dilemmas

Finally, tactics can be designed to signal and appropriate ethical norms that are shared between challengers and the regime. If those observing the repression of a movement share certain values with dissidents, such as justice, proportionality, or equality, then they are more likely to find the movement's frame resonant. Alternatively, if values are shared between elites and the opposition and can be cued through the creative choreography of collective action events, repression may become less likely, or splits may develop within the regime as agents of the state struggle with how to resolve contradictions between state policy and their own ethical systems.

Agents of the regime are often placed in a problematic ethical dilemma when ordered to carry out repression against unarmed disciplined nonviolent protesters. Carefully choreographed actions can amplify this dilemma by making it more difficult for them to overlook ethical or religious proscriptions against killing or harming unarmed opponents. The dilemma can dissuade regime leaders from using repression or can lead to divisions within the ranks of the regime, as some find it prohibitively difficult to violate their own norms. In instances when repression does occur, the coercion can be made to appear as asymmetrical as possible, further violating ethical norms. In the instance of repression during the commemoration of Jan Opletal in Czechoslovakia, protesters made their commitment to nonviolent discipline clear by chanting, "We have bare hands." When security forces attacked protesters, the incident galvanized the nation.

Activists can tap into prevailing understandings of spirituality, citizenship, and gender. While conducting nonviolent trainings in Nashville during the equal accommodations campaign, Jim Lawson described an instance when a friend of his had been tied to a tree to receive a beating from a group of white racists. He began to recite the Lord's Prayer, provoking an argument among the attackers about the propriety of beating someone who was praying. The argument among the attackers undermined their ability to act collectively and diffused the situation (York 2000).

In the case of the Rosenstrasse wives in Berlin during World War II, German women who were intermarried with male Jews demanded the release of their husbands, who had been interned. Despite SS troops firing warning shots over the crowd, the women would not disperse. Ackerman and DuVall (2000, 237) explain, "They knew the soldiers would never fire directly at them because they were of German blood. Also, arresting or jailing any of the women would have been the rankest hypocrisy: According to Nazi theories, women were intellectually incapable of political action. So, women dissenters were the last thing the Nazis wanted to have Germans hear about, and turning them into martyrs would have ruined the Nazi's self-considered image as the protector of motherhood." Interestingly, in this case it was both *challenging* the regime's ideology concerning women and taking advantage of patriarchal norms that managed to reduce the likelihood of repression. The intermarried women of Berlin became activists out of their individual commitments to their husbands, not as part of some larger strategic campaign. However, the effect remains significant. Nazi officials knew that violent attacks on German women risked violating fundamental norms of German culture, not to mention revealing flaws in Nazi ideology.

Activists can take strategic advantage of cultural norms to enhance frame resonance by choreographing their actions in ways that emphasize the innocence and nobility of nonviolent activists in juxtaposition to the brutality of the regime. During the movement to overthrow the Guatemalan ruler Jorge Ubico in 1944, nonviolent protests, often by students, were met with beatings, guns, and arrest. During demonstrations, campaigners faced guns and tear gas. Women dressed in mourning prayed at the church of San Francisco in Guatemala City before undertaking a peaceful silent march, highlighting the contrast between the violence of the forces and the legitimacy of the insurgents. The military fired on the crowd and killed Maria Cincilla Recinos, making her a martyr and icon for the movement. Guatemalans launched a massive general strike in response (Muñoz 2009). The Mothers of the Plaza de Mayo in Argentina deployed a similar performance of mourning as they publicly demonstrated and pressed the military junta to release information about their disappeared children and husbands. In both of these cases, traditional tropes from the local culture were employed to show potential allies and recruits that those calling for change were in fact simply reflecting shared values (Bouvard 1994; Malin 1994; Navarro 2001).

Similarly, student civil rights activists in the lunch counter sit-ins in Nashville were careful to appear as upstanding citizens, wearing their "Sunday best" clothes when engaging in sit-ins or marches. The well-dressed, well-mannered, educated young people (segregated by gender, so as not to take on interracial romance issues) deliberately appeared in stark contrast to the ruffians who beat them up and even the police officers who arrested them. Many Nashvillians were outraged at the sight of fine young college students being rounded up, jailed, and brought into court. If white local ruffians were to harass the protesters, and when arrests were imminent, the students wanted to ensure that the images captured in the media and absorbed by other bystanding African Americans would clearly show that norms of respectability and citizenship were being violated. The arrests of these students led to the galvanizing of African American resistance and the success of widespread economic boycotts (Johansen and Martin 2008).

Campaigns for social change may be more successful when they engage in repression management with attention to cultural themes—choreographing and framing actions that enhance the probability that repression will backfire and increase the credibility of and participation in the movement. This framing can occur both before and after the transformative events of repression (see Shultziner, chapter 3): preemptive choreography as a part of strategic planning may help actionists to shape the kind of repression they face or, more probably, to set the stage for how the event is perceived by relevant actors when it occurs. Of course, these actions are not one sided, but part of a framing contest between insurgents and elites; some authorities are fully conscious of the paradox of repression and have gone beyond brute force to use what we call "smart" repression, which we take up in the next chapter.

After repressive events take place, civil resisters may facilitate the paradox of repression by amplifying the moral outrage (Moore 1978) or arousing moral concern (Collins 2009) through effective framing. Repression does not backfire unless relevant audiences know about it and find it objectionable, potentially triggering negative attitudes toward repressive structures and their representatives, on the one hand, and positive responses toward the resistance, on the other. If a movement's goals are perceived as resonating with significant elements of its cultural context, elites are more likely to defect, and potential activists more likely to mobilize. The cultural capital of a nonviolent insurgency can be enhanced by civil resisters' active attention to the cultural elements of a conflict, leading to increased participation and greater chances of success.

References

Ackerman, Peter, and Jack DuVall. 2000. *A Force More Powerful: A Century of Nonviolent Conflict*. New York: Palgrave.

Alexander, Jeffrey C. 2004. "Cultural Pragmatics: Social Performance between Ritual and Strategy." *Sociological Theory* 22: 527–73.

Ash, Timothy Garton. 1993. *The Magic Lantern: The Revolution of '89 Witnessed in Warsaw, Budapest, Berlin, and Prague*. New York: Vintage Books.

Benford, Robert D., and David A. Snow. 2000. "Framing Processes and Social Movements: An Overview and Assessment." *Annual Review of Sociology* 26: 611–39.

Bouvard, Marguerite Guzman. 1994. *Revolutionizing Motherhood: The Mothers of the Plaza De Mayo*. Wilmington, DE: Scholarly Resources Inc.

Collins, Randall. 2009. "Social Movements and the Focus of Emotional Attention." In *Passionate Politics: Emotions and Social Movements*, edited by Jeff Goodwin, James M. Jasper, and Francesca Polletta, 27–44. Chicago: Univ. of Chicago Press.

Eyerman, Ron. 2006. "Performing Opposition or, How Social Movements Move." In *Social Performance: Symbolic Action, Cultural Pragmatics, and Ritual*, edited by Jeffrey C. Alexander, Bernhard Giesen and Jason L. Mast, 193–217. New York: Cambridge Univ. Press.

Gamson, William A. 1995. "Constructing Social Protest." In *Social Movements and Culture*, edited by H. Johnston and B. Klandermans, 85–106. Minneapolis: Univ. of Minnesota Press.

Goffman, Erving. 1959. *The Presentation of Self in Everyday Life*. Garden City, NY: Doubleday.

———. 1974. *Frame Analysis: An Essay on the Organization of Experience*. New York: Harper & Row.

Isaac, Larry W., Daniel B. Cornfield, Dennis C. Dickerson, James M. Lawson, and Jonathan S. Coley. 2012. "'Movement Schools' and Dialogical Diffusion of Nonviolent Praxis: Nashville Workshops in the Southern Civil Rights Movement." In *Nonviolent Conflict and Civil Resistance*, edited by Sharon Erickson Nepstad and Lester R. Kurtz. *Research in Social Movements, Conflicts and Change* 34: 155–84.

Jasper, James M. 2010. "Cultural Approaches in the Sociology of Social Movements." In *Handbook of Social Movements across Disciplines*, edited by Bert Klandermans and Conny Roggeband, 59–109. New York: Springer. http://link.springer.com/chapter/10.1007/978-0-387-70960-4_3.

Johansen, Jørgen, and Brian Martin. 2008. "Sending the Protest Message." *Gandhi Marg* 29: 503–19.

Kern, Thomas. 2009. "Cultural Performance and Political Regime Change." *Sociological Theory* 27: 291–316.

King, Martin Luther, Jr. 2005. *Threshold of a New Decade: January 1959–December 1960*. Edited by Clayborne Carson, Tenisha Armstrong, Susan Carson, Adrienne Clay, and Kieran Taylor. Vol. 5 of *The Papers of Martin Luther King, Jr.* Berkeley: Univ. of California Press.

Kriseová, Eda. 1993. *Václav Havel: The Authorized Biography*. New York: St. Martin's Press.

Kurtz, Lester R. 2008. "Gandhi and His Legacies." In *Encyclopedia of Violence, Peace, and Conflict*, edited by Lester R. Kurtz, 837–51. Amsterdam: Elsevier. http://works.bepress.com/lester_kurtz/1/.

Lakey, George. 1973. *Strategy for a Living Revolution*. New York: Orbis Books.

Lyng, Stephen G., and Lester R. Kurtz. 1985. "Bureaucratic Insurgency: The Vatican and the Crisis of Modernism." *Social Forces* 63: 901–22.

Malin, Andrea. 1994. "Mother Who Won't Disappear." *Human Rights Quarterly* 16 (1): 187–213.

Martin, Brian. 2007. *Justice Ignited: The Dynamics of Backfire*. Lanham, MD: Rowman & Littlefield.

Moore, Barrington. 1978. *Injustice: The Social Bases of Obedience and Revolt.* New York: Macmillan.

Muñoz, Aurora. 2009. "Guatemalans Overthrow a Dictator, 1944." *Global Nonviolent Action Database*. https://web.archive.org/web/20150222183111/http://nvdatabase.swarthmore.edu/content/guatemalans-overthrow-dictator-1944.

Navarro, Marysa. 2001. "The Personal Is Political: Las Madres De Plaza De Mayo." In *Power and Popular Protest: Latin American Social Movements*, edited by S. Eckstein and M. A. Garretón Merino, 241–58. Berkeley: Univ. of California Press.

Schock, Kurt. 2005. *Unarmed Insurrections: People Power Movements in Nondemocracies*. Minneapolis: Univ. of Minnesota Press.

Sharp, Gene. 1973. *The Politics of Nonviolent Action*. 3 vols. Boston: Porter Sargent.

———. 2005. *Waging Nonviolent Struggle: 20th Century Practice and 21st Century Potential.* Boston: Porter Sargent.

Smithey, Lee, and Lester R. Kurtz. 1999. "We Have Bare Hands: Nonviolent Social Movements in the Soviet Bloc." In *Nonviolent Social Movements*, edited by Stephen Zunes, Lester R. Kurtz, and Sarah Beth Asher, 96–124. Malden, MA: Blackwell.

Smithey, Lee A. and Michael P. Young. 2010. "Parading Protest: Orange Parades in Northern Ireland and Temperance Parades in Antebellum America." *Social Movement Studies* 9, 393–410.

Snow, David A., Jr., E. Burke Rochford, Steven K. Worden, and Robert D. Benford. 1986. "Frame Alignment Processes, Micromobilization, and Movement Participation." *American Sociological Review* 51, 464–81.

Sørensen, Majken Jul, and Stellan Vinthagen. 2012. "Nonviolent Resistance and Culture." *Peace and Change* 37, 444–70.

Tarrow, Sidney. 1988. "Old Movements in New Cycles of Protest: The Career of an Italian Religious Community." In *International Social Movement Research*, edited by Bert Klandermans, 201–304. Greenwich, CT: JAI Press Inc.

Thomas, William Isaac, and Dorothy Swaine Thomas. 1928. *The Child in America: Behavior Problems and Programs*. New York: A. A. Knopf.

Turner, Victor. 1967. *The Forest of Symbols: Aspects of Ndembu Ritual*. Ithaca: Cornell Univ. Press.

Vinthagen, Stellan. 2015. *A Theory of Nonviolent Action: How Civil Resistance Works*. New York: Zed Books.

Woehrle, Lynne M., Patrick G. Coy, and Gregory M. Maney. 2008. *Contesting Patriotism: Culture, Power, and Strategy in the Peace Movement*. Lanham, MD: Rowman & Littlefield.

York, Steve. 2000. *A Force More Powerful* (film). PBS documentary directed by Steve York, narrated by Ben Kingsley. Distributed by Films for the Humanities and Sciences, Princeton, NJ. http://www.aforcemorepowerful.org/films/index.php.

8

"Smart" Repression

Lee A. Smithey and Lester R. Kurtz

Repression by authorities against challengers has become an increasingly common subject of study among scholars of social movements. Most of us are familiar with newspaper photos and videos of protesters being attacked with water hoses, dogs, or chemicals, or beaten by helmeted baton-wielding police officers, or even shot by riot-gear-clad law enforcement. Indeed, many of the most iconic pictures of social movements capture moments of shocking repression. Vicious attacks on demonstrators often backfire, however, if the repression is seen as unjust or disproportionate, bringing shame on the regime and increased support for the movement (Smithey and Kurtz 1999).

It is not only scholars of social movements who have become increasingly aware of this paradox of repression, but also some authorities who are confronting social movements in ways that attempt to avoid the backfire that so often accompanies repression. In this chapter, we turn our attention to that phenomenon: the increasing use by elites of what we call *"smart" repression*—that is, the use of tactics by authorities that are deliberately crafted to demobilize movements while mitigating or eliminating a backfire effect. Some may initially find the concept of smart repression confounding or even unsettling. The term is meant to invoke the same paradox that one finds in references to technology, such as "smart" bombs (precision-guided munitions), which military experts argue reduce collateral damage and make warfare more effective strategically and acceptable politically. Authorities use smart repression to frame or even forestall dramatic confrontations that might undermine their legitimacy. By modulating away from the most heavy-handed tactics, such methods attempt to make popular mobilization less likely, either by making repression incrementally less outrageous or by invoking familiar norms (such as law and order) to make resistance literally unthinkable or unpalatable. In both cases, the ability of authorities to maintain legitimacy is paramount.

Sometimes the repression of dissidents by the state—even if violent—is considered legitimate because of the state's unique institutional role. German sociologist Max Weber ([1920] 1978) famously asserted that what distinguishes the state is its claim to the legitimate use of physical force within a given territory. His dictum seems to have become more prevalent as the preservation of law and order becomes increasingly militarized. As police officers adopt the clothing, protective gear, and weapons of soldiers, they look and respond less and less like the "peace officers" they were once considered to be (see Birmingham and Vitale 2011).

Christian Davenport (1995) looked at the question of when regimes decide to use negative sanctions against social movements, examining fifty-three states in a time series analysis from 1948 to 1993. He concluded that the decision by political leaders to repress dissent was related not so much to the frequency of challenges as to the variety of strategies used by dissidents to challenge governmental authority and whether the regime was democratic (democracies being less likely to impose negative sanctions). Davenport (1995, 702) found that "regimes are more inclined to respond repressively to deviance from the cultural norm and multiple strategies of mass political behavior. In these situations, the regime has to confront conflict that is in violation of its code of acceptable dissent as well as confront different strategies of political conflict, each with its own method of recruitment and impact upon the domestic political economy." What Davenport (2007) calls the "punishment puzzle" is not easily answered: why do "governments respond to behavioral threats with some form of repression despite lack of evidence that repressive behavior is effective at quelling dissent" (Davenport and Inman 2012, 630)? This question is not our focus here, but it is relevant because to counter repression or its effects it is helpful to know what causes the repression. It might be, some suggest, that authorities have to act but have limited options in their repertoire (Davenport and Inman 2012; Kalyvas 2003; Valentino, Huth, and Balch-Lindsay 2004; Ackerman and DuVall 2000).

However, regimes are not held in place simply by brute force, as Gandhi (1999) observed, but by the cooperation of their subjects (forced or otherwise). In recent years, we have observed both increased violent repression (and technologies of repression) but also an increase in smart repression, which includes the modulation of tactical responses by authorities to maximize their ability to demobilize social movements while avoiding the public outrage that violence can evoke.

Authorities sometimes focus on low-risk tactics, just as dissidents do. Moreover, in the classic carrot-stick tension, regimes reward cooperation while they sanction dissidence. As nonviolent civil resistance becomes a major force in contemporary geopolitics, however, a number of regimes have searched for new techniques of repression in an effort to outsmart nonviolent dissidents, who are those most likely to create conditions fertile for the backfire effect.

Such elite strategies increasingly involve intelligence gathering about movement organizations that resembles Foucault's ([1975] 2012, 221) concept of "disciplinary techniques" in which the "traditional, ritual, costly, violent forms of power . . . fell into disuse and were superseded by a subtle, calculated technology of subjection." Indeed, the original French title of Foucault's 1975 book was *Surveiller et Punier: Naissance de la Prison*, literally "to watch and punish," which implies the same kind of rational investigative approach to resistance campaigns—as opposed to raw repression—that we address later in this chapter.

Smart repression is not limited to political regimes but can also be found in the corporate world—as evidenced by public relations specialist Denise Deegan's (2001) handbook *Managing Activism: A Guide to Dealing with Activists and Pressure Groups*, written to help organizations plan for—and mitigate the effects of—"activist attacks." Her introduction begins by bemoaning the negative impact of activists on corporations like Shell, which was forced to spend £38.5 million extra on disposing of a sea rig because of Greenpeace's campaigns, and McDonald's, which was compelled to spend 10 million pounds in court costs suing activists accusing the company of animal rights abuse and exploitation of workers. Deegan advises not to counter with force, but to prepare for and respond to activists intelligently: "if dealt with in the right manner, activists have been shown to change their approach from aggressively confrontational to cooperative" (2–3). She argues that, by understanding and negotiating with activists, it is possible to both influence their strategies and demobilize them.

In an intriguing and escalating contest, both regimes and dissidents often seek to outsmart the other with regard to repression. How do regimes and other elites (like corporate officers) try to *prevent* the backfire effect with smart repression, and how do resisters try to anticipate such measures in order to cultivate defections and support for the movement?

Brute Force versus Smart Repression

Here we find an interesting divergence: even as authorities continue to use physical force and violence, ranging from massive police efforts to herd and sweep up protesters to the use of live ammunition, we also perceive a growing awareness of authorities regarding the limitations of such tactics. Regimes have come a long way since the British Raj was caught off guard by Gandhi and the Indian independence movement. Authorities seem to be increasingly conscious of the thresholds across which physical force repression may backfire. Perhaps they always have been, but there is little research that reveals in any qualitative way how authorities make difficult decisions about the use of repression. The literature on repression focuses on instances of physical force or intimidation by security forces but tends to ignore deliberate efforts by authorities to avoid provoking backfire.

Although students of movements usually focus on the protester perspective, the other crucial side of the contest has been addressed by some scholars. Goldstone and Tilly (2001), for example, argue that authorities seek to combine repression and concession in ways that are most likely to pacify an opposition movement. Tarrow (2003, 149) says that regimes can use a strategy of "selective facilitation and repression" to drive wedges between moderates and radicals, what Haines (1984) calls the "radical flank" question (cf. Schock and Chenoweth 2010). This narrative that labels one group of insurgents as radical and the other moderate is a common tactic of elites (see Alridge 2006), who have a clear preference for dealing with one group rather than the other, which is why President Johnson would invite Dr. King, but not Malcolm X, to the White House. Mistrust sometimes emerges within a resistance movement as moderates are seen to have sold out to the powers that be. Examining cases from the Nonviolent and Violent Campaigns and Outcomes (NAVCO) data set comparing violent and nonviolent campaigns (see Chenoweth and Stephan 2011; Stephan and Chenoweth 2008), Schock and Chenoweth (2010) found that, when a radical flank existed, nonviolent campaigns were less likely to succeed. Radicals, freed from the moderating influence of their former comrades, are more likely to use violence and create a plausible excuse for further repression of all dissent by the authorities. In this way, authorities sometimes can shift the thresholds of public outrage to avoid the paradox of repression. This clever use of selective facilitation and repression suggests authorities can be quite aware of the risks of overt repression and appreciate the important subjective dimensions of repression and protest within which the fundamental battle over legitimacy is waged.

A Continuum of Demobilization

If we are to understand the paradox of repression, we also need to explore how elites sometimes attempt to avoid triggering it. There is some evidence—although it is obviously difficult to get accurate information—that intelligence and military agencies are attempting to construct tactics of smart repression.[1] This chapter represents our

1. Not all of these efforts are covert, however—in fact, Eric L. Nelson (2013) has explored "the intentional subversion of social movements by agents of the

initial foray into a deeper consideration of repression and whether the paradoxical dynamic that is often called backfire operates in the same way across a variety of forms of repression, a topic taken up fruitfully by Jennifer Earl (2003, 47), who suggested looking at "three key theoretical dimensions of repression . . . (1) the identity of the repressive agent; (2) the character of the repressive action; and (3) whether the repressive action is observable."

Keeping those elements in mind but focusing on the second and third, we suggest, as a point of departure, that a continuum of demobilization (Table 8.1) ranges from the most violent forms that rely on inducing fear among challengers and potential movement participants, on the one hand, to intentional attempts to encourage people to internalize a regime's legitimacy, on the other. We expect the type of repression used to affect the dynamics of a conflict and the probability of its backfiring on the regime. As one moves to the right of the continuum in Table 8.1, one encounters less direct threat, violence, and intimidation and a diminishing likelihood of public outrage and mobilization.

We propose that this continuum represents a range of attempts employed by movement opponents to demobilize protest. Nodes to the left of the continuum align more strongly with traditional ideas about repression, while nodes toward the right represent attempts to induce self censorship among would-be activists by disseminating privileged narratives that favor authorities and become internalized in the general populace (see Gramsci 1998). Whether these activities should always be defined as repression remains unclear.

---

organization upon which the social movement is trying to force change" (163). He reviews "thirteen tested and theoretical methods of subversion . . . [that] were designed to induce petit or grand failure into targeted social movements" (172), some of which we discuss below. It is interesting to note that Nelson explicitly avoids discussing the morality or appropriateness of these types of deliberate subversion of a movement, concluding with a warning that "organizational attorneys should be consulted before any subversive program is implemented" (172).

TABLE 8.1 A Continuum of Demobilization

←————————————————————————————————→

Overt Violence	*"Less-lethal" Methods*	*Intimidation*	*Manipulation*	*Soft Repression*	*Hegemony*
Executions	Pepper spray	Indirect threats	Co-optation	Framing contests	Latent repression
Shooting unarmed demonstrators	Active Denial System	Harassment	Selective facilitation	Ridicule	Spontaneous consensus
Assassinations	Laser and acoustic devices	Surveillance	Dilemma actions	Stigmatization	Self censorship
Beatings	"Non-lethal" munitions	Intrapsychic wounding	Resource depletion	Defamation	Election fraud
Torture	Tasers		Information suppression	Silencing	
Arrests			Thwart recruiting efforts	Diversions	
			Disinformation	Media manipulation	
			Making faux concessions	Arranged counterprotest	
			Divisive disruption		
			Censorship		

Source: Lee A. Smithey and Lester R. Kurtz

Overt Violence

The most dramatic forms of repression that attract the bulk of media and popular attention include instances of public physical force: assassinations and executions, baton charges and beatings, arrests, water jets, dogs, and the iconic example of live fire injuring or even killing demonstrators. Overt violence can have the functional effect of removing protesters from the streets as they are incapacitated or arrested and removed to detention facilities. However, its primary effect is *deterrence*—it lies in provoking fear and making an example of a few in order to inhibit the participation of others in protest. Although this is the most likely type of repression to provoke backfire, it can also sometimes actually demobilize or even extinguish a movement that is unable to manage the repression effectively, as did the June 4, 1989 massacre at Tiananmen Square in Beijing, which effectively shut down the Chinese movement at that time. Movement leaders slipped underground or into exile, and demonstrators learned to self censor for fear of harsh repercussions.

Authorities who anticipate using overt violence to demobilize a movement may prepare for the use of force in order to mitigate its negative effects. Here we may see something like a macro-level use of what social psychologist Albert Bandura (1999) identifies as "mechanisms of moral disengagement" that individuals use to justify to themselves the prospect of harming others, and to avoid self-sanctioning for engaging in behavior people know is morally wrong. In this case, it is not so much the belief that violent repression is wrong, although that may be part of the thinking of at least some law enforcement, security, or military personnel. What is most significant is their wish to avoid the stigma of engaging in behavior that may be defined as unjust or disproportionate on the part of significant segments of the public, or even elites or other members of the security forces. The psychological consequences of the use of violent repression by authorities and their agents—what Rachel MacNair (2002) refers to as Perpetration Induced Traumatic Stress (PITS)—may also inhibit elites' use of violent repression (see chapter 4 in this volume).

Authorities may therefore try to deflect criticism before, during, or after the use of violence by dehumanizing its targets, using euphemisms or advantageous comparisons (if we do not do this, something even worse will happen), blaming the victim, or otherwise discounting the negative consequences of violence (Martin 2007, 134–35). Much of this repression management (see Smithey and Kurtz 2010) may be carried out through statements to the press about the danger potentially faced by dissidents if they are not demobilized. They may be marginalized or even dehumanized, stigmatized, labeled, and referred to in derogatory terms, tactics we will discuss in more detail below.

Studies of violence by Stanley Milgram (1974) and Grossman and Siddle (2008) show that it is easier to harm others when one is physically or psychologically removed from the victim and operating under instructions from authorities. Sometimes the targeting of more vulnerable groups in a society by law enforcement (either deliberately or as a result of systematic discrimination and the makeup of the police force) may sustain a greater degree of ongoing control over those populations. That may also backfire, however, as the wave of protests starting in 2014 against the killing of African Americans by US police officers demonstrates. Smart tactics of repression will take these kinds of dynamics into account.

"Less-lethal" Methods

Interestingly, many military and domestic police forces are increasingly interested in what the US military calls "non-lethal" or "less-lethal" methods for controlling dissidents, including plastic bullets and baton rounds, tasers, pepper spray, and ways of moving individuals or crowds of people. This may be especially helpful to authorities in democratic countries where their actions are under more effective scrutiny, and even more so when an independent press can disseminate information about repression and potentially cultivate what Gamson (1992) calls an "injustice frame" (see Benford and Snow 2000).

Perhaps, in part, because of the dangers of PITS, as well as a consciousness of the bad press generated by lethal methods, soldiers have generated a demand for less-lethal options that can help reduce instances of civilian casualties. The US Joint Non-Lethal Weapons Directorate in Quantico, Virginia, oversees the US military's research and development in the field. According to the program's website, the "Department of Defense defines non-lethal weapons as weapons, devices, and munitions that are explicitly designed and primarily employed to incapacitate targeted personnel or materiel immediately, while minimizing fatalities, permanent injury to personnel, and undesired damage to property in the target area or environment. Non-lethal weapons are intended to have reversible effects on personnel and materiel" (Non-Lethal Weapons Program, US Department of Defense 2013).

Military contractors have developed an "Active Denial System," a device that emits electromagnetic energy that creates a painful sensation in a human target but allegedly does no lasting physical harm. The "Mobility Denial System" involves a nearly frictionless viscous fluid that makes it virtually impossible to walk or drive. Conversely, another method involves a sticky gluelike substance that can be dispersed to impede targets' mobility. Other devices fire rubber pellets, sponge projectiles, or plasma energy to repel or deter their targets (Mihm 2004).

Non- or less-lethal methods are presumably attractive to security forces because they spare the user from the traumatic psychological effects of committing violence and help minimize the public relations fallout associated with more violent methods. That said, the impact of non-lethal methods on public perception may vary from context to context, including the extent to which a movement is able to frame the use of these methods and the way they are portrayed in the media. The use of non-lethal weapons like pepper spray and tear gas, along with nighttime raids to clear encampments, backfired in the case of the Occupy movement. Images of pepper-spraying officers went viral on the Internet, and TV commentator Keith Olbermann unleashed a satirical diatribe against New York Mayor Bloomberg, comparing him and Police Commissioner Raymond Kelly with other historical and ruthless US officials, such as Governor Wallace, who used tactical police violence in attempts to shut down civil rights and antiwar movements in the 1960s (Olbermann 2011).

Intimidation

Intimidation often amounts to the *threat* of direct violence, which may be physical, verbal, or written, but also includes such tactics as harassment, surveillance, tax investigations, and other subtle efforts to demobilize activists without the use of direct violence. While clinging to the option of violence under a claim of legitimacy (manufactured or not), security officials are also at least roughly aware of the costs of using direct violence. Most would prefer to deter popular resistance without actually using violence.[2] Consequently, they project strength through deploying superior numbers, displaying weapons, and wearing body armor. Nevertheless, walking the line between effective repression and repression that backfires requires a fine calibration of threat, and thus activities that fall toward the right end of our continuum (Table 8.1) become important in providing a wider range of options to facilitate repression management by authorities.

Nelson (2013, 170) suggests that intimidation can involve either overt actions (which, of course, run the risk of backfire) or "less overt acts such as threats to sue, arrest, and evict. It can also be more subtle, with implications left to the target's imagination." He identifies more subtle forms of intimidation or even overt surveillance. Sometimes community or civil relations officers in more familiar uniforms are deployed to mitigate or modulate intimidatory measures. Nelson notes that "vehicles with agents parked in front of a target's residence, or place of work, and publicly following that person can be unnerving" (170). Authorities can also attempt to avoid the paradox of repression by short-circuiting the confrontations they feel call for repression through *indirect* threat and redirection. If few people

2. This is a ubiquitous preference in warfare and violent conflict (Grossman and Siddle 2008; Collins 2008; Waal 2000). Individual combatants often "posture" to avoid or at least postpone actual violence.

attend contentious events, the popularity of the movement is diminished, protesters appear increasingly marginal and out-of-step with the public, and there may be fewer witnesses to direct repression when it occurs (depending on how well the media covers the event).

On three specific days in December 2011, Russian authorities required schools to hold exams in a poorly veiled attempt to discourage young people from joining protests demanding fair elections. This case provides an opportunity to illustrate the category of indirect threat in our continuum (Table 8.1). Besides the advantages of redirecting students, teachers, and parents away from protest, the indirect use of educational institutions meant that the regime could disguise its social control and leverage indirect threats. Missing exams (taking them or giving them) could result in professional reprimand, failing grades, and the possibility of poor future prospects. Potential movement activists must weigh the costs of their participation, which are not limited to confrontations with the police. If, however, such subterfuge remains concealed, authorities can spread repression and their culpability across various institutions, thus minimizing the dangerous attribution of repression at the top of the regime that might produce backfire.

Nelson (2013, 170) notes the effectiveness of what he calls "intrapsychic wounding," citing Emile Durkheim's concept of the collective consciousness. Intrapsychic wounding involves inflicting trauma that undermines the "beliefs, hopes, values, and thought characteristics of a group." Nelson observes that "the Middle East countries roiled by the Arab Spring had been controlled, for decades, by dictators who stifled dissent through small scale, individualized actions. People were frequently arrested, beaten, falsely convicted, penalized and punished, fired from jobs, prohibited from attending school, or raped" (171). In the final analysis, Nelson contends, "analytically, aggregate-induced wounding, rather than large scale/single massive event wounding, is probably the more efficient and less risky form of intrapsychic subversion" (171).

Brian Martin and Truda Gray (2005, 157) note that "defamation actions often serve as a form of legal intimidation, suppressing free speech"; these actions are therefore also a form of smart repression.

Moreover, they note, "threats of defamation suits are more frequent than suits themselves, and can have the same effect. In Australia, where defamation laws are quite favourable to plaintiffs, defamation law is an especially powerful tool against free speech (Pullan 1994)." Targets of defamation have tactics at their disposal to counter defamation suits or their threats, which Martin and Gray identify as exposing the action, validating the target, interpreting it as censorship, avoiding or discrediting the courts, and resisting intimidation and bribery. Unless activists are prepared to counter defamation, they might be subtly subverted by it.[3]

All of these intimidation tactics are designed to demobilize insurgent or dissident campaigns without the use of overt violence, thus mitigating the possibility of repression backfiring. Even more subtle than intimidation, however, are efforts to manipulate groups or their individual members, often covertly.

Manipulation

Another set of demobilization techniques involves manipulating dissidents and their organizations through such tactics as co-optation, facilitations, "demonstration elections" (including election fraud), information suppression, suppressing recruiting efforts, and engaging in dilemma actions (creating a situation that gives individuals or groups a choice between two negative options). Manipulations involve attempts to undermine, divide, divert, or distract social movement organizations or their pool of potential recruits.

Selective facilitation is one strategy often used to manipulate movements, playing more radical and more moderate groups off of each other with "the selective facilitation of some groups' claims and the selective repression of others" (Tarrow 2011, 209). The problem

3. The utility of defamation in this section revolves around the ability of authorities to provoke fear among activists. In a later section on soft repression we note how defamation or stigmatization may help authorities win framing battles where the target is the general public.

for governments using this tactic is that it can "push radicals into more sectarian forms of organization and more violent forms of action," especially if there is a "decline in mass support and polarization inside the movement" (209). When combined with partial demobilization, it can even produce terrorism (della Porta 1995).

Authorities may attempt to divert or co-opt human resources and leadership away from social movement organizations by offering attractive alternative pathways, such as career moves, to address their social concerns *within* the halls of power, where power is traditionally believed to reside. Activists may be invited to serve on policy-making commissions or establish new government-funded programs. Coy and Hedeen (2005) explain: "Channeling refers to efforts by the dominant group to undermine and redirect the challenging movement's leadership and power base away from substantive challenges to the dominant groups or system and toward more modest reforms" (416). Once a sense of progress through institutional channels has been established, continued access, credibility, and participation can become movement goals in and of themselves, a process that Coy and Hedeen call "the paradox of collaboration" (417). Furthermore, the movement's former sense of urgency can dissipate, since the business is being taken care of within official institutions.

Co-optation is a frequent strategy authorities use to diffuse dissent. Goldstone and Tilly (2001) explore how people in power combine repression and concession simultaneously or alternately in order to raise the cost of dissidence and increase the rewards for collaborating with the status quo for activists or potential resisters. Of course, this carrot-and-stick approach has a long tradition that is a well-worn strategy of smart repression. The Arab states—especially Saudi Arabia—used this combination to diffuse protest after the eruption of protests in Tunisia and Egypt in 2011. Mehran Kamrava (2012, 97) argues that "at the same time as GCC states have resorted to heightened levels of repression to ensure their political survival, they have also sought to strengthen their rule by pumping massive amounts of money into the economy." The Saudis spent $130 billion to give civil servants two months' extra salaries, built half a million additional units of low-income housing, and increased their financial support for religious organization (cf. MacFarquhar 2011).

Nelson (2013, 168) identifies another manipulation tactic against social movements as "resource depletion," which is the opposite of what movement scholars call resource mobilization. This, Nelson says, can take the form of:

- targeting the money, machines, and mobility of a group;
- seizing assets or property (e.g., by filing civil litigation that requires a group to spend limited resources defending themselves);
- introducing computer viruses; or
- "accidentally" blocking a car to prevent transportation to an event, creating what Nelson calls a "*petit* failure" of the movement.

Authorities will often suppress information flow among insurgents, especially by blocking access to the Internet or cell phones. Dubai hosts an annual TeleStrategies conference where American and European companies show their latest technologies for blocking websites and targeting web traffic (Nelson 2013, 164–65). Authorities can also "suppress recruiting efforts," according to Nelson (165), by identifying situations in which potential recruits become vulnerable to movement recruitment, such as life turning points like divorce and unemployment. This tactic is enhanced with subversion methods like reducing recruiting opportunities: authorities can reduce contact between activists and potential recruits by physically removing opportunities for them to meet, through house arrest, communications blockages, or actually relocating them, if possible (165–66). Of course, this type of repression can move well beyond simple manipulation into intimidation or even milder forms of direct violence (like arrests).

"Dilemma actions" are tactics that set up one's opponents so that they are forced to choose between two unattractive alternatives. Long a favorite of movement activists, these tactics were conceptualized by Lakey (1973, 103–8; cf. Lakey 1987) as early as 1968, when he described a dilemma action deployed by activists campaigning against chemical weapons who repeatedly tried to plant a pine tree at Edgewood Arsenal in Maryland. Each time the military authorities arrested activists and their tree, they violated norms about the value of life and nature and highlighted the activists' framing of the arsenal as place of death and destruction. After several confrontations, the military authorities chose to allow a tree to be planted, consenting to the permanent presence of the activists' frame. As Lakey (1973, 107) explains, "in symbol language, when the tree said life, all Edgewood could say back was death, no matter how daintily it picked its phrases."

Though Lakey introduced the concept of dilemma demonstration, it was not until Sørensen and Martin's (2014) article that it received systematic treatment. They devoted attention to how movement activists can choreograph dilemma actions, but their approach is instructive as to how such dilemmas can be set up by authorities as well. Authorities may, for example, place nonviolent activists in a dilemma by calling for civility and calm. To the extent that methods of nonviolent disruption are used, the activists may become vulnerable to charges of having violated their own principles. If they abandon their strategy, they potentially lessen their impact and lose momentum, and the authorities will have successfully demobilized the movement.

Another manipulative technique identified by Nelson (2013, 169) is what he calls "divisive disruption," which may involve using *agent provocateurs* who infiltrate the movement and foment violent actions, or attack "the trust among a group's leaders, perhaps through rumor, a planted letter (or e-mail), or even a photoshopped picture placing one or more in compromising circumstances."

Finally, censorship is another time-honored demobilization tactic. The Roman Catholic Church developed the most elaborate such institutional mechanism, the *Index of Forbidden Books*. The problem was that when a book was placed on the index, its sales soared! The backfire was so acute that, at one point, a cardinal even put the *Index of Forbidden Books* itself on the index!

Soft Repression

Repression includes hegemonic practices that undermine dissent through counterframing and propaganda. In a chapter on soft repression, Myra Marx Ferree (2005) identifies three forms of cultural subversion by non-state targets of social movements: ridicule, stigma, and silencing. She usefully critiques a long tendency among social movement scholars to focus on states as the targets of social movements, and she distinguishes the strategies of state versus non-state actors (such as corporations), with the latter less likely to use the state's methods of physical force retaliation but nonetheless act against movements to defend their interests (cf. Linden and Klandermans 2006, 213–28).

Whereas hard repression involves the mobilization of force to control or crush oppositional action through the use or threat of violence, soft repression involves the mobilization of nonviolent means to silence or eradicate oppositional *ideas.* "The distinguishing criterion of soft repression," Marx Ferree (2005, 141) contends, "is the collective mobilization of power, albeit in nonviolent forms and often highly informal ways, to limit and exclude ideas and identities from the public forum." Our concept of smart repression is similar, and for our purposes, the nonviolent aspect of soft repression feeds into these methods' capacities to avoid backfire. Indeed, there has been increasing interest in what Joseph Nye (1990, 2004) dubbed "soft power," that is, "the ability to get what you want through attraction rather than coercion or payments" (2004, x).

A parallel development emerged in the Iraq and Afghanistan conflicts under the direction of General David Petraeus, with a shift toward counterinsurgency intelligence (COIN) as a focus of US military operations, which a COIN strategist says is "75 percent hearts and minds, just 25 percent combat" (Kaplan 2014, 89). Recognizing the potential backfire of an intimidating and violent military presence countering an insurgency, the COIN approach measured success not by "how many enemy troops you kill but how many townspeople or villagers are spontaneously providing intelligence about where the enemy is, . . . how many community leaders openly support the government . . . and how much spontaneous economic activity is going on in a town (reflecting the sense that it's safe to go out on the streets)" (Kaplan 2014, 89).

Women's movements are demobilized, Marx Ferree (2004) notes, in three ways that raise the cost of becoming associated with identities or groups that challenge the status quo. *Ridicule* occurs on an interpersonal level in daily life as individuals are mocked and degraded as the boundaries of privilege become reinscribed for all present. *Stigma* refers to a broader dynamic of devaluing groups via negative stereotypes that undermines attempts to maintain a movement and recruit new members. *Silencing* occurs as mass media outlets deliberately make biased decisions about what speech to allow and which to exclude. In the process, movement arguments become lost, and the urgency and salience of the movement declines in the eyes of potential participants.

The media constitute a particularly important platform where framing contests between the regime and the movement play out in public. The regime obviously has the upper hand in most instances, because officials usually have easier access to the media than do resisters. It is also, paradoxically, the space where resistance becomes visible precisely when the regime tries to crack down on protesters or the media itself. Without the media, the backfire effect would not take hold. Consequently, authorities may aim to choreograph protest events covered by the media in ways that silence or distract from dissent.

In 2002, the United States Office of Presidential Advance (2002) within the Bush administration released a *Presidential Advance Manual* with instructions on how to minimize any disruptions created by protesters, since the president had been hounded by them whenever he made public appearances. The version obtained by the American Civil Liberties Union (ACLU) was heavily redacted, but it emphasized preventing demonstrators from coming near an event where the president might appear. "Rally squads," preorganized counterdemonstrators, would surround and drown out any demonstrators who managed to get through the elaborate screening system into the venue. Moreover, the manual emphasizes (in bold face): "Remember—*avoid physical contact with demonstrators!*" (35). Event organizers are advised that they should "not do anything or say anything that might result in physical harm to the demonstrators. Before taking action, the advance person must decide if the solution would cause more negative publicity than if the demonstrators were simply left alone" (35). The next thirty pages of the document are redacted and so do not appear in the version released to the ACLU, perhaps to prevent readers from learning their smart antidemonstrator tactics.

The media also plays a key role in the construction and maintenance of hegemony, or latent repression, by repeating the images, ideas, and talking points provided by elites in order to construct what Gramsci calls "spontaneous consensus" (Gramsci 1992–1996). A striking example of this process was revealed in November 2011, when the MSNBC program *UP w/ Chris Hayes* obtained a memo from a lobbying firm, Clark Lytle Geduldig & Cranford (Geduldig et al. 2011), to the American Bankers Association. The unsolicited memo proposed that the firm assist the association by conducting "survey research and message testing, opposition research, targeted social media monitoring, coalition planning, and advertising creative and placement strategy development." The opposition research component was offered to "identify opportunities to construct fact-based negative narratives of the OWS [Occupy Wall Street] for high impact media placement to expose the backers behind this movement." The lobbyists surmised, "If we can show they have the same cynical motivation as a political opponent it will undermine their credibility in a profound way." In this case, negative media representations were intended to make the Occupy movement less palatable to Republican politicians, who might embrace it under pressure from the populist Tea Party movement. The ploy might fall neatly under Marx Ferree's (2005) "stigma" category of soft repression.

A general reading of media coverage of the Occupy movement suggests other similar attempts to portray its participants as marginal and undesirable. In the context of standoffs between police and protesters in cities across the country, we believe this framing battle was related to the probability of repression backfiring as municipal authorities struggled to deal with encampments on public and private property. Reporting characterized Occupy activists as lazy, unhygienic, homeless, and strung out. Whether these portrayals can be traced to the governmental authorities who were under pressure to end protests and clear camps interests us, though as the lobbying firm's memo suggests, the source of negative representations in the media can be shadowy.

In some cases, authorities can simply exclude the media from important contentious events. For example, in a coordinated effort to demobilize the Occupy movement in November 2011, eighteen US mayors held a conference call with federal officials, according to Oakland Mayor Jean Quan ("Occupy Wall Street" 2011). A Justice Department official reportedly told a reporter that federal law enforcement officials advised US cities to use riot gear to intimidate the protesters, but Ellis claimed, "the FBI reportedly advised on press relations, with one presentation suggesting that any moves to evict protesters be coordinated for a time when the press was the least likely to be present" (Wells 2011). Under the FBI's advice, movement voices would, by design, be silenced and repression unreported.

Nelson (2013, 168) identifies "expertly directed, incessant proactive manipulation of media" as a key tactic for subverting a social movement. This may involve

- taking control of media away from the movement preemptively, using media experts;
- manipulating the media "to cast disparaging light on the movement" in order to damage its constructed public image, and alternatively portraying the protested organization as wholesome and worthwhile;
- denying protesters the legitimization provided by meetings with public or institutional officials (if you have to have meetings, "they must be off-camera, unannounced, and, if suspected, be neither confirmed or denied,");
- using subversion efforts that are both proactive and rapidly reactive.

The media can also be used to stigmatize dissident groups, their members, or their leadership. In his discussion of this tactic of stigmatization, Nelson (2013, 168–69) cites Erving Goffman's (2009) work on "spoiled identity" as providing clues as to how to discredit a movement by besmirching its public image.

We appreciate Marx Ferree's (2005) broadening of the study of repression, and we believe (as her article allows) that the strategies she attributes to non-state actors are not exclusive of state authorities, who of course also wield security forces against social movement activists. The various framing strategies that soft repression represents may also be considered "smart" in our formulation because they can take place nonviolently in a range of contexts (e.g., press conferences, news outlets, schools, churches), away from the *sturm und drang* of street protest. More importantly, they can precede direct repression and make it seem better justified and thus less likely to backfire. Nelson (2013, 166) notes that authorities can "develop attractive alternatives" in order to divert potential recruits from movement participation to something less threatening to the status quo. One example Nelson puts forth is what he calls "reverse honeypots operations." Infiltrators in a movement can volunteer to set up websites that would then include tiny hyperlinks in the text that would go undetected but cause Google to link the pages to a movement organization, manipulating Google searches so that other sites would be more likely to show up in a search, diverting potential activists from the movement's site (166). Another tactic of movement subversion Nelson identifies is tempting members to leave a movement by making emotional appeals, for example, with an alternative that distracts people from movement participation, diverting them into other activities. To counter a radical animal rights group, for example, its members might be recruited to engage in rescuing orphaned puppies.

Nelson (2013, 166–67) calls a more aggressive version of this tactic "reverse recruiting," which exposes participants to demoralizing information such as "contradictory evidence or beliefs" to draw them away from the movement. Instead of simply blocking information flow, authorities can disseminate misinformation or disinformation. This tactic might also involve "disseminating believable disinformation" or misinformation that discredits movement leaders or weakens the group, thus increasing personal risks for, and costs of, participation.

Perhaps a more subtle manipulation is what Nelson (2013, 167) identifies as operationalizing "secure/*faux* concessions" that make it appear that the movement has succeeded when it has not. Nelson warns, however (providing an example from Cornell University, whose alleged deception was discovered by protesters), that "the truth of things must remain a carefully guarded secret," if this tactic is to succeed.

Hegemony

The most advantageous type of repression for a regime is that which does not look like repression at all, what we might call the "latent repression" of hegemony, as Antonio Gramsci (1992–1996) has described it. Overt repression of the sort that most often results in backfire is often a consequence of the failure of more "soft" or subtle means of repression. As Bates (1975, 353) notes, "to the extent that the intellectuals fail to create hegemony, the ruling class falls back on the state's coercive apparatus which disciplines those who do not 'consent,'" and which is "constructed for all society in anticipation of moments of crisis of command . . . when spontaneous consensus declines."

In the previous subsection, we addressed how authorities and elites try to manage their own repression in the service of protecting their legitimacy that is often won through the manufacture of consent (Herman and Chomsky [1988] 2011). Postmodern theorists such as Michel Foucault (1980) have revealed the subtle and nuanced ways in which elites wield power by instituting and privileging narratives that become so deeply internalized that they preempt alternative narratives and make the thinkable unthinkable or out of reach of critical thought (cf. Gaventa 1980).

Herbert Marcuse (1974, 94) makes a similar point in *Eros and Civilization*: society defends against threats with "a strengthening of controls not so much over the instincts as over consciousness, which, if left free, might recognize the work of repression in the bigger and better satisfaction of needs." Dissent is co-opted, and people self censor their protest, channeling their discontent into consumerism; here, there is no need to send in the troops to quell demonstrations because potential insurgents are busy shopping, engaging in purchased leisure activities, or working to make the incomes required to "fulfill themselves" with purchases that reinforce the robustness of the very system that stirs their discontent. This may be the "smartest" form of repression of all, the hegemony that we identify on the far right end of our spectrum of repression.

Regimes often rely on nationalism to connect political agendas with deeply held collective identities. The state becomes "father," "mother," "home," and to challenge it either seems incongruent or produces shame and guilt. Under the most effective hegemonic regimes, challenging authorities and elites rarely even occurs to enough people to mobilize resistance that would provoke resistance and backfire. Our focus has been on how authorities deal with those who publicly and nonviolently challenge the status quo, but we include hegemony in our continuum of demobilization (Table 8.1) because it represents the most insidious form of demobilization and is often a product of successful soft repression. Hegemonic power is established throughout a population, but it also presents challenges for activists, who are not immune to the seduction of going along to get along.

Conclusion

One of the keys to the success of a social movement campaign seems to be its ability to manage repression, trying to enhance the potential of its backfiring to the benefit of the movement. The challenge is always significant, as people in power who are trying to demobilize a movement usually have more resources, more access to the media, and sometimes even some legitimacy among the regular populace. They at least have the ability to make people fear them (see Popovic, Milivojevic, and Djinovic 2006), if not love them, as the policy Machiavelli advised the prince to follow suggests.

The task of repression management is even more daunting when the repression is "smart." If it is more subtle rather than overtly violent and brutal, or if the regime has sufficiently convinced others that it is legitimate and the dissenters unworthy, or that the cost of insurgency is simply too high, then managing it becomes more complicated. In our effort to untangle the paradox of repression, we have found smart repression to be particularly puzzling, and this has been a preliminary effort to understand how regimes might employ it and dissenters might counter it.

Some might argue that methods of demobilization toward the right end of our continuum (Table 8.1), such as media strategies and hegemony, do not amount to repression but rather constitute attempts to undermine and demobilize a movement before the need for repression arises. Alternatively, others, such as Marx Ferree, consider these more cultural strategies to be repression in a different sphere. Whether the police are trying to intimidate or beat protesters out of physical public space, or whether spokespersons are seeking to "exclude ideas and identities from the public forum," power is being wielded for social control and to resist challengers. The former position perhaps defines repression too narrowly, while under the latter all contention becomes either repression or resistance (cf. Goodwin and Jasper 2012).

Regardless of whether nonviolent attempts to undermine challengers amount to repression, such efforts still bear on more traditional understandings of repression. The framing battles in which authorities and social movements engage shape the cultural field of public expectations and legitimacy where backfire takes place. Each side wants to shift the threshold across which the paradox of repression is triggered. Authorities want to keep repression (physical or cultural) under the radar as much as possible and to portray challengers as illegitimate or in some way deserving of overt repression, if the latter becomes necessary. Social movement activists want to delegitimize authorities and reveal repression and injustices so that dramatic instances of repression are more likely to become tipping points at which backfire occurs. In short, each side wants to prepare the ground on which repression occurs.

Perhaps one of the reasons the study of repression has focused on physical acts of intimidation and violence by the state is because these are dramatic events that capture press attention and titillate popular audiences. Smart repression is "smart" because it aims to either head off confrontation by making mobilization more difficult through hegemonic strategies of silencing and reeducation or by making direct repression less outrageous and thus less likely to provoke movement organizing and nonviolent action. Either approach makes backfire more complicated. In these framing contests, both authorities and activists seek to shift the threshold at which the paradox of repression is activated in their favor.

Understanding the concept of smart repression can help nonviolent activists reflect more clearly on the impulses and fears that deter them from taking action, and it can guide them in choreographing actions that highlight violations of civil liberties, even when they do not necessarily involve bodily repression. (For example, some activists cover their mouths with tape to focus public attention on ways in which some citizens and their concerns are silenced.) Maintaining nonviolent discipline remains paramount under conditions of smart repression in order to illustrate a clear contrast between the legitimacy of people power and authoritarian attempts to silence democratic voices. Not surprisingly, social movement activists have developed their own strategies for raising the likelihood of repression backfiring. Although the elite may have more resources at its command, it often lacks the creativity or the versatility of a nonviolent civil resistance. Nonviolent activists have shown a growing aptitude (perhaps bolstered by the increasing availability and use of social media and media production tools) for engaging in creative framing battles that make repression more likely to backfire on authorities.

References

Ackerman, Peter, and Jack DuVall. 2000. *A Force More Powerful: A Century of Nonviolent Conflict*. New York: Palgrave.

Alridge, Derrick. 2006. "The Limits of Master Narratives in History Textbooks: An Analysis of Representations of Martin Luther King, Jr." *The Teachers College Record* 108 (4): 662–86.

Bandura, Albert. 1999. "Moral Disengagement in the Perpetration of Inhumanities." *Personality and Social Psychology Review* 3: 193–209.

Bates, Thomas R. 1975. "Gramsci and the Theory of Hegemony." *Journal of the History of Ideas* 36 (2): 351–66.

Benford, Robert D., and David A. Snow. 2000. "Framing Processes and Social Movements: An Overview and Assessment." *Annual Review of Sociology* 26: 611–39.

Birmingham, Chi, and Alex Vitale. 2011. "Riot Gear's Evolution." *New York Times*, Dec. 3. http://www.nytimes.com/2011/12/04/opinion/sunday/riot-gears-evolution.html?_r=3.

Chenoweth, Erica, and Maria J. Stephan. 2011. *Why Civil Resistance Works: The Strategic Logic of Nonviolent Conflict*. New York: Columbia Univ. Press.

Collins, Randall. 2008. *Violence: A Micro-Sociological Theory*. Princeton, NJ: Princeton Univ. Press.

Coy, Patrick G., and Timothy Hedeen. 2005. "A Stage Model of Social Movement Co-Optation: Community Mediation in the United States." *The Sociological Quarterly* 46 (3): 405–35.

Davenport, Christian. 1995. "Multi-Dimensional Threat Perception and State Repression: An Inquiry into Why States Apply Negative Sanctions." *American Journal of Political Science* 39 (3): 683–713. doi:10.2307/2111650.

———. 2007. *State Repression and the Domestic Democratic Peace*. Cambridge: Cambridge Univ. Press.

Davenport, Christian, and Molly Inman. 2012. "The State of State Repression Research since the 1990s." *Terrorism and Political Violence* 24 (4): 619–34. doi:10.1080/09546553.2012.700619.

Deegan, Denise. 2001. *Managing Activism: A Guide to Dealing with Activists and Pressure Groups*. London: Kogan Page.

della Porta, Donatella. 1995. *Social Movements, Political Violence, and the State: A Comparative Analysis of Italy and Germany*. Cambridge; New York: Cambridge Univ. Press.

Earl, J. 2003. "Tanks, Tear Gas, and Taxes: Toward a Theory of Movement Repression." *Sociological Theory* 21 (1): 44–68.

Foucault, Michel. [1975] 2012. *Discipline and Punish: The Birth of the Prison*. Translated by Alan Sheridan. Originally published as *Surveiller et Punir: Naissance de la Prison*. Knopf Doubleday.

———. 1980. *Power/Knowledge: Selected Interviews and Other Writings, 1972–1977*, edited by Colin Gordon, translated by Colin Gordon, Leo Marshall, John Mephan, and Kate Soper. New York: Pantheon Books.

Gamson, William A. 1992. *Talking Politics*. New York: Cambridge.

Gandhi, Mahatma. 1999. *The Collected Works of Mahatma Gandhi* (electronic book). 98 vols. New Delhi: Publications Division Government of India. Accessed February 18, 2018. https://web.archive.org/web

/20180218032747/http:/www.gandhiashramsevagram.org/gandhi-literature/collected-works-of-mahatma-gandhi-volume-1-to-98.php.

Gaventa, John. 1980. *Power and Powerlessness: Quiescence and Rebellion in an Appalachian Valley*. Chicago: Univ. of Illinois Press.

Geduldig, Sam, Steve Clark, Gary Lytle, and Jay Cranford. 2011. "Proposal: Occupy Wall Street Response." Memorandum for the American Bankers Association. Nov. 24. https://web.archive.org/web/20111125005940/http://msnbcmedia.msn.com/i/msnbc/sections/news/CLGF-msnbc.pdf.

Goffman, Erving. 2009. *Stigma: Notes on the Management of Spoiled Identity*. New York: Simon and Schuster.

Goldstone, Jack A., and Charles Tilly. 2001. "Threat (and Opportunity): Popular Action and State Response in the Dynamics of Contentious Action." In *Silence and Voice in the Study of Contentious Politics*, edited by R. Aminzade, J. A. Goldstone, D. McAdam, E. Perry, W. H. Sewell Jr., S. Tarrow, and C. Tilly, 179–94. New York: Cambridge Univ. Press.

Goodwin, Jeff, and James M. Jasper. 2012. *Contention in Context: Political Opportunities and the Emergence of Protest*. Stanford, CA: Stanford Univ. Press.

Gramsci, Antonio. 1992–1996. *Prison Notebooks, I–II*, edited and translated by Joseph A. Buttigieg and Antonio Callari. European Perspectives: A Series in Social Thought and Cultural Criticism. New York: Columbia Univ. Press.

———. 1998. "Hegemony, Intellectuals, and the State." In *Cultural Theory and Popular Culture: A Reader*, 2d ed., edited by John Storey, 210–16. Harlow, England: Pearson Education/Prentice Hall.

Grossman, Dave, and K. Siddle. 2008. "Psychological Effects of Combat." In *Encyclopedia of Violence, Peace, and Conflict*, edited by Lester R. Kurtz, 1796–1805. Amsterdam: Elsevier.

Haines, Herbert. 1984. "Black Radicalization and the Funding of Civil Rights." *Social Problems* 32 (1): 31–43.

Herman, Edward S., and Noam Chomsky. [1998] 2011. *Manufacturing Consent: The Political Economy of the Mass Media*. New York: Knopf Doubleday.

Kalyvas, Stathis N. 2003. "The Ontology of 'Political Violence': Action and Identity in Civil Wars." *Perspectives on Politics* 1 (3): 475–94.

Kamrava, Mehran. 2012. "The Arab Spring and the Saudi-Led Counterrevolution." *Orbis* 56 (1): 96–104.

Kaplan, Fred. 2014. *The Insurgents: David Petraeus and the Plot to Change the American Way of War*. New York: Simon and Schuster.

Lakey, George. 1973. *Strategy for a Living Revolution*. New York: Orbis Books.

———. 1987. *Powerful Peacemaking: A Strategy for a Living Revolution*. Gabriola Island, BC: New Society.

Linden, Annette, and Bert Klandermans. 2006. "Stigmatization and Repression of Extreme-Right Activism in the Netherlands." *Mobilization* 11: 213–28.

MacFarquhar, Neil. 2011. "In Saudi Arabia, Royal Funds Buy Peace, for Now." *New York Times*, June 8. http://www.nytimes.com/2011/06/09/world/middleeast/09saudi.html.

MacNair, Rachel M. 2002. *Perpetration-Induced Traumatic Stress*. Westport, Connecticut: Praeger.

Marcuse, Herbert. 1974. *Eros and Civilization: A Philosophical Inquiry into Freud*. Beacon Press.

Martin, Brian. 2007. *Justice Ignited: The Dynamics of Backfire*. Lanham, MD: Rowman & Littlefield.

Martin, Brian, and Truda Gray. 2005. "How to Make Defamation Threats and Actions Backfire [Public Right to Know Conference, August 2004]." *Australian Journalism Review* 27 (1): 157–66.

Marx Ferree, Myra. 2005. "Soft Repression: Ridicule, Stigma, and Silencing in Gender-Based Movements." In *Repression and Mobilization*, edited by Christian Davenport, Hank Johnston, and Carol Mueller, 138–55. Minneapolis: Univ. of Minnesota Press.

Mihm, Stephen. 2004. "The Quest for the Nonkiller App." *New York Times*, July 25, 38.

Milgram, Stanley. 1974. *Obedience to Authority: An Experimental View*. New York: Harper & Row.

Nelson, Eric L. 2013. "Subversion of Social Movements by Adversarial Agents." *International Journal of Intelligence and CounterIntelligence* 26 (1): 161–75. doi:10.1080/08850607.2013.732445.

Non-Lethal Weapons Program, US Department of Defense. 2013. "Non-Lethal Weapons FAQs." Accessed Jan. 20, 2018 http://jnlwp.defense.gov/About/Frequently-Asked-Questions/Non-Lethal-Weapons-FAQs/.

Nye, Joseph S. 2004. *Soft Power: The Means to Success in World Politics*. New York: Public Affairs.

———. 1990. "Soft Power." *Foreign Policy* 80 (Autumn): 153–71.
"Occupy Wall Street: Night Thins Zuccotti Park Crowd." 2011. *BBC News*, Nov. 16. http://www.bbc.co.uk/news/world-us-canada-15761454.
Olbermann, Keith. 2011. "Keith Olbermann Condemns Bloomberg, Occupy Wall Street Raid." *Huffington Post*, Nov. 16, 2011. http://www.huffingtonpost.com/2011/11/16/keith-olbermann-michael-bloomberg-occupy-wall-street_n_1096898.html.
Popovic, Srdja, Andrej Milivojevic, and Slobodan Djinovic. 2006. *Nonviolent Struggle: 50 Crucial Points*. Belgrade: CANVAS.
Pullan, Robert. 1994. *Guilty Secrets: Free Speech and Defamation in Australia*. Glebe, Australia: Pascal Press.
Schock, Kurt, and Erica Chenoweth. 2010. "The Impact of Violence on the Outcome of Nonviolent Resistance Campaigns: An Examination of Intermovement Radical Flank Effects." Annual Meeting of the International Peace Research Association, Sydney, Australia.
Smithey, Lee, and Lester R. Kurtz. 1999. "We Have Bare Hands: Nonviolent Social Movements in the Soviet Bloc." In *Nonviolent Social Movements*, edited by Stephen Zunes, Lester R. Kurtz, and Sarah Beth Asher, 96–124. Malden, MA: Blackwell.
———. 2010. "Repression Management and the Arts of Nonviolent Strategy." Presented at the International Studies Association annual meeting, New Orleans, LA.
Sørensen, Majken Jul, and Brian Martin. 2014. "The Dilemma Action: Analysis of an Activist Technique." *Peace and Change* 39 (1): 73–100.
Stephan, M. J., and E. Chenoweth. 2008. "Why Civil Resistance Works: The Strategic Logic of Nonviolent Conflict." *International Security* 33: 7–44.
Tarrow, Sidney. 2003. "Paradigm Warriors: Regress and Progress in the Study of Contentious Politics." In *Rethinking Social Movements: Structure, Meaning, and Emotion*, edited by Jeff Goodwin and James M. Jasper, 39–46. Lanham, MD: Rowman & Littlefield.
———. 2011. *Power in Movement: Social Movements and Contentious Politics*, 3d ed. New York: Cambridge Univ. Press.
United States Office of Presidential Advance. 2002. *Presidential Advance Manual*, redacted ed. https://www.aclu.org/files/pdfs/freespeech/presidential_advance_manual.pdf.

Valentino, Benjamin, Paul Huth, and Dylan Balch-Lindsay. 2004. "'Draining the Sea': Mass Killing and Guerrilla Warfare," *International Organization* 58: 375–407.

Waal, Frans B. M. de. 2000. "Primates: A Natural Heritage of Conflict Resolution." *Science* 289: 586–90.

Weber, Max. [1920] 1978. *Economy and Society: An Outline of Interpretive Sociology*. Edited by G. Roth and C. Wittich. Los Angeles: Univ. of California Press.

Wells, Matt. 2011. "Occupy Wall Street: Zuccotti Park Re-Opens—As It Happened." *Guardian*, Nov. 15. http://www.theguardian.com/world/blog/2011/nov/15/occupy-wall-street-zuccotti-eviction-live.

9

Egypt

Military Strategy and the 2011 Revolution

Dalia Ziada

Introduction

The relationship between military forces' involvement and the success of a nonviolent revolution has been an interesting topic for academic researchers for years. But studying this topic within the context of the Arab Spring is relatively new. The novelty of the topic, the special nature of the Arab World, and the complicated history of violent conflicts and their influence on the progress of liberal democracy in the region make the need for studying the relationship between military forces and nonviolent movements in this part of the world both urgent and challenging. The Egyptian revolution suggests that the military, as one of the main pillars of support for the ruling regime, can determine the success or failure of a social uprising. The relationship that developed between the military and insurgency throughout the eighteen days of protests proved a critical factor in the fall of the regime. President Hosni Mubarak's regime depended heavily on two main weapon-carrying pillars of support: the police forces whose existence depended on the existence of the regime, and the military forces who enjoyed financial and institutional independence. As the use of violence by police forces during the first three days of the revolution backfired into more heated protests, the military chose to avoid violence and show their will to understand and contain insurgency.

The Arab Spring started before 2011 as a potential Middle East Spring. The Tunisian and Egyptian revolutions were not the first uprisings against dictatorship in the Middle East. In June 2009, young pro-democracy activists in Iran ran and maintained massive protests all over the country, which had effectively shaken the throne of the ayatollah (Pletka and Alfoneh 2009). Internet-savvy young activists, under thirty years old, who represented more than 60 percent of the Iranian population, launched and organized the nonviolent uprising in Iran. Activists in Egypt, myself included, followed the developments in Iran with much hope that "if the revolution succeeds in Iran, the next revolution will take place in Egypt."[1] There were many similarities between the struggle for democracy and youth movements in both countries. However, the brutal interference of the military in Iran, especially the Islamic militia known as Basij Forces, helped the Mullahs there contain the uprising and remain in power.

Sixteen months later, the Tunisians started a nonviolent revolution that ended Ben Ali's rule in less than one month, followed by an Egyptian revolution that brought down Mubarak's thirty years of dictatorship within only eighteen days. The military's cooperation with nonviolent movements in Tunisia and Egypt during the 2011 revolutions essentially guaranteed the movements' successes. "Cooperation" does not necessarily mean that the military believed in the goals and legitimacy of the revolution, but even the "negative cooperation" that included choosing not to kill protesters was enough to bring down the dictators by allowing the movements to continue to mobilize and undermining the legitimacy of the regimes.

After Egypt, there were other massive nonviolent uprisings in Yemen, Libya, and Syria, each with varied responses by the military and insurgents. If we compare successful Arab nonviolent insurgencies

1. I was personally involved in helping the Iranian activists use proxy tools to avoid being tracked by security forces, especially on Twitter. Egyptian bloggers were extremely interested in the Iranian revolution, as we believed that the success of the revolution in Iran would inspire a stronger revolution in Egypt.

with those that failed, the key difference is the military's response to the uprising. In the successful cases, the movement chose nonviolent strategies, and the military chose not to use extensive violent repression. By contrast, in Libya and Yemen, revolutionaries used violence to defend themselves against the brutality of Saleh's and Gaddafi's armies. In short, violent insurgencies and state repression are common, even during the recent and remarkable period of nonviolent resistance across the Arab world.

Although in this chapter I focus on strategic decisions made by nonviolent protestors, military leaders, and President Mubarak, it is worth noting that the situation in Egypt was ripe for change. A range of conditions helped the nonviolent movement succeed in record time. In Iran's 2009 revolution, the protesters were highly organized and skillfully applied nonviolent tactics and strategies against the regime. But their revolution failed because the proper conditions were not present, and the movement's momentum was not strong enough to overcome them. The conditions were much more favorable in the Egyptian case; they included international pressure not to use violence against protesters, the independence of the military institution, and the legitimacy of the nonviolent movement against the police forces and the politically and economically corrupt regime they protected. At the same time, a narrow conflict-of-interest gap lay between the military and the people, especially toward the end of the eighteen days of the revolution. Several of these conditions contributed to the restraint exercised by the Egyptian military toward nonviolent protesters and ultimately the military's role in deposing Mubarak.

Divisions within the Regime

The Egyptian military's decision to refrain from repressive action represents a form of repression management that has implications for movement and military strategists alike. The lesson for nonviolent activists is that the military forces that usually protect a regime might decide to refrain from repressing a movement, and nonviolent activists might try to cultivate that option. What makes a military decide to take the side of the people against a dictator in a nonviolent conflict?

Studying the Egyptian 2011 revolution can help us understand what motivated the Egyptian military to disobey, cooperate with nonviolent protesters, and abandon Mubarak, the president of the state and supreme commander of the armed forces.

The Egyptian revolution was a concerted nonviolent struggle between the nonviolent protesters and military forces who chose to put down their traditional weapons. The military's restraint, an attempt to control the revolution, brought them into conflict with President Mubarak. Mubarak interpreted the military leaders' preference not to use violence and to accommodate protesters nonviolently as a strategic attempt to protect the regime against the nonviolent protesters, but as Mubarak made concessions under pressure, he lost confidence in his own army. The more compromises Mubarak offered in order to contain the revolution and remain in power, the more legitimacy the passive military gained, and the wider the protests became.

Fearing that the military was double-crossing him, Mubarak started to make decisions that threatened the minister of defense and other military leaders. Perhaps motivated by the possibility of losing his last pillar of support—the military—Mubarak apparently tried to isolate the minister of defense. By then, however, the military had already won considerable popular legitimacy. The military no longer depended on Mubarak and was thus able to abandon him and ultimately take over his office, all with popular support.

Analysts have developed four main propositions about why the military joined the challengers to Mubarak's regime in Egypt.

1. Military leaders had a personal interest in undermining Mubarak's plans to groom his son Gamal for the presidency (see Claude 2010; Hashim 2011), so they chose to take advantage of the revolution to achieve that goal.
2. The military is an independent institution, and was not necessarily dependent on Mubarak's patronage. Military leaders chose to abandon Mubarak to preserve their legitimacy and their power, on the one hand, and to preserve the well-being of the state, on the other hand.

3. The decision to disobey Mubarak's orders to kill the protesters was motivated by international pressure, especially from the friends and patrons of the Egyptian military leaders in the US military.
4. The positive historical relationship between the military officers and the people made it harder for the military to kill the people and easier to disobey Mubarak.

I return to these propositions with more details and further explanation at the end of the chapter.

To analyze the Egyptian military's decisions, I draw on my own experience of the revolution as a participant observer in the resistance as well as a familiarity with the growing literature on nonviolent strategies and tactics, with a special focus on mechanisms used to undermine military power, one of the most crucial pillars of support for most dictators. The theories of Gene Sharp, and the work of the International Center on Nonviolent Conflict (ICNC) in Washington, DC, and the Center for Applied Nonviolent Action and Strategies (CANVAS) in Belgrade figure prominently and help us to understand the triangle of power relations among a dictator, the military, and the people in a nonviolent conflict. I also select information from interviews I conducted with key actors, including military officers and insurgents.

The Birth of the Nonviolent Movement

The struggle to bring down Hosni Mubarak and establish a liberal democratic state that respects human rights and civil freedoms started long before the revolution. The appearance of Gamal Mubarak on the political scene in 2003 as a potential successor to his father encouraged the organized struggle for change by political dissidents. Several nonviolent movements formed, the most prominent of which were Kefaya in 2004 and "April 6" in 2008. Meanwhile, civil society across the Middle East was getting stronger, thanks to the international interest—after the War on Saddam Hussein in Iraq—in enhancing pro-democracy and human rights nongovernmental organizations (NGOs) through funding and capacity-building initiatives.

In an attempt to distract people from joining anti-Mubarak campaigns or human rights NGOs, and to please international powers by feigning support for freedom of expression, the Egyptian government provided citizens with affordable access to mobile phone, Internet, and TV satellite services. The year 2004 marked a revolution in the communications sector in Egypt, led by the minister of communication, Ahmed Nazif, who was appointed a few years later as prime minister and kept that position until Mubarak fired him during the 2011 revolution. Unexpectedly, cheap access to the Internet helped dissidents, NGOs, opposition political parties, and pro-democracy movements to better organize and form more influential networks. In 2005, a vibrant community of bloggers started to flourish as the main source for credible information about Mubarak regime's corruption and violations of human rights and civil freedoms.

Mubarak's Illiberal Democracy

The state's performance, which exhibited simultaneous democratic impulses alongside authoritarian practices, often confused Egyptians as well as international observers. For example, while the government was giving affordable access to the Internet and refused to block any websites, agents of the state arrested bloggers and cyber dissidents and detained and tortured them for expressing antiregime opinions. While the state ran parliamentary elections regularly and allowed tens of political parties and individuals to contest the seats of the upper and lower houses of parliament, leading members of the ruling National Democratic Party (NDP) and Mubarak's loyal affiliates from other so-called opposition parties dominated the parliament. While the government did not formally challenge the opening of human rights NGOs, it severely harassed and indirectly banned the activists working for those NGOs from participating in public activities.

Under Mubarak, Egypt could have been considered neither a democracy nor an autocracy, but rather a living example of Fareed Zakaria's (2003) concept of "illiberal democracy." According to Zakaria, the Athenian definition of democracy as "the rule of people" through the process of selecting their government is "meaningless" if it is not supported by constitutional liberalism that would guarantee the fairness and openness of practicing democracy. He wrote that "if a country holds competitive multiparty elections we call it 'democratic.' When public participation in a country's politics is increased—for example through the enfranchisement of women—this country is seen as having become more democratic" (18–19). Ironically, Mubarak undertook a smart initiative in 2009 by allocating sixty-four seats in the lower house of parliament for women in hopes of increasing women's participation in the 2010 parliamentary elections (American Islamic Congress 2010). Thus, he skillfully hit two birds with one stone: on the one hand, he polished the image of his regime in the eyes of the international community by showing that he was getting "more democratic" and supportive of women's rights; and, on the other hand, his reallocation of parliamentary seats would weaken the Muslim Brotherhood bloc, which occupied one-third of the seats, by filling more seats with women loyal to the NDP and the current regime.

Simultaneously, the regime did not shy away from adopting "illiberal" practices, as it denied international observers access to parliamentary or presidential elections, claiming that allowing international observation on domestic elections would "infringe the national sovereignty" (Dunne and Hamzawy 2010). In addition, grassroots movements and NGOs were indirectly banned from observing elections under the Emergency Law, in effect since 1980. "This law grants the president extraordinary powers to detain citizens, prevent public gatherings, and issue decrees with little accountability to Parliament or the people" (Rutherford 2013, 1).

Consequently, major opposition leaders and political parties, including the bloc of opposition intellectuals from different political affiliations and, namely, the National Association for Change, decided to boycott the parliamentary elections that took place at the end of 2010, only two months before the revolution. El-Wafd Party and the Muslim Brotherhood group reluctantly allowed their candidates to compete against the NDP candidates.

Mubarak's Eroding Pillars of Support and Repression

Before 2004, Mubarak relied on four main pillars of support—the judiciary, the parliament, the military, and the police—that helped him to stay in power through a centralized authoritarian state that wore a democratic mask. Mubarak also nurtured additional, but less important, pillars of support like the ruling NDP, the business community, and the state media.

In 2010, Mubarak attempted to manipulate the parliamentary elections but had to do so without the help of one of his four main pillars of support, the judiciary, which had abandoned him during the 2005 presidential and parliamentary elections by exposing the forgery of results by the NDP. Soon after the 2005 elections, a strong nonviolent movement was launched to call for the independence of the judiciary and the rule of law (see, for example, Aly 2012).

The independent judges movement was strongly supported by human rights NGOs, the Kefaya movement, and the bloggers community. Together, they formed a massive nonviolent front that began to irritate Mubarak and threatened his credibility in the international community. In response, Mubarak authorized the police forces, especially state security forces (through the renewal of the Emergency Law) to harass activists, torture them, and arrest whoever acted as a threat to the regime.

Over the following five years, the brutality of police forces increased. They tortured civilians in police stations, in the streets, and even in their homes. State security forces arrested bloggers and activists and tortured them to collect information about their movements and organizations, or put them in jail for years without bringing charges against them. This sustained repression over the years triggered a growing consciousness within civil society about the need to resist the Mubarak regime.

The Rise of the Nonviolent Movement

As Mubarak lost the judicial system as a critical pillar of support, he had to rely more heavily on the Emergency Law and the brutality of the police to enhance his position. Meanwhile, public interest in ending corruption and dictatorship rose. In an effort to counter this persistent repression intelligently and strategically, young activists used the Internet not only to organize but also to learn about nonviolent strategies. International organizations interested in empowering Egyptian civil society helped NGO members travel to the United States and Europe to acquire new skills and transfer knowledge about nonviolent struggle to their fellow activists at home. From 2007 to 2009, several activists became educated about the history and theory of nonviolent civil resistance against corrupt regimes through the Fletcher School for the Advanced Study of Nonviolent Conflict and the International Center on Nonviolent Conflict, in addition to participating in training workshops on the application of those theories organized by CANVAS.

In 2008, after the decline of the Kefaya movement following internal conflicts among its leaders, the April 6 movement formed and started to apply nonviolent tactics to challenge Mubarak's regime. The logo of the movement (the right-hand fist) was adapted from the logo of the Serbian nonviolent movement Otpor that had brought down Milosevic and a few years later had established CANVAS. The founders of the April 6 movement were formerly young members of Kefaya and the campaign to support the young liberal candidate Ayman Nour, who ran for presidency against Mubarak in 2005. Ayman Nour came close to victory over Mubarak, but a few months after the elections, Mubarak put him in jail, though his campaign remained strong.

Meanwhile, the controversy over the viability of using nonviolent action to bring down Mubarak started to emerge among thinkers, academics, and civil society members. The young activists who had received CANVAS (Rosenberg 2011) and ICNC trainings held several training workshops and conferences and translated books from Gene Sharp and Peter Ackerman around the topic of nonviolent action (Stolberg 2011). In 2008, I translated a 1960s comic book about the Montgomery bus boycott into Arabic and used it in a number of workshops that I held in Egypt about the concept of nonviolent action. In 2011, several analysts credited the translation of this book for inspiring young people in the Arab world to adopt nonviolent tactics to undermine dictatorial regimes (Mendel 2009; Vesely-Flad 2011; Cavna 2011).

Repression Sparks the Revolution

In August 2010, the Egyptian community was terrified and outraged by the story of Khaled Said, a young man from Alexandria who was beaten to death by two policemen outside a cyber café. Khaled was a twenty-eight-year-old musician who had refused to be searched by two policemen who stormed into the cyber café he was visiting. This was not the first incident of police torturing innocent citizens, but it was the most shocking because the victim was not a "criminal, a terrorist, or a thug"[2] and yet was publicly beaten in the street. Said's murder angered young people, who were suffering from economic and political marginalization and who realized, after the murder of a young man who looked very much like themselves, that they were helpless in the face of police brutality.

A few days after Khaled Said's death, a Facebook page was created to call for the punishment of his killers and an end to the state of emergency, and to urge police forces to stop using violence against civilians. In cooperation with other youth movement organizations, especially the April 6 movement and human rights NGOs, the Khaled Said page contributed to the organization of some small rallies in Cairo and Alexandria that were properly covered by bloggers and independent local and international media.

Around the same time, it seemed Gamal Mubarak had already established himself as a politician and was preparing to run for the presidency in 2011. To guarantee a victory, he abused his position as the head of the Policies Committee in the ruling NDP and interfered

2. The government used to justify the brutality of the police and the extension of the emergency of state by falsely claiming that they were only targeting terrorists, criminals, and thugs. But ordinary citizens would not be touched.

not only in the organization and planning of the 2010 parliamentary elections but also in faking poll results so the majority of seats went to his loyal affiliates from the business community and NDP.

Mubarak's National Democratic Party won 83 percent of the seats and gave the remaining seats to loyal individuals and members of so-called opposition parties that had negotiated a secret deal with the Mubarak regime (News Editor 2010). Opposition groups, NGOs, and civil rights movements called for the annulling of the results under allegations of fraud. The European Union and United States also criticized the Egyptian state for those results, but the regime responded by rejecting their criticism as international interference in Egypt's affairs. Arguably, the forgery of the 2010 parliamentary elections undermined the legitimacy of Mubarak's regime and broke another very important pillar of his support, the parliament.

The NDP and state media were secondary pillars of support for Mubarak. They were less important and much weaker than the aforementioned primary pillars of support. Although Mubarak tried to rely on the secondary pillars, they could not keep him standing for more than a few days. The protesters nonviolently coerced Mubarak to dissolve the NDP after the disintegration of the police forces. The blogging community had already undermined the credibility of state media long before the revolution by exposing its lies and offering a more credible source of news. Even when Mubarak tried to block Internet service on the eve of January 28 to distract the revolution, and to block the news from the international community, the tactic backfired against him as more people went to the streets to join protestors, after they lost access to the Internet. The inability of elders to communicate with their young family members, who were participating in the revolution, compelled parents to go to the focal points of protest to make sure their children were alright.[3]

3. In chapter 5 in this volume, Beyer and Earl address the way in which online repression can invoke greater offline mobilization.

Repression Management in a Triangle of Nonviolent Conflict

By the end of 2010, Mubarak was relying on only two of his most crucial pillars of support, the military and the police, after he had already lost support from the parliament and judiciary. By the beginning of 2011, the Khaled Said Facebook page called for nationwide protests against police brutality on the annual police anniversary, January 25. The protest was planned to challenge police repression and call for an end to the state of emergency and the systematic torture of civilians by policemen. The Tunisian Revolution's success in bringing down Ben Ali on January 14 encouraged activists in Egypt to see the planned antipolice protests on January 25 as a potential spark for an antiregime revolution. Triggered by anger over police brutality and jealousy over the success of Tunisian activists, the January 25 protests turned into a nonviolent revolution that brought down Mubarak in eighteen days.

After the protesters succeeded in defeating the police forces in four days, they had to face the military, Mubarak's only remaining pillar of support. Unexpectedly, the military declined to use violence against the nonviolent protesters, a decision that helped to ensure the movement's success in bringing down Mubarak.

Strategic Contention between the People and the Military

To weaken and damage the four main pillars of support around Mubarak, the Egyptian nonviolent movement used strategies of conversion and nonviolent coercion. The military employed strategies of accommodation and co-optation to control the revolution. In this section, I focus on how nonviolent strategies were employed against the police and military forces, and how the military forces worked to protect themselves from becoming targets of the revolution by encouraging a spirit of solidarity and accommodating some of the protesters' demands. It is also important to understand the power relationships between the regime, the nonviolent movement, police forces, and military forces to understand why the military and activists behaved as they did.

Power Relations

Mubarak was a military man who had participated in the 1973 war against Israel and was one of President Sadat's most loyal officers; in 1980, Sadat appointed him vice president. After Sadat's assassination in 1981, Mubarak was automatically upgraded to the office of president. According to military rules established by President Nasser after the 1952 revolution that put the military in power, the president of the state is the supreme leader of the armed forces.

Over the course of his presidency, Mubarak gradually minimized the role of the military in public life, but he did so without diminishing or withdrawing any of their powers. The regime barred the media from discussing the military's budget, size, or the extent of its power. In Mubarak's illiberal democratic state, the military played a clear role in keeping things under control without necessarily interfering in day-to-day decision-making processes. The ambiguity of the relationships between the military and Mubarak's administration helped maintain the positive image the military had developed since the 1973 victory over Israel. The Egyptian military was also used for nontraditional missions, such as providing humanitarian aid during disasters. Two major incidents, the earthquake in October 1992 and the bread crisis in 2008, solidified the positive relationship between the people and the military during the Mubarak era.

Mubarak also established a very good relationship with the police forces and turned them into an apparatus for his own protection rather than an authority serving the people. As soon as he took over the presidency in 1981, he announced the state of emergency, purportedly to deal with terrorist organizations responsible for the assassination of Sadat ("Egypt's State of Emergency" 2012). The state of emergency gave police forces cover for the mistreatment of civilians, unjustified arrests, torture, and detention without charge. In the 1990s, with the rise of violent jihadist movements that executed terrorist attacks in Cairo and Upper Egypt, the regime gave police forces license to become more brutal in dealing with suspects.

When the nonviolent movement emerged in 2004, the police were instructed to deal with the dissidents. The state security department was trained to deal with terrorists and was not prepared to handle nonviolent dissidents differently (Hardin 2011). They used violence against nonviolent protesters, harassed bloggers and journalists, closed human rights NGOs, and threatened pro-democracy activists.

The brutality of police forces toward activists and ordinary citizens damaged the relationship between the people and the police forces. The 2010 killing of Khaled Said at the hands of police became the tipping point in this relationship of hatred and fear between the people and police forces. Indeed, the January 25 revolution was initially planned as a protest on police brutality on the police anniversary (Logan 2011).

Overwhelming the Police Forces

During the January 2011 revolution, the nonviolent protesters took only four days to force the police to suspend their operations. In dealing with police forces, the nonviolent protesters used two of Gene Sharp's four mechanisms: *conversion* and *coercion*. The protesters focused on the conversion of the police, who surrounded the protesters and were ordered by their officers to throw tear gas bombs and beat protesters with sticks. George Lakey describes conversion as a process by which "the opponent, as the result of the actions of the nonviolent struggle group or person, comes around to a new point of view which embraces the ends of the nonviolent actor" (Lakey 1968, 12). According to Gene Sharp (2005, 416–17), conversion is the tactic with the highest potential for failure because it is impractical in most cases and depends on a number of factors that make it too complicated to work: "The factors influencing conversion include the degree of conflict of interest and the social distance between the contending groups, the personalities of the opponents, shared or contrasting beliefs and norms between the groups, and the role of third parties. . . . [F]or various reasons, including unsatisfactory fulfillment of the above influential factors, conversion efforts may only partially succeed or may fail completely."

The Egyptian protesters thought it would be easy to convert the policemen through creating mutual understanding and empathy with them. For example, in Tahrir Square, I witnessed protesters offering food and water to police and soldiers and speaking to them about the legitimacy of the protests and the nonviolent movement. In fact, protesters' attempts to convert policemen did not work because soldiers' fear of punishment if they disobeyed their commanding officers was greater than their love, empathy, and understanding of the protesters.

Protesters used nonviolent coercion to greater effect. According to Sharp, "in nonviolent coercion, the opponents are not converted, nor do they decide to accommodate to the demands. Rather, shifts of social forces and power relationships produce the changes sought by the resisters against the will of the opponents" (2005, 418–19). The nonviolent protesters in Egypt's revolution launched massive nonviolent and highly organized protests and rallies at several locations all over the country at the same time, which distracted police forces and thus weakened them. The careful organization of large rallies and the protesters' commitment to reacting nonviolently to police attacks strained the forces' abilities to handle the massive simultaneous protests all over Egypt and put the regime under pressure by paralyzing routine social and economic operations and activities.

On the fourth day of the revolution, January 28, the police received orders from the military to leave all main squares as the military forces prepared to deal directly with the protests. The tattered relationship between Egyptians and police forces and the urgency to end police repression superseded citizens' fear of escaping prisoners, who broke out of prison during revolution. Rather than begging for police forces to return to work, people organized themselves to defend their houses against any potential attacks by escaped prisoners and made sure not to disturb the flow of the revolution in Tahrir Square and other focal points in different cities.

The Military and the People Convert and Accommodate One Another

The hard-won victory of nonviolent protesters over the violent police forces was not enough to bring Mubarak down, as he continued to rely on another stronger pillar of support, the military. The regime sent

TABLE 9.1 Tug of War: Military versus Protesters

	Military	*People*
Beginning	Pro-Mubarak and against the revolution	Against Mubarak and against the military
First day in Tahrir	Accommodation strategy	Conversion strategy
Camel Battle	Neutral about Mubarak	Favorable to military (Military≠Mubarak)
Removing Tantawy	Against Mubarak and pro-revolution	Against Mubarak and pro-military
Fall of Mubarak	Cooperation	Cooperation

Source: Dalia Ziada

military forces to contain and eventually end the revolution on the evening of January 28, just a few hours after the police received orders to withdraw from squares. The next fourteen days marked an intense confrontation between the protesters and the army (Table 9.1). Apparently, the military learned from the tragic defeat of the police forces and decided not to use violence against the protesters while staying on the fence in terms of abandoning Mubarak.

Conversion

The military put aside their traditional weapons and instead sought to contain the movement and ultimately to end the revolution. The military first appeared in Tahrir Square in Cairo, Suez, and Alexandria on the night of January 28, a few hours after the police forces withdrew. According to eyewitnesses at Tahrir Square, including myself, there was a strong feeling of caution when the tanks descended from Kasr Elnil Bridge heading toward Tahrir Square and State TV Building. "Some people expected the tanks are coming to kill us, and everyone was asking what should we do about it," explained one of the protesters outside State TV Building on that night.[4] "Almost everyone agreed to

4. Interview with Mai Ibrahim, one of the protesters who was at Tahrir Square on the night of January 28, by Dalia Ziada, Cairo, January 28, 2011.

stand still and continue the fight till the end." After a few moments of silence, "protesters rushed in front of the first tank shouting, 'God is great,' and making clear that any further forward movement would be over shattered bodies" (Contenta 2011). A few moments later, an unknown person chanted the slogan that has since become the icon of the revolution: "The people and the army are one hand!" Protesters repeated the chant until a collective sense of confidence developed and people's fear evaporated (Wedeman 2011). According to eyewitnesses from Suez, similar slogans were chanted there, but no one knows who started them.

As both the protestors and the military signaled to one another the potential for cooperation and solidarity, strong emotions of empathy were created among the protesters and the military soldiers and young officers, who were sent to control the revolution. The long positive relationship between the people and the military and the lack of any apparent conflict of interests between them helped the military succeed in co-opting the movement instead of repressing it, and yet the narrowness of the social and age gap between the two groups increased the potential for converting young officers into revolutionaries. In fact, some of those young officers formed the April 8 movement of military officers (Fathi 2012), which appeared after the fall of Mubarak to warn people against the intentions of the Supreme Council of Armed Forces (SCAF) to fully hijack the revolution.

Accommodation

The military succeeded in redirecting the ire of Egyptian citizens away from themselves, but the protesters were able to maintain the momentum of the revolution by continuing the nationwide rallies and protests calling for the end of Mubarak's presidency. While some protesters chanted "people and the army are one hand," their colleagues were chanting "people want Mubarak down." The military chose to accommodate the resistance movement by pressuring Mubarak to offer some concessions to the protesters, including dissolving the cabinet and government, hiring a vice president, pledging that he would leave office at the end of his term in 2011, and ensuring that his son,

Gamal, would not run for the presidency. Even more, the military pressured Mubarak to give away one of his secondary pillars of support by dissolving the National Democratic Party and annulling the results of the 2010 parliamentary elections.

Accommodation was an effective mechanism of success for the military in the nonviolent struggle with protesters. According to Gene Sharp, "in accommodation, the opponents are neither converted nor nonviolently coerced. The opponents, without having changed their minds fundamentally about the issues involved, resolve to grant at least some of the demands of the nonviolent resisters" (Sharp 2005, 417). The ability of nonviolent activists to persist despite the repression by police, played an important role in military leaders' decisions to accommodate the movement, but they also most likely chose to accommodate as part of a strategy that Sharp (418) describes as "adjusting to opposition within their own group, and acting to prevent the growth of that opposition." By choosing to accommodate, SCAF succeeded in controlling potential dissidence in the military and winning more legitimacy that helped generate more supporters for the military's actions later. Thus, while military leaders were avoiding using repression that might backfire and generate greater civilian resistance, they were also managing potential dissent within their own ranks.

While the military was busy avoiding repression and engaging protesters, Mubarak appeared to feel abandoned. He yielded to the military's pressure and offered a number of concessions, but the protesters insisted on bringing him down. The more concessions he offered, the more legitimacy he lost, and the more legitimacy the military won, locally and internationally. Mubarak apparently could not understand why the military disobeyed his orders to shoot protesters and preferred to contain the situation without violence. The fear of being abandoned by his military pushed Mubarak to make use of his two secondary pillars of support (state media and the NDP) to protect himself.

Mubarak broke his last solid pillar of support in a deceptive attempt to repress activists in Tahrir Square. On February 2, Mubarak ordered the leaders of the dissolved NDP to incite the owners of tourist camels and horses from the pyramids area to carry swords and attack protesters in Tahrir Square (Beaumont and Shenker 2011). Mubarak was planning to scare protesters out of Tahrir Square and arouse suspicions toward the military and the new prime minister, Ahmed Shafiq, who promised no protester should be hurt (Fagge 2011). But in fact, this move backfired by strengthening the relationship between the military and protesters, who together fought against the armed camel and horse riders. At the same time, it aroused the suspicions of SCAF leaders that Mubarak was trying to discredit them. Consequently, they decided to stop informing him of their plans and began to adopt a policy of neutrality. Mubarak then seemed more suspicious of the intentions of SCAF and escalated divisions between them, deepening the prisoner's dilemma that was coming to define their relationship (Youssif and Mosa'ad 2012).

The protesters' determination to bring down Mubarak escalated after the camels and horses battle. Meanwhile, the military continued to adopt a position of neutrality out of fear of being deposed along with Mubarak. On February 9, Mubarak made the mistake that turned his last friends into foes. He sent a DVD to State TV for immediate release. In the video, Mubarak recorded his decision to remove General Tantawy, the minister of defense, who was the highest-ranking officer in SCAF and one of Mubarak's most loyal officials. The director of the news sector at State TV was shocked when he watched the video, and he called SCAF leaders immediately to inform them about it. After consulting with General Tantawy, General Etman, the director of the Morale Affairs Department of the Egyptian military, asked State TV to broadcast a video that showed SCAF being convened for the first time without Mubarak (Khattab 2011). Two days later, Omar Suleiman, Mubarak's vice president and former head of Egypt's intelligence, appeared on State TV to announce Mubarak's resignation and decision to transfer power to SCAF (Fox News Insider 2011).

Thanks to the military's strategy of accommodation instead of repression, the people embraced Mubarak's transfer of power to the military. Even political groups that rejected the rule of the military were compelled to accommodate and accept this transfer of power.

Military leaders had both avoided triggering the paradox of repression and had won sufficient support among the nonviolent resistance to ensure their continued authority.

Factors Influencing the Military's Strategy

Very few have studied the motives behind the Egyptian military's decision to abandon Mubarak and side with the protesters. Four factors influencing the military leadership's defection from Mubarak were presented at the beginning of this chapter: (1) self-interest, (2) independence and professionalism, (3) external pressure by third parties, and (4) positive relationships with protestors.[5] I will focus now on the last two of these factors, as they bear directly on SCAF's decisions not to engage in violent repression.

Third Party (International Pressure)

The third proposition holds that the military's decision not to shoot the protesters was motivated by their allies in the US Army. The Egyptian and the American military have long maintained strong relationships. Since the peace agreement with Israel in 1970s, the United States has been committed to providing $1.3 billion annually to the Egyptian military (Sharp 2012). The independence of the military institution in Egypt and its large US subsidy helps explain why there was international interest in communicating directly with the Egyptian SCAF rather than contacting Mubarak after the military got involved on January 28.

The Egyptian military sends young and mid-rank officers to the United States to receive training not only on warfare but also on civil issues (e.g., human rights, democracy, peace) and nontraditional roles of the military in non-wartime. The older, higher-ranking officers, particularly from SCAF, used to travel to the United States once every

5. The three propositions are derived from the sparse literature and articles available on the topic as well as interviews I conducted with experts, politicians, and activists.

year to meet with top leaders at the Pentagon. When the revolution started in January 2011, the leaders of SCAF were in the United States for their annual meeting with Pentagon leaders, and they had to cut their visit short and return to Egypt on January 27.

In an interview, the US Joint Staff Spokesperson told me that "General Sami Enan and a military delegation were in Washington, DC, for the US-Egypt annual Military Cooperation Commission meetings in January 2011. These meetings aimed to advance the peace and security of both nations by discussing security assistance, military training, and industrial defense cooperation. Meetings of this kind are a routine part of the long-standing military-to-military relationship of the United States and Egypt."[6]

He explained further that when the protests erupted in Egypt, the Egyptian military leaders discussed the issue with their US military counterparts before ending the meeting to go back to Egypt. According to the Joint Staff Spokesperson, "the US military leaders discussed a number of topics with Egyptian military leaders in this meeting to include the political-military situation in Egypt. Although, it would not be appropriate to discuss the details of those conversations, the US military, to include the Chairman of the Joint Chiefs of Staff (at the time) Admiral Mike Mullen, publically and repeatedly encouraged the Egyptian military to refrain from violence against the protesters and commended them on their professionalism and restraint."

Although the US military urged the leaders of the Egyptian army to refrain from killing the protesters and encouraged them to avoid violence, they emphasized that the army should not let Mubarak down. General Sami Enan—Egyptian Army Chief of Staff—assured his counterparts at the US military that the Egyptian Army would not abandon Mubarak in the same way that the Tunisian Army defected from Ben Ali (Bhalla 2011). Further, the US Joint Staff Spokesperson said to me, "I can tell you that at no point did the US advocate the overthrow of President Mubarak but rather emphasized the need for

6. Interview with US Joint Staff Spokesperson, Dalia Ziada, January 2012.

genuine change to meet the demands of the protestors and expressed the confidence the US had in the Egyptian military to see Egypt through its governmental transition." US support for the Egyptian military is consistent, regardless who is the head of the state, which provided the military with latitude to side with the protesters rather than protecting the Mubarak regime.

Positive Relationship with the People

The Egyptian military is historically more biased toward the people than the ruler, sensitizing its leaders to the risks of using violence against civilians and predisposing its leaders to become allies. "The fact that the Egyptian army is a conscript force drawn from all segments of society also seems to have contributed to its identification with demands of the protesters" (Lutterbeck 2011, 27). The armed forces are one of the most respected institutions in Egypt. It is the only institution that was not accused of corruption during the Mubarak era. The distance and ambiguity that surrounded the military's relationship with Mubarak helped in maintaining the positive image of the military that has prevailed since the 1973 victory over Israel.

The Egyptian military was also trained in carrying out nontraditional missions, such as providing humanitarian aid in times of disaster. Two major incidents, the earthquake in October 1992 and the bread crisis in 2008, solidified the positive relationship between the people and the military during the Mubarak era (News Editor 2008). The power relationship between the people and the military, compared with the power relationship between the military and the regime, made it easier for the military to choose to align with the protesters and stop supporting Mubarak's regime.

Conclusion

The Egyptian military learned from the defeat of the police forces, whose violence against protesters backfired. Military leaders understood that the nonviolent protesters were no longer fearful and would not be controlled by the use of violent force or physical coercion. Therefore, the military chose to put aside its traditional weapons and attempted to manage the growing nonviolent movement by avoiding violent repression. As protesters began to identify with the military, its leaders sought to accommodate the movement by pressuring Mubarak to offer concessions, including dissolving the NDP, annulling parliamentary election results, pledging not to renew his term (and barring his son from the presidency), changing the government, and hiring a new prime minister.

Conversely, Mubarak took a more repressive approach aimed both at repressing movement activists and intimidating and delegitimizing the military. Inciting the camels and horses battle and attempting to remove the head of SCAF backfired as the military responded by removing their support, contributing to Mubarak's fall on February 11, 2011, while SCAF stepped up to take his office.

The Egyptian revolution of January 2011 provides a useful case through which to study the relational nature of power that informs much of the work in this volume. The configuration (in this case a triangle) of relationships between multiple actors shaped their strategic choices and the outcome of an iconic nonviolent struggle. It started as a struggle of a nonviolent movement responding to violent repression by police forces. In four days, the nonviolent movement defeated police by using methods of nonviolent coercion and attempts to convert police and induce defections. Over the next fourteen days, the revolution turned into a nontraditional conflict between the nonviolent protesters and the military that led to the military avoiding repression and working to accommodate protesters and thus align with the nonviolent revolution. Mubarak's attempts to challenge military leaders compelled them to go further and push the president out by accommodating the movement's immediate goals of deposing Mubarak.

The military was Mubarak's last pillar of support, and his regime fell when they abandoned him. This chapter attempts to answer the complicated question of why the Egyptian military decided to eschew the violent strategies typical of their profession. Unlike the violent police forces that were defeated by the nonviolent movement within only four days of massive nonviolent protests, the military was able to manage the protests by avoiding violence and accommodating some of the movement's demands, thus ultimately enacting the kind of "smart" repression that Smithey and Kurtz describe in chapter 8 in this volume. When the military first intervened on January 28, a few hours after the police withdrew, the leaders of SCAF decided not to use violence against the protesters because they realized the movement had reached a level of confidence and momentum that would not respond to further repression. Consequently, the military decided to put aside their traditional weapons and adopted strategies that enabled them to control the protests and gain legitimacy independent from the presidency.

Both the Egyptian military and the nonviolent civil resistance movement attempted to shape the struggle over Mubarak's presidency. Activists, drawing on well-established knowledge about nonviolent civil resistance, drew on a range of tactics and methods to press the Mubarak regime for reforms and to withstand repression by police forces loyal to the president. More to the point, the initial police repression backfired and encouraged the Egyptian military to be cautious about making a similar mistake. Military leaders instead exercised restraint in an understudied form of internal repression management. By reaching out to activists who exercised nonviolent discipline and by accommodating to some of their interests, the military engaged in a political dance with activists that resulted in a bloodless end to Mubarak's regime.

References

Aly, Abdel Monem Said. 2012. "State and Revolution in Egypt." Crown Center for Middle East Studies, Brandeis Univ., Waltham, MA. http://www.brandeis.com/crown/publications/ce/CE2.pdf.

American Islamic Congress. 2010. *A Modern Narrative for Muslim Women in the Middle East: Forging a New Future*. Washington, DC: American Islamic Congress.

Bhalla, Reva. 2011. "Dispatch: 'Day of Rage' in the Middle East" (video report). Jan. 25. http://www.stratfor.com/analysis/20110125-dispatch-day-rage-middle-east.

Beaumont, Peter, and Jack Shenker. 2011. "Egypt's Revolution Turns Ugly as Mubarak Fights Back." *Guardian*, Feb. 2. http://www.guardian.co.uk/world/2011/feb/02/egypt-revolution-turns-ugly.

Cavna, Michael. 2011. "Amid Revolution, Arab Cartoonists Draw Attention to their Cause." *Washington Post*, Mar. 7. http://voices.washingtonpost.com/comic-riffs/2011/03/arab_cartoons.html.

Claude, Patrice. 2010. "WikiLeaks: L'armée égyptienne ne veut pas d'une succession dynastique." *Le Monde*. http://www.lemonde.fr/documents-wikileaks/article/2010/12/13/wikileaks-l-armee-egyptienne-ne-veut-pas-d-une-succession-dynastique_1452924_1446239.html.

Contenta, Sandro. 2011. "Protesters Stand Their Ground as Tanks Roll into Tahrir Square." *Toronto Star*, Jan. 30. http://www.thestar.com/news/world/article/930658--protesters-stand-their-ground-as-tanks-roll-into-tahrir-square.

Dunne, Michele, and Amr Hamzawy. 2010. "Does Egypt Need International Election Observer?" *Carnegie Commentary*, Oct. 14. http://carnegie-mec.org/publications/?fa=41733.

"Egypt's State of Emergency Ends after 31 Years." 2012. *Telegraph*, May 31. http://www.telegraph.co.uk/news/worldnews/africaandindianocean/egypt/9303195/Egypts-state-of-emergency-ends-after-31-years.html.

Fagge, Nick. 2011. "Camel Charge in the Battle for Cairo." *Telegraph*, Feb. 4. http://www.dailytelegraph.com.au/news/camel-charge-in-the-battle-for-cairo/story-e6freuy9-1225999796755.

Fathi, Yasmine. 2012. "Egypt's '8 April Officers' Remain in Political Limbo." ahramonline, Sept. 12. http://english.ahram.org.eg/NewsContentP/1/52144/Egypt/Egypts--April-officers-remain-in-political-limbo.aspx.

Fox News Insider. 2011. "VP Suleiman Speaks on State TV, Saying Mubarak Steps Down" (video). Fox News Network, Feb. 11. https://www.youtube.com/watch?v=nVt4XITH-gM.

Hardin, Luke. 2011. "US Reported 'Routine' Police Brutality in Egypt, WikiLeaks Cables Show." *Guardian*, Jan. 28. http://www.guardian.co.uk/world/2011/jan/28/egypt-police-brutality-torture-wikileaks.

Hashim, Ahmed. 2011. "The Egyptian Military, Part Two: From Mubarak Onward." *Middle East Policy* 18 (4): 106–28.

Khattab, Mohamed Saad. 2011. "Backstory of Mubarak's Last Hours in Office: The President Attempted to Remove Tantawy, So SCAF

Decided to Abandon Mubarak." [In Arabic.] *Sawt Al-Oma*, July 24, print edition of the newspaper.

Lakey, George. 1968. "The Sociological Mechanisms of Nonviolent Struggle." *Peace Research Reviews* 2 (6): 12.

Logan, Lara. 2011. "The Deadly Beating that Sparked Egypt Revolution." *CBS News*, Feb. 3. http://www.cbsnews.com/2100-18563_162-7311469.html.

Lutterbeck, Derek. 2011. *Arab Uprisings and Armed Forces: Between Openness and Resistance*. Geneva Center for the Democratic Control of Armed Forces, Geneva, Switzerland.

Mendel, Noah. 2009. "Can a Comic Book about MLK Change the Middle East (At Least a Little)?" *History News Network*, May 10. http://www.hnn.us/articles/80834.html.

News Editor. 2010. "Egypt Election: Hosni Mubarak's NDP Sweeps Second Round." *BBC*, Dec. 7. http://www.bbc.co.uk/news/world-middle-east-11935368.

———. 2008. "Egypt Army to Tackle Bread Crisis." *BBC*, Mar. 17. http://news.bbc.co.uk/2/hi/middle_east/7300899.stm.

Pletka, Danielle, and Ali Alfoneh. 2009. "Iran's Hidden Revolution." *New York Times*, Jun. 16. http://www.nytimes.com/2009/06/17/opinion/17pletka.html.

Rosenberg, Tina. 2011. "Revolution U: What Egypt Learned from the Students Who Overthrew Milosevic." *Foreign Policy*, Feb. 16. http://www.foreignpolicy.com/articles/2011/02/16/revolution_u.

Rutherford, Bruce K. 2013. *Egypt after Mubarak: Liberalism, Islam, and Democracy in the Arab World*. Princeton, NJ: Princeton Univ. Press.

Sharp, Gene. 2005. *Waging Nonviolent Struggle: 20th Century Practice and 21st Century Potential*. Boston: Extending Horizons.

Sharp, Jeremy. 2012. "Egypt: Transition under Military Rule." *Congressional Research Service Reports*, RL33003, Jun. 21, Washington, DC. https://digital.library.unt.edu/ark:/67531/metadc94010/.

Stolberg, Sheryl Gay. 2011. "Shy US Intellectual Created Playbook Used in a Revolution." *New York Times*, Feb. 16. http://www.nytimes.com/2011/02/17/world/middleeast/17sharp.html?pagewanted=all.

Vesely-Flad, Ethan. 2011. "The Untold Story of How a FOR Comic Book Inspired Egyptian Revolutionaries." Fellowship of Reconciliation, Feb.

2. http://forusa.org/blogs/ethan-vesely-flad/martin-luther-king-egypt-fellowship-reconciliation/8479.

Wedeman, Ben. 2011. "Protesters Swarm Egyptian Army Vehicle" (video). *CNN.* http://cnn.com/video/?/video/world/2011/01/28/egypt.cairo.tank.protesters.cnn.

Youssif, Ahmed, and Nevin Mosa'ad. 2012. "The Arab Nation 2011–2012: Complexities and Horizons of Change." [In Arabic.] Center for Arab Unity Studies, Beirut, May.

Zakaria, Fareed. 2003. *The Future of Freedom.* New York: Norton.

10

Repression Engendering Creative Nonviolent Action in Thailand

Chaiwat Satha-Anand

Introduction

On November 18, 2012, more than one hundred people boarded the skytrain from Siam Center station in Bangkok to Mor Chit station, a trip that takes about twenty minutes. Then they took the train back to the Siam Center station and went to the posh Siam Paragon shopping complex in downtown Bangkok. Although the temperature in Bangkok that day was between 26 and 34 degrees Celsius (80–93° F), all of them were wearing winter clothing, complete with overcoats, jackets, hats, shawls, gloves, and even blankets. When they arrived at the shopping complex, they went to feast at the ice cream parlor.

The group is called "Red Sunday," and its leader is Sombat Boonngamanong, a forty-five-year-old activist who has done much by way of creative nonviolent resistance in fighting for democracy in contemporary Thailand. Red Sunday carried out this "flash mob" to protest against a rally led by a retired army general who mobilized more than 50,000 people in a call to "freeze Thailand" by preventing elected officials from taking office. The general's supporters intended to allow only selected "good" officials to run the country for five years because they believed that Thailand is not ready for democracy. Sombat explained that while he accepted the right of the general and his supporters to rally, he disagreed with their message and wanted to "tease" the general's plan, which would not only freeze the elected politicians but also the rights of ordinary people who had elected them. Red Sunday's flash mob was so captivating that every major Thai news agency reported this creative nonviolent action.[1]

This chapter is about Sombat and his group and their actions, particularly in the period after violent government repression in May 2010 and before the general election held in July 2011. The Red Sunday movement was born from repression that left more than ninety people dead and more than one thousand wounded. I explore how it is possible that such a creative nonviolent movement could have arisen out of the ashes of violence and repression. I also argue that, at the time, Sombat and his comrades prevented a highly polarized Thai society from falling into a dangerous civil war. It was Red Sunday and their creative nonviolent actions that prevented the Red Shirts from becoming a violent movement after it was violently suppressed in 2010 by the military force under the administration of Prime Minister Abhisit Vejjajeeva. The Red Sunday movement had opposed the September 19, 2006, coup and the government of the Democrat Party, demanding a dissolution of the house and a national election.

There are several ways one could try to understand the Red Sunday movement. One could focus on its leadership and how someone becomes such a leader, or one could look primarily at the movement's nonviolent actions from various sophisticated theoretical perspectives and analyze the ways in which their humorous tactics work and conclude that it has become "the key ingredient for a constructive nonviolent struggle" (Sombatpoonsiri 2016, 143).[2] Here, I want to focus on understanding how and why such creative and compelling strategy could emerge as a result of violent repression. I argue that this

1. See, for example, *Matichon* online [in Thai], November 22, 2012, 21. (http://www.matichon.co.th).

2. This research was carried out by Janjira Sombatpoonsiri under the Senior Research Scholar multilayered three-year projects on "Nonviolence and Violence in Thai Society," which I headed from 2011 to 2013, funded by Thailand Research Fund (see Sombatpoonsiri 2015; Sombatpoonsiri 2016, 127–48).

nonviolent resistance became possible as a result of how the political space left from repression interacted with alternative leadership from within the movement and a history of nonviolent resistance in Thai society. The nonviolent tactics chosen by Sombat and his group shaped the longer-term strategy of the movement, in turn providing hope for those who were repressed by the regime and, most important, encouraging them not to choose the path of violence.

This chapter begins with a brief historical portrait of resistance in Thai politics that serves as a larger context for nonviolent resistance by the Red Sunday group after repression. Then I will discuss selected nonviolent resistant actions by Sombat and his group, especially those that appeared right after the violent suppression. I will emphasize the role of creativity or the ability of activists to develop unexpected but powerfully meaningful and persuasive actions that compel people to abandon fear and participate in popular nonviolent movements. The creativity of these nonviolent actions will be examined in light of the "cleansing" effect of violent repression, Thailand's history of nonviolent resistance, and the ways creativity works in transforming conflict.

Portrait of Resistance in Thai Society: A Calendar

In the article "Why So Much Conflict in Thailand," Tonnesson and Bjarnegard (2015, 132–61) from the Peace Research Institute in Oslo point out that Thailand is the only country in East Asia with three more or less simultaneous deadly conflicts—in the streets of Bangkok, at the border with Cambodia, and in the southernmost provinces. Tonnesson and Bjarnegard look at the causal mechanisms that allow these conflicts to feed on one another, highlight the significance of national conflict on both the northeastern border and the peripheral deadly conflicts in the Deep South of Thailand, and caution that they might play out in other conflicts as well. It could be argued that the turmoil is a result of the political change and conflict of the past decade.

In the early 2000s, a new political party was created under the leadership of Thaksin Shinawatra, a billionaire telecommunications tycoon, politician, and former policeman who had led his party to victory in four consecutive elections in 2001, 2004, 2008, and 2011 (the last two times under very restrictive circumstances and with the party's de facto leader in absentia after his government was ousted in the coup on September 19, 2006). Thaksin's victories and the responses to them by the losing elites—which included those associated with the palace, the army, the judiciary, and some parts of the bureaucracy and the business sector—has engendered a polarized Thai society with unprecedented and widespread animosity.

The three interlocking deadly conflicts mentioned above—ethnic violence in southern Thailand, border conflict with Cambodia in the Northeast, and the protests and violence during the last few years in Bangkok and elsewhere in the country—have been historical consequences of three interrelated phenomena: the unfinished nation-state project, the unfinished regional project, and the unfinished democratic project. Echoing Tonnesson and Bjarnegard, I argue that it is the unfinished democratic project that holds the key to unlock all three deadly conflicts. The border conflict with Cambodia would not have turned deadly if not for the intensity of the conservative nationalist drive that pits the two countries against each other (Pawakapan 2013). The unrest in southern Thailand, with its legitimation deficit problem, could not be solved except by treating it as a national problem that demands a strong political will necessary to overcome structural impediments and design an innovative political arrangement between Bangkok and the restive south. Both conflicts could be best dealt with in a more democratic environment, but the limits of Thai democracy have been contested since 1932, when Thailand (Siam at the time) ceased to be an absolute monarchy.[3] The Red Sunday movement could be best construed when placed in the context of the interplay between repression and resistance in Thailand during that time.

3. The military carried out another coup on May 22, 2014, installing General Prayut Chanocha as the prime minister. At the time of this writing, it seems that the military government has successfully silenced most actions opposing it using strict laws and other methods against most activists, including Sombat himself. The Red Sunday leader is not imprisoned, but due to all kinds of pressures, his activities have been restricted.

June 24, 1932: A group of young civilian and military bureaucrats, many of whom were educated abroad in France, staged a peaceful revolution (some would call this a coup) to put an end to absolute monarchy and usher in the era of democracy. Under the new political arrangement, the king ruled under the Thai constitution. The legacy of June 24, 1932, is still a subject of debate even today. On one side are those who believe that the country was not yet ready for electoral democracy at the time, and that the officials' seizure of power from the monarch was an act of treason. They believe that King Rama VII, who was educated in England, would have given a democratic constitution to the Thai people in time, and that the revolution simply replaced one ruler with many. On the other side of the debate are those who believe that the 1932 revolution constituted the advent of a new era ushered in by commoners, particularly Dr. Pridi Bhanomyong, who two years after the revolution, founded Thammasat University. Such differences of opinion aside, it is a fact that no one was killed or wounded during this important transition, partly because the soldiers were tricked[4] to rally behind the Khana Rasadorn (Citizen Group) who carried out the action on that fateful day.

October 14, 1973: After World War II, Thai society was ruled by successive military governments. The country continued to modernize because of a strong and institutionalized bureaucracy, so much so that it was called a "bureaucratic polity." In the context of ideological struggle, passionate student movements, and anti(Vietnam)-war protests, a group of Thai students from Thammasat University staged a mass protest to demand the drafting of a constitution and a democracy. The nonviolent student movement shut down the university,

4. For example, some military leaders of the 1932 revolutionary group took control of a key military unit in Bangkok by falsely claiming that there was a riot in the city, and then using their higher rank to order the unit commander to commit his force to them. Another member of the 1932 group, the commander of Military Cadet School, ordered the cadets to join others at the Rama V Plaza in Bangkok where the revolutionary group congregated by telling them that they were there for a training parade (Mektrairat 2010, 304–5).

organized mass demonstrations, and blocked the main avenue in the city. It was said that the military fired the first shot leading to violence in which 77 people were killed and 857 wounded. After the military junta, headed by field marshal Thanom Kittikachorn resigned and left the country, the king appointed the rector of Thammasat University to be the new prime minister, while a new constitution was drafted and approved, and the age of free elections began with the flowering of various ideologies (Kongkirati 2005). The event was considered a great democratic success—even Greek students at the time were shouting "Thailand! Thailand!" during their own political protests.

October 6, 1976: If the 1973 demonstrations echo the fourth episode of George Lucas's *Star Wars* saga, then October 6, 1976, mirrors the fifth, *The Empire Strikes Back*. During the three years after the October 14, 1973, incident, the student movement basked in its victory, and some parts moved further left along the ideological spectrum. Both the right and the left became radicalized in the atmosphere of freedom. When Thanom returned to Thailand one day in October 1976, the students staged nonviolent protests at Thammasat University to demand his expulsion. On the morning of October 6, Thammasat University was attacked by paramilitary troops and thugs. The brutality of repression was unmatched by any other political event in modern Thai history. Students inside were massacred, people were dragged out of the university to be burned alive and hung from the tamarind trees, and bodies of young men and women were mutilated, all in broad daylight, in the middle of the city, on ground many consider holy since it is surrounded by sacred temples and holy objects. And there were people watching, grinning, clapping their hands at the brutality committed before their very eyes. The elected government went into hiding, the constitution was voided, and a new ultraconservative government took power. Many students left the city to join the Communist Party of Thailand (CPT) in armed struggle. October 6, 1976, entered into the Thai collective memory as wounded history. For the most part of the last three decades, it was treated with silence, perhaps because of shame of many parties about the role they played in the tragedy (Winichakul 2010).

February 1991: Three years after its formation, a coalition government headed by the first elected prime minister—himself a former general and diplomat from a most prominent Thai political dynasty—was ousted by a coup. The leaders of the takeover cited the usual accusations: corruption and undue interference in the bureaucracy by the politicians, among others. The coup makers imprisoned the prime minister for a few days and invited Anand Panyarachun, a former master diplomat and successful businessman who himself was persecuted after October 6, 1976, to lead one of the most professional and transparent governments the country has seen. Anand later became very popular within Thai civil society.

May 17–18, 1992: When a leader of the 1991 coup, General Suchinda Kraprayoon, decided to take the helm as the prime minister in March 1992, despite giving his word that he would not, a group of Thai civil society members rose up under the leadership of Major General Chamlong Srimuang. Chamlong was to become a most successful Bangkok governor and later a leader of the Yellow group fighting to oust Thaksin. The protest used the nonviolent battle cry "Ahimsa-Ahosi" (nonviolence-forgiveness), but it was met with violent suppression. Forty people were killed and 736 more wounded, with some fifty people missing. But the protesters and the people did not yield. There were incidents of burning buildings, but by and large it was another case of nonviolent resistance. This time they won, and the military retreated to the barracks after the king intervened. A process to draft a new constitution began, this time involving the widest public participation. Five years later, the 1997 constitution, the most democratic in Thai history, was born (Satha-Anand 1999). The cycle of electoral politics began anew with many people believing that the era of coups d'état was over.

September 19, 2006: The 1997 constitution aimed to tackle a persistent problem of governing Thailand, namely, the instability of the coalition government. It put in place mechanisms to strengthen political parties with electoral regulations. At the time, Thaksin created the Thai Rak Thai party and with that constitutional platform led his party to victory in the 2001 election. More important, he consolidated his power both within the party and in the parliament, giving birth to a very strong and stable government. His populist policies and daring and decisive style of governing endeared him to the rural poor, but his poor human rights record and use of violence antagonized those whose voices he relegated to the margins. Failing to get rid of Thaksin at the polls, large civil society groups from right and left organized themselves and staged protests to oust the prime minister. The anti-Thaksin group called themselves "Yellow Shirts," taking their name from the color associated with Monday, the day on which the king was born, and protested against the government. They claimed that they were protesting because the prime minister was no longer a loyal subject, and they called for the military to step in.

The military intervened on September 19, 2006. A new government was established with a prime minister who was a former military general and a privy councilor close to the king, and the great polarization of Thai society, simmering under the surface, burst into the open. A new constitution was drafted and born in 2007, this time designed so that independent organizations, such as the anticorruption panel and the constitutional court, could monitor and effectively curtail abuses. Many later said that while they were critical of Thaksin's close association with the capitalist/globalized project and poor human rights record, it was the coup that made them decide to resist the military and its supporters, including the Democrat Party under Abhisit Vejjajeeva, who many believed became the prime minister of a coalition government in 2008 with assistance from the military (Chiangsaen 2011).

It was against this backdrop that the Red Shirts emerged. Sombat Boonngamanong, who would later lead the Red Sunday movement, thought that those opposing the coup needed a symbol. He suggested the color red because he believed it was highly visible and represented the color of the sun, a natural power source. Another leader from the resistance group extended the idea to vibrant and visible "red shirts," and thus the Red Shirts as a political entity was born.

April–May 2010: The Red Shirts movement mobilized both in Bangkok and in the provinces, especially in the North and Northeast, Thaksin's party stronghold. They moved to Bangkok with a demand to dissolve the parliament and called for a new national election, since they considered the Abhisit government illegitimate. The government tried to negotiate with the red-shirted protesters, but when the effort failed, violence ensued. The Red Shirts employed common nonviolent resistance techniques, such as occupying the streets with tens of thousands of people and more than a hundred thousand at the peak of the protests. There were "problematic" nonviolent actions, such as when the protest leaders used three hundred liters of blood donated by approximately 70,000 donors to splash at the government house, the Democrat Party headquarters, and the private home of Prime Minister Abhisit on March 16–17, 2010 (Cohen 2012, 216–33). When the threat of government repression became imminent, some leaders said on stage before a large crowd of protesters, "If you [the military] seize power, our people will burn the whole country. Burn, brothers and sisters—I will take responsibility myself."[5] Another leader also said, "If they threaten to suppress us, don't prepare much. Just come with a glass bottle. Come collect your gasoline, fill the glass bottle up to 75 cc or 1 liter. If a million of us come to Bangkok with a million liters of gasoline, I assure you—Bangkok will become a sea of fire."[6]

The protest ended in violence, and Bangkok was engulfed in flames, especially in business districts. Some believe fires were started by the protesters, while others claim that they were set by unknown parties after the protest was called off and most of the leaders were in police custody. Here are some statistics of this most violent suppression in Thai history:

5. Speech of a Red Shirt leader, Nattawut Saikua, who was later a deputy minister of commerce in the Yingluck government (2011–14), given at the protest site in Bangkok, April 8, 2010.

6. Speech by Arismun Pongruangrong, a popular singer who is also a Red Shirt leader who spoke from a stage during the demonstration on January 29, 2010.

- The government used more than 50,000 troops and fired more than 100,000 real bullets to deal with the protesters.
- There were ninety-four deaths, ten of them government officials; more than 1,400 people were wounded. Six of those killed were women while the youngest fatality was twelve years old ("Truth for Justice" 2010, 14–15).

Three points emerge from this brief portrait of resistance over the last eighty years of Thai political history. First, there is a strong tradition of resistance against dictatorship in Thai society. Second, the story of resistance in Thai society has been primarily nonviolent (with some elements of violent protest included, as is common with resistance movements around the world), and nonviolent resistance is often met with violence. Third, after repression there were times when resisters chose armed struggle to continue their resistance.

It is in this context that the Red Sunday group takes on such significance in the history of resistance in Thai society, and perhaps elsewhere. Unlike past instances of resistance, the group's actions were initiated to prevent the broader movement from turning violent after state repression, as a form of repression management. The next section will explore what Sombat and his group did to manage the response to repression, and how they did it.

Creativity Unleashed: The Day(s) After

"I cried every day. I continued to cry for weeks. Just sitting by myself and then tears came out," said Sombat of his immediate reaction to the violent suppression of the Red Shirts in May 2010, but Facebook became his salvation. As one of the top five Facebook authors in the Thai Internet world, where he goes by the name "Dalmatian Editor" (Bor Gor Lai Jud), Sombat has many followers. "I was trying all the time. Never quit fighting. After May 19, I am outside—I hid in the internet world and proposed the idea 'Red Sunday' to the public. I thought of this by myself and then proposed it. If you look at my Facebook, you will know—it's a one-man show. I am a radical individualist because every Red Shirts member has equal energy, depending on how one manages the energy. . . . It was full of anger, very painful. If you cannot handle the enormous energy in your heart, you will hurt yourself in the end. If you cannot release it, you will be stressful" (Panpong 2010, 148).

His way of "releasing the energy," once he had expressed his ideas through his Facebook page, was to start the Red Sunday nonviolent resistance, beginning with a coffee-drinking group of five people talking about democracy.[7] They met to challenge the emergency law which prohibited political gatherings at the time. Then, on June 26, 2010, Sombat led his people to tie red ribbons around the Raj Prasong Square sign post at Raj Prasong intersection, the site of the Red Shirts' demonstration and later violent suppression. Sombat was arrested and kept at a Border Police camp outside Bangkok until July 9 when he was released on bail.

He told an interviewer that he was not in prison.

> It was a house in the Border Police camp. I could use the phone, have visitors . . . read newspapers, watch TV. I also sneaked in my phone to play Facebook inside . . . I could connect the struggle inside with the outside world because I was not lying idle. I think all the time how I would fight from inside the camp. I even think that if they release me, I would go and tie the red ribbon again. I must say that I did not plan to be arrested and did that. . . . When I came out, I knew that I was in a position to fight on when I saw *Matichon Weekly* [an influential news magazine] with my photo on its cover. I then continued with my tying the red ribbon activity at Raj Prasong (Panpong 2011, 152–53).

Sombat went to Raj Prasong every Sunday with others. On July 11, two days after he was released, he was tying red ribbons there with fifty other friends. A week later, on July 18, he went to perform the same

7. This is clearly intentional and, therefore, slightly different from some of the examples of what happened in Eastern Europe that prefigured the Solidarnosc movement, which led to the end of the Soviet empire (Goldfarb 2006).

act, but this time more than one hundred riot police blocked the area and arrested one of the members on a charge of making loud noise. Ultimately, the authorities decided that they had had enough with the red ribbon action menace and removed the sign post on which the resistors tied their ribbons.

On July 25, the Red Sunday group staged an aerobic dance with more than five hundred people near a city park. Then, on August 1, they performed a show at the democracy monument that reenacted a scene where actual killings took place in May, but with masked protesters dressed as ghosts. These ghosts carried banners reading "There were dead people here," a reference to the famous line from M. Night Shyamalan's film *The Sixth Sense*. On August 8, Sombat led five hundred people in a 700-meter run around peace park. On August 15, there was a red rice picnic for about one thousand people at a park (red rice is often served in prison). On August 22, Sombat led his friends to northern Thailand to perform activities in Chiang Mai; this was the first time the Red Sunday group held an activity outside of Bangkok. On August 29, Red Sunday engaged some two thousand participants in a "walking tour at shopping centers" called "patriotic shopping." The action was meaningful because the May 2010 killing took place in a square surrounded by posh shopping malls, and given the number of these malls in Bangkok, it is safe to assume that Bangkokians love to shop.

On September 5, Red Sunday went to the Eastern province of Chonburi to participate in the "Red in the Sea" activity. On September 12, sixty bicycle riders rode along a "bloody path" near Saladaeng Intersection, another site of a violent attack, during which one of the group's militant leaders was killed. On September 19, the fourth anniversary of the 2006 coup, and the fourth month after the suppression, Sombat led more than 10,000 people back to Raj Prasong Square and released 10,000 balloons into the sky and tied 100,000 red ribbons in the area. Far more people participated than either the organizers or the police expected.[8]

8. *Khao Sod* (newspaper), September 20, 2010. [In Thai.]

It could be argued that some of these activities are directly related to repression, such as the "there were dead people here" show, while others, such as the aerobic dance in the park and "Red in the Sea" activity, are not. However, both sets of actions service different but important functions in relation to repression. Nonviolent resistance *after* repression is different from that carried out in the face of repressive force. Nonviolent resistance after repression must reignite the fighting spirit of protesters affected by violence by making them feel that they can continue to fight. The aerobic dance in the park was a form of resistance that could be considered a protest without being seen as a protest, since it was a normal everyday activity in a public space.[9] This type of resistance is often necessary as a lower-risk platform of symbolic acts that can prepare for further resistance after repression, once protesters have regained their confidence.

When Sombat was asked what he was trying to do, he answered:

> After the suppression of the protest, I was thinking of how to reclaim symbolic space because the point that can connect the people must be through symbols, otherwise I don't know how to salvage the disintegrated mass protesters. Everyone kept symbols hidden. No one knows who is who? Who is still fighting? How are we doing? To use the symbol of "red" is to plant a flag, to insist to continue to wear red shirts. It reflects the mobilization of fighting spirits. I want to salvage all this. So I propose "Red Sunday" since it is what the people could do together. To put on their red shirts together again after violent suppression, their image tarnished. We must show our presence that we still are "Red Shirts." I use Facebook activities to project a unified image of Red Shirts movement to do relaxing activities. . . . I believe I have provided people with "mental" support.[10] To help mobilize those who were vanquished to return. Now those who

9. See a discussion of this nonviolent action using the concept of "excorporation" in Sombatpoonsiri (2015, 178–201).

10. The Thai word he used here is *jit-jai*, which could be translated as *mind* or *morale*, or even *spirit*.

> have fallen could get back on their feet. This is what I and the Red Sunday group have done. (Panpong 2011, 153–54)

Sombat believes that instead of large-scale demonstrations and protests, symbolic campaigns should be used ferociously with sufficient intensity to "pressure the government to lose its nerves." It is important to point out that, for him, the opening of such a symbolic battle front is not meant to supplement nonviolent tactics but to become a main battle front that could lead to effective changes. And for him, "If this is intended to be the main battle front, it will be fun" (Panpong 2011, 153–54).

Later on, Sombat explained some of the reasons why he preferred to use these symbolic campaigns. He noted that, as a thespian, he is interested in the ways emotions engender actions. In politics, a common emotion used to foster actions such as political resistance has been rage. But an emotion that is no less powerful than rage is humor. His strategy has always been to engage in conflict through humor, to "tease" the authorities without fomenting rage. He also maintained that Thai society is rich with such treasures, which allow those who use such tactics to get away with it without much risk.[11]

But how has the movement sustained itself, since many of these creative nonviolent actions were carried out using very short time frames and with flashy nonviolent styles, compared to the massive demonstrations or occupation of public space seen in earlier surges of resistance? Sombat introduced the idea of *Kaen Norn*, or horizontal leaders.[12] Using the Red Sunday activity of tying 100,000 red ribbons at Raj Prasong Square as an example, he explained that the sheer number of people who came out to participate exceeded his wildest dreams.

11. Sombat's comment at a public forum to report on the three-year research project on Nonviolence and Violence in Thai Society, titled "Nonviolent Space/Way for Thai Society," at the Faculty of Political Science, Thammasat University, Bangkok, August 6, 2013.

12. I believe Sombat would prefer the terms "laid-back leaders" or "lying-down leaders."

The organization of the protest became "self organization" (his term), moving from bottom up without leadership, without major activities. Nothing was clear, but there were many participants.

> Its mood, feeling and tone were different from all other demonstrations. It has its own personality. There was no stage to give speeches, no leader, no agenda as to who will do what, nothing, even I could not do anything. . . . When the police came and told me to stop the activity, I told him that I could order no one. It was a flash mob. . . . There is a theory that mobilizing a mob is not that difficult, downing it is much more difficult. But for us, it was spontaneous. They came by themselves and they left themselves. No one told them anything. It was self-organized, which cannot be directed. A strange thing happened—the red spider web.[13] I assure you that no one has thought about this before, no one dares to. But when a large group of people congregate, with the same feeling, it just so happened. . . . It is fresh performance, live arts. I just tie red ribbons around the poles, but how did the red spider web appear? I am puzzled. . . . It was the quality of the mass, at a particular point, it just appears. It is "suchness" and I think it's great (Panpong 2011, 155–57).[14]

What was fantastic about the more than 10,000 people who turned out on September 19, 2010, was that they were no longer afraid. Once freed from fear, the emergency law became a joke. Law was used to instill fear, but "the Red Sunday movement used humor, symbols to pierce its back. It turns the Emergency Law, which was an instrument of fear, into a clown. . . . It is a mental fight, an invisible and rule-changing game. We recovered with speed. But we were in the standing

13. I believe he used this phrase to capture the fact that the leaderless protest he described has become a spontaneous network of popular power that keeps expanding not unlike a spider web.

14. The explanation Sombat gave here resonates with the Hegelian notion of quantity changing into quality. But the term "suchness" he used is a Buddhist term. The Buddha calls himself *Tathakhata* (in Pali) which means the One who lives and has gone as such or "Suchness."

moment, not offensive. . . . From now on, I would try to find ways to move/walk on, not to stand up. I am trying to change the people into operators" (Panpong 2011, 158).

To do this, Sombat sold shirts and funded a school to train people to become *Kaen Norn*, or "lying down leaders." The school teaches four things: recheck perspectives on democracy to see the commonality among the Red Shirts; discuss how to market democracy focusing on target groups, their behavior, and communication techniques; explore how to organize and manage democratic organizations; and design activities without relying on traditional actions, such as speeches or concerts (Panpong 2011, 161–63).

When I read Sombat's interviews and spoke with him, I came to understand that repression played a role in the development of Red Sunday's creative nonviolent actions. Five centuries ago, Machiavelli wrote in *The Prince*:

> It was therefore necessary for Moses to find the people of Israel, in Egypt, slaves and oppressed by the Egyptians, so that the former, in order to come out of servitude, might dispose themselves to follow him. For Romulus to become king of Rome and founder of that fatherland, it was necessary that Romulus not be confined in Alba, that he should have been exposed at birth. It was necessary that Cyrus should find the Persians discontented in the empire of the Medes, and the Medes soft and effeminate because of a long peace. Theseus could not demonstrate his virtue if he did not find the Athenians dispersed. These occasions consequently made these men happy, and their excellent virtue enabled them to recognize that occasion whence the fatherland was ennobled and became most happy. (Machiavelli [1532] 1997, 21–22)

But if Machiavelli is right in saying that repressive conditions are necessary for a new beginning to emerge, how did this happen in the Red Sunday case? Let me continue with a more modern theory of violence. This time, it is Frantz Fanon's wisdom that is useful.

Fanon maintains that not only does violence destroy the formal colonial structure, but it also frees the alienated consciousness of the native from his/her feeling of inferiority and humiliation, restoring him/her to the fullness of being human. This is why Fanon sees violent resistance as a cleansing force, not unlike the Christian baptism, which terminates a person's past existence as a thing, and initiates a new one as a human being (Hansen 1977, 121–22).[15] But Fanon's theory rests on the petrifying effects of violence on the individual and how his/her (violent) resistance would free him/her. However, what about its effects when the subject is not an individual but a movement?

Combining the thoughts of Machiavelli and Fanon, I would argue that violent suppression by the government incapacitated the Red Shirts movement with fear of violence when all its leaders, some of whom had earlier advocated violent options, were arrested. Those who were left must have been paralyzed with both fear and anger. In this case, violent suppression produced the necessary condition for a new beginning by depriving the movement of its traditional leaders and creating an empty space in which the new portrait of the movement could emerge. Sombat's activity filled the empty space with a new force of creativity, very different from what went before. When the traditional "vertical" leadership of the Red Shirts movement was apprehended, the "horizontal leadership," Sombat's *Kaen Norn*, could emerge in its place. He was able to guide this transformation because he was a part of the original Red Shirts movement and commanded sufficient credibility to propose actions. He was trusted by many as someone who could lead, but this ability could not shine when the other more traditional figures were leading the movement.

Violent suppression produced the empty space necessary for a new beginning, and Sombat's creative ideas about resistance offered means to neutralize the paralyzing effect of repression on the movement by

15. For those who might feel that invoking Machiavelli and Fanon in a discussion of nonviolent actions is sacrilegious, I would say that there are, in fact, those who study Gandhi in light of Machiavelli, and others argue for the "humanist Fanon" that could be compared with Mahatma Gandhi and Nelson Mandela. See for example Panter-Brick (1966) and Presbey (1996).

enabling ordinary people to retain their moral rage and yet refuse to allow themselves to be petrified with fear. His creative nonviolent actions replaced the cleansing effect of violence with a more effective alternative. People could continue to fight, frame the Emergency Law as a joke, keep the resistance going without the loss of lives, and secure critical legitimacy. Many in Bangkok did not agree with the Red Shirts and their disruptive techniques, but they also found the violence used against the Red Shirts deplorable.

More important, Sombat's Red Sunday activity arose at a most crucial *time* for the resistance movement. Along with the empty space that follows repression, there is also empty time, the time to choose. Given the history of resistance in Thai society outlined above, the possibility that people might choose armed struggle to continue resistance after violent suppression was quite real. At that very moment, I was worried most about the radicalizing effect of violence, and indeed there were rumors that some had already thought about going underground to prepare for armed struggle. This idea of "going underground" and choosing violent options is not uncommon, however. Take Northern Ireland as an example. The civil rights movement in the 1960s led to the emergence of political violence. In the beginning, despite profound conflict, nobody was killed. Then from 1969 to 1972, 497 people lost their lives. Previously marginal and simplistic arguments in favor of aggressive violence appeared to be vindicated as a result of the state's violent suppression. This allowed the Irish Republican Army to become the major agent of killing (English 2009).[16]

In the empty time, if no one with some level of credibility and fantastic imagination steps up to suggest creative nonviolent actions that are practical and credible, that time will be taken by others with violent strategies and the resistance movement can be lost to violence.

16. In April before violence broke out I wrote an op-ed piece in a newspaper emphasizing the danger of violence ahead and the need for nonviolent confrontation at the time (see Satha-Anand 2010).

Lessons Learned from Creative Nonviolent Actions

When I discussed the possibility of armed struggle after repression with some Thai intellectuals, they pointed out that 2010 was not the same as 1976. At that time, when students and others faced brutal suppression by the Thai state, they took off from the city and headed for the jungle to join the CPT. In 2010, there was no longer a CPT waiting to receive lost fighters. Much of the jungle has been turned into tourist resorts, so it is not likely that armed struggle would arise as a result of repression. Though I can see that the context has changed over the last thirty years, changes also produce new threats. In the twenty-first century, sometimes it takes only one man or a few violent ones to cause serious damage to many lives, as well as political futures. Take Anders Behring Breivik, the perpetrator of the Norway attack that killed seventy-seven people in 2011, as an example. This is perhaps what Arjun Appadurai meant when he warned the globalized world to fear small numbers, who could inflict such horrible damage through violence (Appadurai 2006).

Yet this chapter discusses a case study of creative nonviolent actions that begin with small numbers. This case depends on so many particulars, including a leader, such as Sombat, who is an activist with a background in theater, and who also likes to read how-to books and is fluent with new technology. One must also consider the specific set of political circumstances that gave rise to the Red Shirts movement, which mobilized rural people with those on the left in support of a billionaire, who is an integral part of the globalized capitalist economy.[17] What kind of conversation could such a case study have with the field of resistance, and especially nonviolent resistance?

17. The discussion here is different from Piven and Cloward's classic study (1979) on how poor people's movements could mobilize, organize, agitate, and sometimes win reforms. Though their work points out how poor people's apathy could be transformed into hope as a result of extraordinary disturbance in a larger society, their main focus is clearly on examining the institutional conditions that both create and limit the opportunities for mass struggle.

I believe at least five issues should be considered:

1. histories of resistance,
2. the interaction of polarization and diversity of participation,
3. internal movement cohesion,
4. the relationship between tactical and strategic nonviolent actions, and
5. the importance of symbolic nonviolent actions.

First, Thai society has a long history of resistance that makes it possible to come together now, in both physical space and in cyberspace, to carry out certain political actions. The Arab Spring of 2011 has been compared to the "revolutions" of 1848 because both swept across whole regions with amazing speed and yet yielded limited advances in terms of freedom and democracy. Apart from failing to see differences in one country from another and overrating the Tunisian success, one of the reasons given in the more recent case is that Arab societies were weakly organized and repressed. They lacked organization density, the opposition was weak, and civil society was fragmented, as in Egypt (Weyland 2012).

This type of conclusion can be called into question by some as a lack of understanding of Arab societies resulting from Orientalism and Euro-Centrism, among other things (e.g., Shihade 2012). Others may argue that Thai society is clearly different from "Arab" societies. However, one can see that histories of resistance are important. I am not saying that there will be no resistance without a history of resistance in any society. However, I contend that nonviolent resistance would be easier to organize after violent suppression in a country with a history of resistance, whether violent or nonviolent.

Second, the diversity of participants has been as important as the number of participants for successful nonviolent campaigns, according to Chenoweth and Stephan (2011) in their award-winning book, *Why Civil Resistance Works*. Using the violent struggle of the New People's Army (NPA) in the Philippines as an example, they argue that the NPA was so exclusive due to its Marxist ideology that it lacked the links to the ruling elite that could have been accessed by a much more diverse movement, and thereby decreased the chances of creating divisions within the regime (192–93).

The Red Shirts movement was diverse, with 20 percent white-collar workers, 16 percent small business owners, 12 percent entrepreneurs, 10 percent government officials, and only 1.6 percent farmers (Chiangsaen 2011, 128).[18] Yet this movement could have turned violent despite its diversity, because the Thai context at the time was, and remains, so heavily polarized. How does extreme polarization affect a resistance movement? Can polarization overwhelm the force of diversity and thereby lessen the likelihood of working toward nonviolent actions? What must a movement do to counter the force of polarization, maintain diversity, and open the movement up for nonviolent actions?

Third, violent suppression that undermines a movement's unified structure can foster a highly creative and more committed nonviolent movement. In a study of the Palestinian national movement covering almost a century, Pearlman asked a very interesting question: Why do some activists choose nonviolent tactics, while others favor violent ones? She argues that for a nonviolent movement requires discipline, clear strategic direction, and coordination, which only a unified movement can provide. In fact, she points out that "while the paths to violence are multiple, there is only one prevailing path to nonviolent protest: a path that requires a movement to have or create internal cohesion" (Pearlman 2011, 2).

Looking at the Red Shirts movement from Pearlman's perspective, it is possible to see that a reason why Sombat and Red Sunday could not have greater influence on the Red Shirts movement *before* the violent suppression was perhaps because the movement was so unified and cohesive and therefore did not have sufficient space for alternative kinds of leadership that could move the movement closer to nonviolent strategy. Only *after* the violent suppression all but destroyed

18. This is another reason why the case discussed here is very different from older class-based movements as analyzed by Piven and Cloward (1979).

the movement's unified structure could a highly creative and more committed nonviolent movement such as the Red Sunday emerge. In a way, the May 2010 violent repression could be seen as the "internal transformative event" that affected the ways in which subsequent resistance has taken shape, both in its unexpectedness and nonlinear fashion (Shultziner 2011).

There are several questions that seem relevant here. When is cohesion most necessary for a nonviolent movement? Is it possible to imagine cohesion as a quality that might curtail the nonviolent potential of a movement? Is there anything a nonviolent movement might need in place of cohesion? Judging from the Red Sunday case, there are times when cohesion might be less necessary for a movement to be nonviolent—as when the violent suppression was about to take place. Obviously, there are times when cohesion might be needed more, such as when people need to feel connected to regain their strength and rejuvenate the movement with nonviolent action after violent suppression.

Fourth, tactical decisions may shape a movement's strategic direction. In analyzing six nonviolent revolutions against socialist regimes (China and East Germany), military regimes (Panama and Chile), and personal dictatorship (Kenya and the Philippines) from the mid-1980s to the 1990s, Nepstad (2011) found that in all cases of successful nonviolent revolutions, defections by security forces proved most important as a strategic factor, since they effectively undermine the state's sanction power. In reviewing Nepstad's work, Pearlman (2012) questions whether security force defection is strategic or structural. She pointedly asks how it is possible for behavior to be tactical, strategic, and unintended at the same time. The question is provocative. By the same logic, is Red Sunday's ribbon-tying activity tactical or strategic? When Sombat first went to Raj Prasong Square to tie the red ribbons at the pole on June 26, 2010, was the intent and the effect the same as when he joined 10,000 others to tie 100,000 red ribbons at the same place on September 19, 2010? If the answer is no, then could the same act be tactical at one point in time and strategic at another? Moreover, is it possible, despite Pearlman's question, to imagine an act that is both tactical and strategic at the same time?

Could it be that when the Prophet Muhammad migrated from Mecca to Yathrib (later called Medina) in an act called *Hijrah*—a protest emigration, which is nonviolent action according to Sharp's classification (2012, 148)—the act was both a tactical move, because he and his followers were fleeing persecution, and strategic, in that it led to a new center for the newborn movement? While most writers seem to subsume the importance of nonviolent tactics under those of nonviolent strategy, Iain Atack (2009, 239) has argued that such division is artificial in practice, since the two objectives of limited and broad structural changes often coexist within particular cases of nonviolent campaigns. This is because such nonviolent campaigns often consist of coalitions of different groups with their own objectives, which may be limited among some and extremely broad among others.

My colleagues and I have argued that some tactical nonviolent actions could be consciously used within a much larger strategic objective, while others could be used with a much more limited goal (Satha-Anand et al. 2013). Could it be that it is tactics which inform and perhaps shape a long-term strategy for a resistance movement? For Sombat and the Red Sunday group, the use of social media is tactical, but it is the tactics that shape the ways in which the movement's strategy could be effectively formulated.

Fifth, there are those who might think that the kind of nonviolent resistance influenced by Gene Sharp's work privileges the use of noncooperation and other structurally oriented strategies over symbolic actions used by Sombat and the Red Sunday group. Sombat's motivation aside, I argue that there are at least four reasons why such common wisdom about Sharp's thoughts needs to be carefully reconsidered.

1. In the nonviolence literature influenced by Gene Sharp, I would argue that there is not one but at least two Sharps in action: "hard Sharp" and "soft Sharp." Hard Sharp would see that noncooperation is a much more potent weapon while soft Sharp would underscore the ways in which nonviolent protest and persuasion inform, if not shape, noncooperation. In other words, it would be difficult, if not impossible, for a movement to mobilize

its supporters without the use of symbolic action that enables a large number of people to participate in noncooperation that would result in the desired political objective.

2. Those influenced by hard Sharp seem not to fully appreciate the power of creative forms of protest and persuasion, perhaps in their intention to articulate the important fact that nonviolent resistance is not limited to actions in the streets but also includes other "creative and concrete" alternative forms of potent noncooperation, such as boycotting foreign occupiers' goods or withdrawal of money from financial institutions found to support the dictatorial regime that a movement seeks to bring down. Theorists such as James C. Scott (1990) and Jeffrey Goldfarb (2006) have, in contrast, pointed to the importance of "hidden scripts" (Scott) or "small things" (Goldfarb) that serve to empower ordinary people and constitute ways to express disobedience from the ruling regimes.
3. Noncooperation may work best with a specific group with a strong common interest, such as a trade union. When unions strike, it is clear (to many of them) that they are in a class relation with industrialists' whose interests are always in opposition to their own. The workers can therefore be mobilized more easily through an articulation of common class interest. But noncooperation may work less well in more diverse settings, unless movement participants are creatively mobilized into understanding that disobedience is possible, that it is empowering to them, and that it could undermine the existing regime's sources of power.
4. In the case of Thailand, perhaps not unlike many other Asian societies, it is important to understand that society is a "regime of images."[19] In such a social world, the struggle in the theater

19. It should be noted that Peter Jackson (2004) originally uses this term to mean an internally differentiated form of power that exerts systematically different types of control over actions in both public and private spheres.

of image assumes paramount importance. Symbols, symbolic actions, and artistic creativity operate so powerfully, perhaps even more than any other concrete actions. For example, to prevent deforestation, it is debatable whether boycotting wood products would be more powerful than placing yellow robes around trees in a Buddhist ritual of "ordaining trees," which would then make it more difficult for those Buddhists who want to cut those trees down to follow through with their plans (Satha-Anand 1997).

Conclusion: Creativity and Nonviolent Actions

The challenge going forward is to understand how creativity works in deadly conflict. In a study on how creative options emerge to transform conflicts, Tatsushi Arai (2009) uses sixteen episodes of conflict-resolution creativity. These include the problem-solving workshop to address the Indonesia-Malaysia-Singapore conflict, the binational ecological zone in the disputed Peru-Ecuador border area, and Gandhi's first satyagraha campaign in South Africa from 1906–1914. Arai proposes that creativity is defined as "unconventional viability," where an actor or actors involved in conflicts learn to formulate unconventional resolution options and/or procedures for change, while a growing number of others come to perceive it as a viable way of coping with their problems from their collective and subjective perspectives.

In this chapter, I have argued that Sombat and his group's creative nonviolent actions were initiated to fill empty space produced by repression, in a moment of empty time when choices were to be made by people filled with pain and anger. The creative nonviolent actions initiated by the Red Sunday group served as a form of repression management that offered "unconventional viability" to those who were crushed by violent suppression. Because the actions proposed by Sombat and his group were viable and unconventional, they could fill the empty space and steal the empty time at the right moment and thereby prevented the Red Shirts movement from becoming violent, a path which could have torn Thai society apart, possibly resulting in a fierce civil war.

> The lesson may be painful but it is the best thing given to us by the crisis. Don't ignore it and (try to) reap the lessons after the (violent) event. . . . Three years ago, I returned to Raj Prasong (where the violent repression took place against the Red Shirts) to say that "Be not Afraid." This year, I am returning to the same place to say: "Do not forget."
>
> —Sombat Boonngamanong[20]

References

Appadurai, Arjun. 2006. *Fear of Small Numbers: An Essay on the Geography of Anger*. Durham: Duke Univ. Press.

Arai, Tatsushi. 2009. *Creativity and Conflict Resolution: Alternative Pathways to Peace*. New York: Routledge.

Atack, Iain. 2009. "Some Reflections on Transformative Nonviolence." In *Building Sustainable Futures: Enacting Peace and Development*, edited by L. Reychler, J. F. Deckard, and K. H. Villanueva, 239–44. Bilbao: Univ. of Deusto.

Chenoweth, Erica, and Maria J. Stephan. 2011. *Why Civil Resistance Works: The Strategic Logic of Nonviolent Conflict*. New York: Columbia Univ. Press.

Chiangsaen, Uchain. 2011. "The Origin of 'Red Shirts' as a Counter Movement." [In Thai.] *Fa Diew Gan* 9: 133–34.

Cohen, Erik. 2012. "Contesting Discourses of Blood in the 'Red Shirts' Protests in Bangkok." *Journal of Southeast Asian Studies* 43: 216–33.

English, Richard. 2009. "The Interplay of Non-violent and Violent Action in Northern Ireland, 1967–1972." *Civil Resistance and Power Politics: The Experience of Non-violent Action from Gandhi to the Present*, edited by A. Roberts and T. Garton Ash, 75–90. Oxford: Oxford Univ. Press.

Goldfarb, Jeffrey C. 2006. *The Politics of Small Things: The Power of the Powerless in Dark Times*. Chicago: Univ. of Chicago Press.

Hansen, Emmanuel. 1977. *Frantz Fanon: Social and Political Thought*. Columbus: Ohio State Univ. Press.

20. Sombat was interviewed at a rally that can be viewed in a YouTube video posted by thefanmai on May 19, 2013 (youtu.be/YpfljR1SN6I, accessed May 25, 2014).

Jackson, Peter A. 2004. "The Thai Regime of Images," *Sojourn: Journal of Social Issues in Southeast Asia* 19: 181–218.

Kongkirati, Prajak. 2005. *And then Appears the Movement: Cultural Politics of Students and Intellectuals before October 14*. [In Thai.] Bangkok: Thammasat Univ. Press.

Machiavelli, Niccolò. (1532) 1997. *The Prince*. Translated and edited by Angelo M. Codevilla. New Haven: Yale Univ. Press.

Mektrairat, Nakarin. 2010. *Siamese Revolution 2475*. [In Thai.] Bangkok: Fa Diew Kan.

Nepstad, Sharon Erickson. 2011. *Nonviolent Revolutions: Civil Resistance in the Late 20th Century*. Oxford: Oxford Univ. Press.

Panpong, Worapoj. 2010. "Sweet-Cool Red campaigner." [In Thai.] In *An Interview of Sombat Boonngamanong*, edited by P. Janwit, 148. Bangkok: Openbooks.

———. 2011. "Sombat Boonngamanong: On the Battle between Humans and God." [In Thai.] *Emergency*, 153–54. Bangkok: Banglampoo.

Panter-Brick, Simone. 1966. *Gandhi against Machiavellism: Non-Violence in Politics*. Delhi: Asia Publishing House.

Pawakapan, Puangthong R. 2013. *State and Uncivil Society in Thailand at the Temple of Preah Vihear*. Singapore: Institute of Southeast Asian Studies.

Pearlman, Wendy. 2011. *Violence, Nonviolence, and the Palestinian National Movement*. Cambridge: Cambridge Univ. Press.

———. 2012. Book Review. "Nonviolent Revolutions." *Perspectives on Politics* 10: 995–98.

Piven, Frances Fox, and Richard A. Cloward. 1979. *Poor People's Movements: Why They Succeed, How They Fail*. New York: Vintage.

Presbey, Gail M. 1996. "Fanon on the Role of Violence in Liberation: A Comparison with Gandhi and Mandela." In *Fanon: A Critical Reader*, edited by L. R. Gordon, T. D. Sharpley-Whiting, and R. T. White, 283–96. Oxford: Blackwell.

Satha-Anand, Chaiwat. 1997. "Two Plots of Nonviolence Stories: From the Streets of Bangkok to the Forests of Thailand." *Social Alternatives* 16: 12–15.

———. 1999. "Imagery in the 1992 Nonviolent Uprising in Thailand." In *Nonviolent Social Movements: A Geographical Perspective*, edited by S. Zunes, L. R. Kurtz, and S. B. Asher, 158–73. Malden, MA: Blackwell.

———. 2010. "Courting Nonviolent Confrontation in Thai House Divided: What Can Be Done?" *Bangkok Post*, Apr. 19.

Satha-Anand, Chaiwat, Janjira Sombatpoonsiri, Jularat Damrongwith-itham, and Chanchai Chaisukkosol. 2013. "Humor, Witnessing and Cyber Nonviolent Action: Current Research on Innovative Tactical Nonviolent Actions against Tyranny, Ethnic Violence and Hatred." In *New Paradigms of Peace Research: the Asia-Pacific Contexts*, edited by Akihiko Kimijima and Vidya Jain, 137–55. New Delhi: Rawat Publications.

Scott, James C. 1990. *Domination and the Arts of Resistance: Hidden Transcripts*. New Haven: Yale Univ. Press.

Sharp, Gene. 2012. *Sharp's Dictionary of Power and Struggle: Language of Civil Resistance in Conflicts*. New York: Oxford Univ. Press.

Shihade, Magid. 2012. "On the Difficulty in Predicting and Understanding the Arab Spring: Orientalism, Euro-Centrism, and Modernity." *International Journal of Peace Studies* 17: 57–70.

Shultziner, Doron. 2011. "Events, Transformative Events, and Democratization: A Theoretical Framework." Paper presented at APSA Annual Meeting, 2011. https://ssrn.com/abstract=1902911.

Sombatpoonsiri, Janjira. 2015. *Laughing at Power: Humor and Nonviolent Protest*. [In Thai.] Bangkok: Matichon.

———. 2016. "Playful Subversion: Red Sunday's Nonviolent Activism in Thailand's Post-2010 Crackdown." In *The Promise of Reconciliation? Examining Violent and Nonviolent Effects on Conflicts*, edited by Chaiwat Satha-Anand and Olivier Urbain, 127–47. New Brunswick, NJ: Transaction.

Tonnesson, Stein, and Elin Bjarnegard. 2015. "Why So Much Conflict in Thailand." *Thammasat Review* 18 (2): 132–61.

"Truth for Justice: Events and Consequences from the Violent Suppression of the Demonstrations, April–May 2010." 2010. People Information Center for Victims of Government Suppression, Bangkok.

Weyland, Kurt. 2012. "The Arab Spring: Why the Surprising Similarities with the Revolutionary Wave of 1848?" *Perspectives on Politics* 10: 917–34.

Winichakul, Thongchai. 2010. "October 6 in the Memory of the Rights: From Victory to Silence." [In Thai.] In *Violence Hides/Seeks Thai Society*, edited by Chaiwat Satha-Anand, 409–512. Bangkok: Matichon.

11

Making Meaning of Pain and Fear

How Movements Assist Their Members to Overcome Repression

George Lakey

Gandhi urged his followers to become fearless. The British Empire, he believed, ruled India only because Indians were afraid of the British. Give up fear, and the British would have to leave. The nonviolent activists I have worked with in dozens of countries are not as ambitious as Gandhi. For most, the goal is not to "give up" fear but to handle fear so it does not prevent effective action. Everyone, however, would agree that the "fear factor" is critical to success in overcoming repression.

This chapter explores ways that activists have found to handle fear, make meaning of pain and suffering, and support risk-taking so that violent repression will not shut down their movements. I will follow sociologist Francesca Polletta (2007) in looking for clues in

In this chapter, I make frequent reference to information that I have garnered from many movements over the years, information I have not seen in documents and cannot cite. Often, this information came from personal observation (for example, Freedom Summer in 1964, where I was a trainer), interviews I conducted (for example, in Serbia, where I led workshops that included Otpor members), conversations (in events in many countries), or correspondence. Where possible, I indicate these sources in the chapter text, references, or footnotes.

the stories activists tell each other, since narrative is crucial for how human beings understand themselves and act powerfully in the world. I will draw intensively from more than half a century's experience as a participant in nonviolent movements, since participation provides an "inside track" to knowledge supplementing information gained from the outside.

Framing Matters

In the world of classical music performance, handling fear is part of the training. After twenty years of a young performer's preparation, the high-stakes competitions can destroy the young adult's dream of a career. A concert pianist told me what he was taught at conservatory: "Turn your fear into excitement." He said the adrenalin became a friend; performance was enhanced. One way activists have overthrown dictators and defeated the Ku Klux Klan has been to turn their fear into excitement. They framed their anticipation of action by using materials at hand in their historical situation and in their movement culture.

Journalists at Cairo's Tahrir Square during the early days of the 2011 Egyptian revolt interviewed participants facing tear gas, beatings, and death. They reported little fear. Instead, participants said they were excited at the enormity of the opportunity to act at last, and they felt joy that so many were acting together. A shared story began to emerge: we have been impatiently holding ourselves back—we who are Egyptians and the center of the Arab world—and we are aware that the Tunisians acted before we did, so our pride and honor compel us to again take leadership and do what we have been wanting to do: throw out this contemptible and embarrassing Mubarak regime. Even the Egyptian activists' sense of humiliation as the center of the Arab world became part of the movement's story, using collective self-esteem as an ingredient for the needed framing of their mass performance of defiance.

Similarly, among African American Baptists in the southern civil rights movement, Jesus came to be nicknamed "the first Freedom Rider." Since for Baptists the emulation of Jesus was a central pivot for self-understanding, these activists could face the possibility of death by following their Lord and Savior. All the more so after 1961, when the Freedom Riders' Greyhound bus was bombed, while the activists were still inside it, in Anniston, Alabama. To escape the fire, the racially integrated team had to exit through the front door into the hands of a mob armed with baseball bats and lead pipes. One Freedom Rider barely escaped death, needing over fifty stitches in his head in a hospital emergency room. The segregationist mob's attack backfired. Many people who learned about the attack on television or in some other way increased their commitment to the civil rights cause, and more volunteered to ride the buses as Freedom Riders. The paradox of repression had been invoked.

In this chapter I offer multiple examples of activists, culture workers, and trainers creating frames and stories that supported collective resilience and redoubled participation in the face of repression. First, I will describe an example of tactical choice and then organizational choice to show how repression management works. In each case, I will relate the choice to how the participants make meaning of a threat and what they believe works in meeting that threat. I will go on to explain how some movements use training to assist participants to face their fears and become resilient in the face of repression, an important dimension of repression management.

Movements create cultures that may or may not help them overcome repression. Strategists and trainers need to think carefully about whether a movement's culture includes stories about pain and suffering that offer a positive and transformative meaning. I will describe how that has in fact been done through

- acts that dramatize the agency of the participants,
- the portrayal of martyrdom,
- placing sacrifice within a narrative of spiritual development, and
- linking risk with self-esteem in the context of a reference group.

One easily overlooked cultural dimension of the paradox of repression is the influence of a movement's theory of change. The activists' story of how they can win their struggle may influence their ability to withstand an opponent's repression. This narrative has at least two aspects: their story about the nature of their opponent, and their picture of potential allies.

Theory of change relates directly to strategy or lack of it. I will present briefly a nonviolent strategic perspective that puts overcoming repression squarely in the center of the narrative, and then apply it by comparing the Egyptian revolt against Mubarak's dictatorship with the 2011 Occupy movement in the United States.

Tactics and Structures

Because this chapter is mainly about the influence of stories in participants' heads, at the outset I want to caution against a view that the successful performance of confrontation depends only on beliefs and stories. Movement organizers also influence participants facing repression through their choice of tactics and structures, which matter, of course, in all forms of combat. Where would military strategy be without the tactical possibility of retreat or the organizational structure of top-down command? What complicates most nonviolent struggles, however, is the lack of highly coercive sanctions to enforce tactical choices and the following of commands. In nonviolent struggle, participants who desert the cause are not executed.

Nevertheless, some nonviolent campaigns have learned how to influence participants' behavior through tactics and structures to increase their ability to overcome repression. To illustrate, I will describe (a) the physical placement of participants as a tactical choice, and (b) the organization of combat units. I will also suggest how these choices may in turn influence the frames and stories that maintain a high standard of performance by participants.

Physical Placement Provides Direction When Multiple Frames Compete

Campaign participants operate in a world of ambiguous and competing frames that can lead to different and even opposite behaviors. In the early days of the anti-Mubarak movement, Egyptians' reports of their feelings suggested that the sheer size of the crowds fueled their experience of excitement, rather than fear. Large numbers, however, can also be problematic. Participants in a large demonstration know they have limited knowledge about what is happening in the bigger picture. A reasonable belief that sits side-by-side with "a very large crowd means support" is "*there are others here who know more about what is happening than I do!*" When demonstrators hear loud noises at the edge of the large crowd as attackers begin their violence, they can abandon their "large-crowd-means-safety" frame and jump to "all of us are about to get slaughtered," stimulating a stampede in the opposite direction.

When two alternative frames conflict in participants' heads, tactics and structures matter. Key organizers in the civil rights movement believed that when protesters run away from the threat of getting hurt they end up suffering even more violence, with more casualties. The Reverend Andrew Young, for years a key lieutenant of Martin Luther King, told a group of us that one way to reduce the risk of a stampede was to get the protesters on their knees to pray. "Yes," he said, "we preachers do pray for divine intervention, but the other reason we have the marchers kneel is that *it is difficult to run on your knees.*" Reduced physical mobility may provide an incentive for participants in a protest to choose the frame that best matches their physical reality, and thus to reduce cognitive dissonance that might be unbearable when men with weapons are attacking. My hypothesis is that, when on your knees, turning to God and the tactile reassurance of fellow protesters offers a better frame, representing safety (even when hearing the Klan's curses and "thwacks" of sticks hitting skulls), than the more problematic frame of breaking free of the group to run on your own.

I have raised this question in a variety of cultures and situations (for example, in the 1950s among French anti-Algerian war activists facing violent police, and in the 1990s among Thai protesters facing the attacks of soldiers), and I have frequently been told that getting a group to sit down close together, whether the group includes a dozen or a thousand, reduces the risk of running, being chased, and then finding that far more are hurt or killed in the end.

Movements sometimes learn survival skills from each other in the face of repression. In the summer of 2013, a mass nonviolent movement of Brazilians demanded governmental reform. A friend sent me a document reportedly being circulated among participants, which stated: "If any vandalism starts, sit down on the ground. Listen, folks who want to participate in the demonstration: try following an idea based on demonstrations in Argentina. When the vandals started to break everything there, the genuine demonstrators sat down, thus making it easier for the police to put down and arrest those who were responsible for these types of worthless actions. We can use this as a form of action in our demonstration, because we want a better city and not a destroyed city."

In India, the raid on the Dharasana saltworks during the 1931 salt satyagraha showed another way of physically organizing nonviolent confrontation to overcome repression (Tedla and Lakey 2011). As it happened, Gandhi was prevented from leading the action by his arrest, so Mrs. Sarojini Naidu took his place. She had thousands of volunteers available for the action, but instead of using her numbers to surround the saltworks and try to overwhelm the armed guards, she organized them into columns moving gradually toward a narrow point of confrontation.

As can be seen in Steve York's (2001) documentary *A Force More Powerful*, portrayed also in the widely seen film *Gandhi* directed by Richard Attenborough (1983), the volunteers stepped forward in small groups to be struck down by lead-tipped bamboo clubs, line after line, hour after hour. A field hospital was set up to care for the wounded; only one death was reported, but many people sustained severe injury. Although reporters on the scene described continued brutality, the participants neither ran away nor fought back violently. The resulting impact of the action makes the Dharasana saltworks raid iconic in the literature of the failure of authorities to shut down the movement through repression (Bondurant 1958, 88–102).

Affinity Groups as Cohesive Structures that Manage Response to Repression

The leadership of the Serbian young people's movement Otpor, formed in 1999, considered how to prepare members to face the risk of injury or death in a country run at that time by dictator Slobodan Milosevic. Otpor backed up its training with another framing: "You are not alone." Because the most feared beatings tended to be carried out not on the street but in the jail after arrest, the young people were told that within minutes of their arrest a lawyer would be summoned, and their peers would gather at the police station to demand fair treatment (York 2001).

If the member was beaten, whether inside jail or out, the procedure was for the member to go to other members and have the injuries photographed. At times, these photographs would be blown up and placed on picket signs to be carried outside the offending police officer's home, reassuring the member of the group's solidarity. The picketing tactic also encouraged the beating's backfiring for the police, since the picture of a bloody student might have repercussions in the family and social circle of the offending officer.[1]

Activists sometimes use the structure of small action groups in mobilizing large numbers to face repression. While reading military combat literature in graduate school during the early 1960s, I found writers emphasizing the value of the small, face-to-face group as the basic fighting unit because of its ability to maintain courage and morale under fire (Collins 2008). Such groups discourage running away when danger threatens. I then noticed the same dynamic operating in some large antiwar demonstrations, where small groups formed as supportive clusters and acted as teams. I used my influence in the rapidly developing nonviolence training network in Europe and the United States to urge the conscious formation of small groups within large confrontations. By the 1970s, in the nonviolent activist

1. Personal communication from Otpor members to the author.

world, these came to be called, with a nod to the anarchist tradition, *affinity groups.*[2]

Affinity groups may be composed of people who come to the demonstration already bonded as friends, coreligionists, neighbors, or coworkers. On the other hand, they may have been formed into affinity groups as part of a training process created specifically for this confrontation. Such groups provide a structure that reinforces a particular frame. They may at times even enforce a nonviolent behavior on participants that are trying to do something judged to be dangerous, like throwing a rock.

Because affinity groups can be crucial to maintaining a performance that overcomes repression, on multiple occasions before large-scale confrontations thousands of demonstrators have been organized into affinity groups as a critical part of the preconfrontation training.

Training for Handling and Growing from Repression

Historical Context

Few if any military leaders would want to lead untrained soldiers into battle, and the trend in social movements is likewise to prepare nonviolent combatants through training. Training provides a systematic way to influence the stories participants bring to the place of action.

The Gandhian movement in India used ashrams (intentional communities) as education and training centers for satyagraha campaigns and to prepare *Shanti Sena* (peace army) volunteers to intervene in riots. The Gandhian methodology was holistic, prioritizing community living, service, meditation, and reflection, with less emphasis on direct action skills (Desai 1980).

A Gandhi-inspired Pashtun independence movement on the Northwest Frontier led by Abdul Ghaffar Khan used marching as an

2. An early description of the affinity group in the context of repression management can be found in my book *Strategy for a Living Revolution* (1973, 72–77). The book is now in print as *Toward a Living Revolution* (2012f, 100–108).

important supplemental training tool; the Pashtuns faced even harsher repression from the British than did most people in India. In each case religion-based frameworks were important for making meaning of suffering; the Pashtuns called themselves servants of God (Bondurant 1958, 131–43).

The US civil rights movement was using experiential training methods like role-play by the 1950s, if not earlier. In role-play, some participants in the group take the role of campaigners while others take the role of violent police or other violent actors. The trainer sets the stage and calls for action; the campaigners perform their agreed-upon tactic, such as sitting down at a segregated lunch counter, and the workshop participants role-play police attacking the campaigners. The trainer stops the role-play when enough material for learning has emerged and debriefs the whole group for lessons learned.

Facing Fears

At the working retreat at George Mason University that brought the contributors of this book together, two of the authors, Dalia Ziada and Jenni Williams (with experience in Egypt and Zimbabwe, respectively), emphasized that nonviolent campaigners need to acknowledge their own fear. The training debrief, where participants reflect on what they have discovered through role-play, can help provide a social context where fear is normalized.

The Student Nonviolent Coordinating Committee (SNCC) and their allies showed the efficacy of training during the training camp for Freedom Summer in 1964. Northern-based college students gathered on an Ohio campus to prepare for a summer of nonviolent confrontation in Mississippi. In two weeklong sessions, groups of about four hundred students were trained and sent. Early in the second training, the leaders informed the students that two members of the previous week's group, plus a SNCC organizer, had just been killed in rural Mississippi. While the students knew that they were volunteering for a dangerous situation, the news that two of their peers were already dead a few days after reaching the combat zone gave rise to intense fear. The trainers, including myself, immediately swung into action along with SNCC workers still in Ohio. Group singing, permission for people to express their grief and fear, and exemplary stories all played a role. We observed that very few students returned home; nearly all stayed through the week and went on to Mississippi to face the Ku Klux Klan (Ohrenschall 2012).

The Chilean opposition to the Pinochet regime in the 1980s executed a similar use of training in a very different culture and political context. A group committed to nonviolent struggle encouraged people to face their fears directly in a three step process: small group training sessions in living rooms, followed by small "hit-and-run" nonviolent actions, followed by debriefing sessions. By teaching people to control their fear, trainers intended to prepare the way for the fall of the dictatorship.

The use of experiential training for combating the Pinochet dictatorship and racial segregation in the United States tallies with the observation of the authors meeting at George Mason University that methods must be found to make confrontation in some way predictable. Williams and Ziada believe that it is important to dispel the fear of the unknown, and reducing that fear is what activists experience when they receive this training. It is not that anyone expects exact replication of the training scenarios, but through repeated simulations the campaigners build trainees' confidence that they will be able to handle the version of reality that they will eventually encounter.

Supporting Resilience

The authors at the George Mason University gathering emphasized resilience and the need to help participants work through the sometimes traumatic impact of the violence they have experienced. A movement's long-term response to repression is influenced by how those wounded early in the struggle cope and heal so as to bring their skills back to the struggle instead of being sidelined, perhaps embittered by their experience.

Supporting resilience is another service that training offers. The first extensively research-based training curriculum for unarmed civilian nonviolent peacekeeping includes methods for immediate response after violence that might have traumatic impact. One example is the critical incident stress debriefing, a normalizing exercise based on the work of Paolo Freire (Hunter and Lakey 2004, 513–15).

I suggest that activists make meaning of their risk-taking and their experience of pain and loss of comrades with materials given in their historical situation and in their movement culture. Activists' stories frame their expectations and support them in performing their nonviolent actions. The George Mason authors' meeting addressed the importance of a movement's culture: surviving repression gets interpreted as an act of solidarity, a show of commitment, and a badge of honor, which in turn enhances participants' self-esteem. Training enhances that process in several ways.

- Trainers, when debriefing the exercises, tell movement stories, transmitting the culture through sharing folklore.
- Trainers elicit from participants their own stories, based on personal experience or inspiring stories they have heard from others.
- Trainers use exercises to increase the bonding in the group, bonding that overflows into storytelling at informal times.
- Trainers invite participants to share their fears and uncertainties as well as their grief and losses, again making meaning in a group setting.
- Trainers ask participants to share with each other their deepest motivations for joining the campaign and taking the risks. Participants in a labor union training I cofacilitated shared so passionately that the company spy in our workshop reported their level of commitment to his boss, who promptly began to negotiate with the union without any need for the action we trained for![3]

The decisive step forward in the proliferation of training for nonviolent action since the US civil rights movement has been creating

3. For a pedagogical overview and detailed descriptions of training methods, see my 2010 book *Facilitating Group Learning.*

the capacity for in-depth training of the trainers themselves.[4] Training for Change, an organization based in Philadelphia, has developed a methodology for doing this and offers a seventeen-day "Super-T" training for both aspiring and experienced trainers. Training for Change is often turned to by other training organizations to upgrade the skills of their trainers.

Anticipating Pain and Suffering: Contributions of Movement Culture

Members of the Serbian young people's movement, Otpor, told me that the movement had a slogan: "It only hurts if you're scared." The linking of fear and pain is of course psychologically astute: when we become ill or have an accident, if we fear the pain, we heighten the pain itself. When we reduce our fear, we reduce the pain as well.

When I interviewed an Otpor member who had been beaten by police multiple times, I asked, "Did you actually find that it only hurt when you were scared?" He smiled. "Well, I was always scared, but I think the slogan did help me not to be so scared, and not to hurt so much." A critical element of making meaning of pain is finding ways to embrace it and turn it into a positive and transformative part of the story.

Two Roles of Self-Esteem in Motivating Increased Risk of Pain and Suffering

Movements often find themselves calling on participants to risk more. As a result, we sometimes see participants performing acts that they

4. The availability of training in nonviolent action was greatly expanded by (1) the US civil rights movement's elevation of the role of training (especially in 1964 with the Mississippi Freedom Summer Project); (2) the Martin Luther King School of Social Change turning its student body into cadres of trainers who fanned out across the United States and made a big difference to the anti–Vietnam War movement; (3) the series of international training conferences (starting in 1965 in Perugia, Italy, which I attended) that put training on the global agenda; and (4) the professionalized approach to nonviolence training developed by Movement for a New Society (1971–88) and the organization Training for Change (1991 to present).

would not have considered a year or two earlier. They move from, for example, picketing outside a discriminatory store to going inside and risking arrest in a sit-in.

Movements support this dynamic when they celebrate those who risk boldly. They shift the meaning of being hurt by repression from victimhood to the experience of, for example, a "heroic nonviolent soldier." They encourage those who are ready to risk more—who may be few in the beginning—and in that way cultivate the contrast between exemplary suffering and minimal suffering.

This stimulates the low-risker's comparison of others' sacrifice with her or his own, a calculus within a frame of self-esteem. When participants think about a dramatic act that risks or involves major suffering (including a long prison sentence) they may ask, "If s/he can do that, what more can I do, at the very least?" Being arrested as a first offender may seem minor by comparison, even if civil disobedience had earlier been dismissed as much too scary.

When the agents of repression increase the level of pain and suffering, they inadvertently "move the goalposts" of what movement participants consider necessary to risk in order to maintain their self-esteem. On the other hand, a very different meaning might be made by individuals who volunteer to substitute for others in situations of very high risk or likely death. There are grave threats against groups whose members have varying vulnerability. During World War II, the German army occupied Norway and installed the Norwegian Nazi leader Vidkun Quisling as head of state. When Quisling moved to Nazify the schools, the teachers resisted collectively (Goldberg 2009). When the struggle escalated, Quisling ordered a limited roundup of teachers for torture in a concentration camp north of the Arctic Circle.

I was told when I taught in a Norwegian high school that the Norwegian police implementing the order were willing to let the teachers in each school decide how to make up the quota of arrestees. In my school (and perhaps others), the faculty met and, instead of drawing lots, met their quota for arrest by discussing criteria such as number of dependents, age, and bodily strength. The discussion was collective as well as in individuals' heads, with a collective framing and an existential collective outcome required. In light of the discussion, enough teachers volunteered to make the school's quota, even though the risk of serious injury and death once turned over to the Gestapo was high. In this kind of situation, self-esteem was framed by individuals' willingness to take the place of others for the good of the whole.

When Risk of Death Nears Certainty

It's one thing for a campaigner to risk death in the midst of repression when being killed is possible but unlikely, and another when death is all but certain. There are both religious and nonreligious traditions that offer meaning to support an individual in the latter situation—the honored history of martyrs. A little-known case in seventeenth-century Massachusetts alerts us to dynamics that deserve further research: How does a group offer sufficient meaning, and the inevitable high esteem, to support volunteers for nearly certain death, while creating a boundary that guards against pathological acts done in the name of a good cause?

When Quakers began to invade Puritan Massachusetts in 1656 to upset its theocratic governance, they believed themselves to be waging "the Lamb's War," a kind of Quaker jihad. The Massachusetts Puritan leadership feared the Quaker invasion, calling Friends "ravening wolves." When they arrived, Quakers were punished for a variety of transgressions: attempting to speak after the sermon in church, making speeches from jail windows during imprisonment, holding illegal public meetings, and refusing to pay fines (Sigmond 2012).

The government developed a series of gradually escalating punishments, first locking Quakers in prison without food, whipping them at the stocks, sending them into exile, then tying them to the back of a cart and whipping them as they were led from one town to another.

Most of the Quakers returned to practice their tactics of disruption. Sixty-year-old Elizabeth Hooton returned to Boston five times after being thrown out, and was whipped four times through neighboring towns. These Quakers saw themselves reviving the faith of the early Christians and were not surprised to be treated as the early Christians were in Rome.

The authorities escalated more, slicing off one or both ears of returning Quakers and burning holes in their tongues. The campaigners persisted, and a growing number of Puritans began to aid the Quakers, with some even converting.

Frustrated, the authorities turned to the gallows. While Quaker William Leddra was being tried and considered for the death penalty, Wenlock Christison, who had already been banished on pain of death, calmly walked into the courtroom. Leddra was hung. While Christison was being tried, Edward Wharton, who also had been ordered to leave the colony or lose his life, wrote to the authorities from his home that he was still there. Christison was hung, and then Wharton in turn.

When Puritan authorities put Mary Dyer on a ship bound for Barbados, they warned her that if she came back she would be hanged. They had been consistent in following through on their threats. She hesitated for a year before returning to Boston. In her journal she worried that she was out of step with the Quaker way, which encouraged a willingness to be killed but not an eagerness for it. She suspected she was experiencing a "lust for martyrdom." After much prayer she concluded that it was God, not ego, that wanted her to return to Boston to "look those bloody laws in the face."

The hanging of Mary Dyer on Boston Common was the beginning of the end of the Puritan theocracy. For us, it marks an example of a boundary set by the Quaker movement to guard against what might be a dangerously extreme behavior in the heat of combat. The movement needs people willing to volunteer to die if need be for "the cause," in this case the abolition of theocracy. When a movement accords esteem to those who volunteer to die, however, how does it draw a line between dying for the cause and dying for the esteem?

Framing Opponents and Allies: The Campaigners' Metastory

Framing the Opponent

Activists carry a metastory, a theory of how change happens. The activists' story about how they will win their struggle can influence the way they do or do not prepare for repression and how they make meaning of repression once it has happened.

One possibility is to believe that there will be no significant repression because the opponent is open to feedback, correction, and change. A characteristic metastory carried by US liberal activists is found in middle school civics textbooks: pluralism, balance of powers, elected officials eagerly listening to their constituents' point of view.

Other activists may anticipate that there will be at least some violent pushback from the authorities, whether government, business, or another kind of opponent. Activists may believe that how they respond to the opponent will influence the outcome of their campaign, and, in that case, their image of the opponent's capacity and willingness to change is significant in forming their strategy.

Opponents are widely diverse in the degree to which they turn to repression to resist the demands of campaigners. The value of gaining an accurate analysis ahead of time is shown in cases where overly optimistic campaigners are shocked into submission when authorities respond with a heavy hand. Middle-class professionals are particularly vulnerable to shock, since their life condition can give them a rosy view of the owning class and a belief that heavy repression will not be used. One corrective for them is to keep checking with marginalized and low-ranked people in their society, who may have a more accurate power analysis than the middle-class professionals do.

Framing Potential Allies

Strategically, successful movement coercion in the face of repression generally depends on widespread participation, which means that other elements of the population who previously were bystanders join the struggle. However, the activist leadership of a campaign in its early stages may ignore these potential allies and tell themselves a story they find more compelling: the field of action has only two players, us and our opponent.

That overriding (although irrational) story comes from years of contestation in which other potential players in the drama are passive, "invisible" to the movement leadership. The activist center is fascinated by the opponent, researches and gossips about the opponent, and watches its every move. To illustrate this in trainings, we sketch a "spectrum of allies" that looks something like half a pie with wedges (Oppenheimer and Lakey 1965), with the two opposite wedges representing us and them, and the wedges in between representing the potential players with varying inclinations to support either one side or the other. (The wedge in the middle is trying for one reason or another not to take sides.) Workshop participants grin with embarrassed recognition when trainers ask: how much attention do you give the wedges that are not on the extremes? They will often acknowledge that, while giving some attention to the wedge closest to them, they mostly remain absorbed in themselves and their opponent. I believe the emotive power of this dualistic story helps account for the difficulty many movements have in creating a fully nonviolent strategy for coercing their opponents. More to the point, when failing to pay attention to the dynamics among the other players, they are less likely to make maximum use of the paradox of repression. They are more likely to forget what repression can do to bring them allies, and more likely to feel they have run out of options and turn to counterproductive, violent tactics against the agents of repression. Then, we observe them moving quickly from violent "self-defense" to using violence as an offensive tactic as well, as in Ukraine in 2013–14.[5] It would help to have a strategic framework that emphasizes the importance of potential allies and the role of the paradox of repression in mobilizing them.

Projecting a Strategy that Makes Full Use of the Paradox of Repression

For reasons I do not understand, we lack multiple developmental models for nonviolent social movements. True, models are never as

5. This dynamic played out on the edge of the US civil rights movement of the 1960s, as I have discussed in the online periodical *Waging Nonviolence* (wagingnonviolence.org) in a series of articles analyzing the Deacons of Defense and the Black Panther Party (Lakey 2012a, 2012b, 2012d, 2012e). For an account of the Ukrainian example, see Girgenti (2014).

complicated as the reality they point to, and they may be misleading. Perhaps it is a worry about making mistakes that explains why we do not have more developmental models, but organizers in social movements are used to making mistakes and can perhaps encourage scholars to be more willing to risk as well.

I suspect that everyone in fact has a model in her or his head of how change takes place, although usually not explicit. We are more likely to learn from revealing and then discussing each other's implicit models than from appearing not to have them. Developmental models are different from analytic models, which are static and ex post facto. Change is the opposite of static, and organizers making decisions are anything but ex post facto. This is one reason for the frequent gulf between peace studies scholars and nonviolent activists: scholars wedded to static cognitive forms invite nonviolent activists to do as the generals of old—to fight the last war again. Of course, what the activists want is to be assisted in fighting this war.

Developmental models that are based on dynamics that exist in reality help nonviolent actors to ground their strategies rather than allow them to remain in mid air, buffeted by emotion and ideological notions. Part of a developmental model's usefulness is that it is a theorist's way of telling a story with a beginning, middle, and end. An example is the Movement Action Plan (MAP) invented by sociologist/strategist Bill Moyer (2001), who was on the national staff of Dr. Martin Luther King Jr. Moyer organized his model into eight stages: (1) a period when few pay attention to a social problem, (2) proving there is a problem, (3) organizing as discontent grows, (4) mass action, (5) demoralization, (6) broad public support, (7) negotiation to a successful institutional or policy change, and (8) pursuing new demands on related problems.

The eight stages of the MAP model have been used successfully by nonviolent movements in a number of countries where the system is amenable to reform. The Institute for World Order sponsored the first publication of a five-stage model I devised in *Strategy for a Living Revolution*, which proposes a story that goes beyond reform to transformation (Lakey 1973). The first four stages are:

1. Conscientization/education/consciousness-raising
2. Organization-building
3. Confrontation ("propaganda of the deed")
4. Mass political and economic noncooperation.

As Moyer did with his model, I built this model from historical materials, noting some dynamics that presented themselves in full display and some others that were less apparent.[6] The stages tell a story that fully anticipates, and gives meaning to, the paradox of repression.

Based on historical failures and successes of movements, I made the following assumptions in sequencing the order of the stages. Mass political and economic noncooperation is necessary in order to open a power vacuum that allows system change, one feature of which might be regime change. In the sequence of stages, I placed mass noncooperation late in the process. The word "mass" needs always to precede "noncooperation" in referring to this stage, because people can carry out Sharp's noncooperation methods on a small group basis as well, but that is not what this stage is describing. It is the *large scale* of mass noncooperation that enables it to force regime change or other major changes (e.g., a giant steel strike that forces steel companies to increase wages when their objective was the opposite, to reduce wages and bust the union). Small- to medium-size group nonviolent confrontation with an opponent will, under some circumstances, lead to mass political and economic noncooperation (through the paradox of repression). Confrontation therefore comes before the mass noncooperation in the sequence.

Confrontation will more likely be successful, producing movement growth rather than shutdown, if the movement is already organized,

6. An example of a dynamic that my reading of history saw fully revealed was the coercive power of noncooperation, as brilliantly shown by Gene Sharp (1973). An example of one only hinted at in the historical materials was the strategic usefulness of the dilemma demonstration as a kind of propellant for the paradox of repression (see Sørensen and Martin 2014 for further analysis; see Lakey 2012c for vivid examples of the dilemma action at work).

since organizational infrastructure is a major antidote to fear and loss of hope. Organization-building therefore needs to come before the confrontation stage in the sequence. Strong organization is more likely to be built by people whose consciousness is already changing with regard to clarity about the opponent and the nature of the injustice. The activist consciousness will be supported if it has generated a just set of alternatives and has come to clarity about the worthiness and power of the oppressed. This stage of consciousness-raising should therefore come before the flowering of organizational infrastructure.

Making the paradox of repression fully beneficial to a movement, therefore, is served by this sequencing. By first engaging in the kind of consciousness-raising I propose, and then building on that attitude and knowledge with a set of strong organizations, the movement maximizes its chance of not only enduring the strong repression reacting to confrontation but also using the repression itself as a movement-building tool. Gene Sharp called it "political jiu-jitsu" (1973, 3:657–703). Briefly stated, this is the developmental logic that justifies the sequence of stages.

For many victories, these four stages of movement activity are sufficient, but it is commonly observed that regime change, for example, may simply be the replacement of one gang of exploiters by another. That is a frequent lament made by observers of the Arab Awakening and the color revolutions. I therefore added a fifth stage to the model, for movements that seek a transformation or liberatory revolution:

5. Parallel institutions

These institutions' growth is rooted in stage two of the model, during which movement organizers are consciously building structures that support the transformational values of the movement—structures like producer and consumer co-ops or nonpatriarchal decision-making procedures. Drawn from the visionary work of stage one, these new "people's institutions-in-embryo" grow during the subsequent stages of the movement's development so that, by the time stage five is reached, they represent skills, practical vision, know-how, and confidence sufficient to replace the failed and corrupted institutions of the old order.

Models are inherently simplistic. While some intellectuals may find this troubling, simplicity is a virtue if one wants a broad-based, democratic, and participatory movement.[7] Comrades working with me have pointed out that the five-stage model can gain complexity without reducing its usefulness in non-elite activist circles by being displayed as a spiral, through which we could work with the very uneven condition of different groups and regions in a given society. Instead of 1-2-3-4-5, the sequence could, for example, be pictured as 1-2-3, 1-2-3, 1-2-3, 1-2-3-4, 1-2-3-4-5.

What If Repression Starts before Stage Three?

Regimes and other defenders of an oppressive order may punish early signs of a movement's development to prevent it from getting to a point of readiness in which stage three, confrontation, can be waged successfully. US-supported police states in Central America in the 1980s, for example, attacked organizers of co-ops (stage two activity) and even nuns and priests, who were helping Christian base communities to analyze the reasons for their poverty (stage one). Historically, for activists in such a situation, it has often seemed impossible to reach the point of movement development where repression will backfire on the regime. Hiding and waiting for a new historical situation seemed the only option.

A new application of nonviolent action has relevance for this situation: third-party nonviolent intervention, also called unarmed civilian peacekeeping. This application helps in two ways: it deters repression and, if used, it increases the cost of repression to the opponent. Either way, it helps movement activists control their fear so they can keep

7. My thinking about the relationship between intellectual rigor and democratic participation has been influenced by the writing of the Harvard sociologist George Caspar Homans, as I discuss in my book *Facilitating Group Learning* (Lakey 2010, 95–101).

operating. In addition, it gives them higher morale because they experience in a concrete way the international solidarity that otherwise is difficult to feel deeply.

In this application, people without an immediate stake in the issues being fought out in a conflict enter the conflict anyway to reduce the incidence of violence. A number of NGOs now include this work in their mission. The first was Peace Brigades International (PBI), which in 1983 brought volunteers from Canada and the United States to Guatemala to explore how to be helpful to local people experiencing a period of intense state terror (Peace Brigades International–Canada 2013). The PBI team was asked by the Mutual Support Group for Families of the Disappeared (GAM), some of whose leaders had been assassinated, if team members would become round-the-clock nonviolent escorts. PBI agreed. After PBI began accompaniment, not a single GAM leader was killed, and the group became the first human rights group to survive the Guatemalan terror (Gonzales 2013a).

As PBI gained confidence in accompaniment, it placed a team under similar circumstances in El Salvador (Gonzales 2013b) and then other countries. In 1989, I was on the first PBI team to provide accompaniment to threatened human rights lawyers in Sri Lanka. Other NGOs offering this service include Christian Peacemaker Teams and Nonviolent Peaceforce (the first to field a corps of paid third-party nonviolent interveners).[8]

A larger-scale use of international volunteers was that of the Canadian group Project Accompaniment, which assisted 25,000 refugees to return safely to Guatemala in the 1990s. The online *Global Nonviolent Action Database*[9] includes other examples of nonviolent interven-

8. The *Global Nonviolent Action Database* (nvdatabase.swarthmore.edu) includes a number of cases of this kind of intervention, some of which were spontaneous and predated PBI's making the method systematic (for examples, see Phalen 2009; Lehman 2011; and Palazzolo 2013). In South Korea the interveners included high officials in the US government (Choi and Welch 2012).

9. This database has so far assembled over 1,400 cases from nearly two hundred countries, researched and written by students at Swarthmore College and

tion that were based on somewhat different strategies but had similar results. Here, I am emphasizing the conscious use of outsiders to raise the stakes for would-be agents of repression such that the authorities' fear of the paradox of repression restrains them from kidnapping and killing activists.

Liam Mahoney and Luis Eguren (1997), who authored the classic academic study of this form of nonviolent action, emphasize its value as a deterrent to repression. It deters because the regime understands that repression will be too costly. The main requirement for the local activists, whose movement is not yet resilient enough to manage on its own, is to be able to perceive the existence of allies outside the immediate field of vision—not a small matter when a movement is threatened! This is all the more notable when, for example, in 1989 the president of the Sri Lankan Bar Association reached out to PBI to request unarmed bodyguards for his human rights lawyers who were being assassinated.

A Developmental Model and the Paradox of Repression

Activists often try to learn from the behavior of other movements, especially regarding their tactics. The danger is in trying to apply tactics to a very different situation; sometimes it works splendidly, and sometimes it is a disaster. I will confine myself to only one example. A debate arose within the US Occupy movement in 2011 about the potential role of violence, especially street-fighting with the police. Some Egyptian activists involved in the movement to overthrow dictator Hosni Mubarak had written an open letter to US activists about their experience, defending the use of street-fighting in Tahrir Square. The Egyptians had great credibility in that moment, and their letter was used within Occupy as evidence for the efficacy of violence, and

collaborating colleges and universities. The author of each can be found along with their case on the website. This public database is searchable and currently used by scholars, writers, and activists around the world.

therefore encouragement for US activists to initiate street fighting at Occupy Wall Street and other sites.

Activists acquainted with the Living Revolution model (Lakey 1973), however sympathetic they might personally be to street-fighting, could see that the Egyptian example had no relevance for them. The difference had to do with timing, which is what strategy is very often about. The street-fighting in Tahrir Square happened in what was for Egyptians late stage four in the model. In Egypt there had already been an intense period of nonviolent confrontation, stage three, which had done its job and moved the entire movement to stage four, massive political and economic noncooperation. Virtually all of Egypt was on strike! At such a moment, the choice of a fraction of people in Tahrir Square to engage in street-fighting could in no way stop the momentum of the movement and the overthrow of Mubarak (Nakhoda and Lawrence 2011).

The Occupy sites in the United States in 2011, in contrast, were engaged in a completely different stage: confrontation, quite early in stage three. The point of stage three is to heighten the contrast between the activists and the agents of repression. Heightening the contrast maximizes the chance of the paradox of repression, in turn triggering entry into stage four. The best way to heighten the contrast between activists and police and/or troops is to maintain a high standard of nonviolent performance, not to undermine the outcome of stage three by street-fighting.[10]

Story, Strategy, and a Celebration of Culture Work

Participants in nonviolent movements make meanings of the risks they take and the injuries, suffering, and losses they experience. They create stories that have consequences for the tactics and strategies they

10. For more on the activists' tactical challenges for managing repression, especially when the authorities are sophisticated enough to know about the paradox of repression and are taking measures to avoid it, see Lakey (2012g).

choose. Their stories influence their ability to take advantage of their opponents' repressive acts. Their stories draw materials from their historical situation and their movement's culture, and in turn change history and build the culture of their movement. Participants' tactical behavior, however, is also influenced by any preparation they may devise—training—and the structures they use in confrontation, such as logistical layouts and affinity groups.

Story, strategy, and tactical behavior intersect at significant points. One is in the view taken of the opponent: what are the chances that the decider might come around to agreement with the campaigners, or at least be willing to change rather than to continue to repress the campaigners? If the campaigners believe they will have to coerce an opponent who remains obdurate, then what story do they tell, if any, about the potential allies who must be mobilized in order to put the coercion into operation?

And how is a movement's strategy itself influenced by the campaigners' metastory of how movements make change, step by step, over a period of time that might be short or long? A historically grounded theoretical model for understanding the dynamics of struggle that is itself developmental in character—that is itself a kind of narrative—logically ought to support the powerful use of the paradox of repression for gaining the movement's goals.

I have made many observations in this exploratory chapter and proposed generalizations that might stimulate systematic research to test their validity. I hope so. Activists who put their bodies on the line deserve strategies that are backed up as much as possible by accurate understandings of the dynamics of nonviolent action. At the same time, I want to celebrate the culture workers who tap their empathy and intuition to create meaning that supports some of the most important decisions an activist can make. The best culture workers try to solve movement problems through their work.

An artist who has worked brilliantly with the problems discussed in this chapter is feminist singer-songwriter Holly Near, who became prominent in the 1960s and 1970s. Near was surrounded by a US culture heavily influenced by Judaism and Christianity, with their iconic stories of sacrifice, but she was wary of that theme because "sacrifice" is often used to hold women in violent relationships. At the same time, she wanted to embolden both women and men to risk, which meant making meaning of the possibility of injury or death. Her solution is well expressed in the following song:

IT COULD HAVE BEEN ME

It could have been me, but instead it was you
So I'll keep doing the work you were doing as if I were two
I'll be a student of life, a singer of song
A farmer of food and a righter of wrong.

(Chorus): It could have been me, but instead it was you
And it may be me dear sisters and brothers
Before we are through
But if you can work for freedom
Freedom, freedom, freedom
If you can work (die, sing, live, work, speak) for freedom I can too.

Students in Ohio 200 yards away
Shot down by a nameless fire one early day in May
Some people cried out angry you should have shot more of them down
But you can't bury youth my friend
Youth grows the whole world round.

The junta broke the fingers on Victor Jara's hands
They said to the gentle poet "play your guitar now if you can"
Victor started singing but they brought his body down
You can kill that man but not his song
When it's sung the whole world round.

A woman in the jungle so many wars away
Studies late into the night, defends the village in the day
Although her skin is golden like mine will never be
Her song is heard and I know the words
And I'll sing them until she's free.

(Chorus): It could have been me, but instead it was you
And it may be me dear sisters and brothers
Before we are through
But if you can work for freedom
Freedom, freedom, freedom
If you can work for freedom I can too.

By Holly Near (Copyright 1974 by Hereford Music.
All rights reserved—used by permission)

The tune and throbbing beat of the song, and her own full-throated singing of it, reflect Holly Near's message.[11] Everything about the song suggests that she is at peace with a painful reality and fully alive in her commitment. In Holly Near's story, the movement participant does not deny the chance that suffering or death may come, nor does she make it an emblem of spiritual or moral elevation. Instead, Near reminds the listeners of the vision—freedom. She calls them to activity—demonstrating, studying, singing. She acknowledges an existential reality: if I fully engage in the struggle, my turn to suffer may come, and that will be a rich opportunity to give my own life deeper meaning.

Holly Near's song exemplifies how successful movements make meaning of the risks they take and the losses they may experience. They share stories that help them take advantage of their opponents' violence, and therefore trigger the paradox of repression. They rely on symbols, group formations, and training experiences to underline their central message when facing repression: the only way out is through.

References

Bondurant, Joan V. 1958. *Conquest of Violence: The Gandhian Philosophy of Conflict*. Princeton, NJ: Princeton Univ. Press.

Choi, Natalia, and Mackenzie Welch. 2012. "U.S. Officials Nonviolently Intervene in South Korea to Protect Leading Dissident Kim Dae Jung,

11. Near's song is available on YouTube (www.youtube.com/watch?v=CadP4dRemYk#aid=P9OniF8daQo, accessed May 30, 2014).

1985." *Global Nonviolent Action Database*. Accessed May 30, 2014. http://nvdatabase.swarthmore.edu/content/us-officials-nonviolently-intervene-south-korea-protect-leading-dissident-kim-dae-jung-1985.

Collins, Randall. 2008. *Violence: A Micro-sociological Theory*. Princeton: Princeton Univ. Press.

Desai, Narayan. 1980. *Handbook for Satyagrahis: A Manual for Volunteers of Total Revolution*. New Delhi: Gandhi Peace Foundation.

Girgenti, Guido. 2014. "Ukrainians Bring Down Yanukovych Regime, 2013–2014." *Global Nonviolent Action Database*. http://nvdatabase.swarthmore.edu/content/ukrainians-bring-down-yanukovych-regime-2013-2014.

Goldberg, Jasper. 2009. "Norwegian Teachers Prevent Nazi Takeover of Education, 1942." *Global Nonviolent Action Database*. http://nvdatabase.swarthmore.edu/content/norwegian-teachers-resist-nazi-takeover-education-1942.

Gonzalez, Sarah. 2013a. "Peace Brigades International (PBI) Protects and Aids Guatemalan Mutual Support Group (GAM), 1984–1989." *Global Nonviolent Action Database*. http://nvdatabase.swarthmore.edu/content/peace-brigades-international-pbi-protects-and-aids-guatemalan-mutual-support-group-gam-1984-.

———. 2013b. "Peace Brigades International Protects Human Rights Activists in El Salvador, 1987–1992." *Global Nonviolent Action Database*. http://nvdatabase.swarthmore.edu/content/peace-brigades-international-protects-human-rights-activists-el-salvador-1987-1992.

Hunter, Daniel, and George Lakey. 2004. *Opening Space for Democracy: Third-Party Nonviolent Intervention, Curriculum and Trainer's Manual*. Philadelphia: Training for Change.

Lakey, George. 1968. "The Sociological Mechanisms of Nonviolent Action." *Peace Research Reviews* 2 (6). Oakville, ON: Canadian Peace Research Institute.

———. 1973. *Strategy for a Living Revolution*. New York: Grossman; San Francisco: W. H. Freeman.

———. 2010. *Facilitating Group Learning: Strategies for Success with Diverse Adult Learners*. San Francisco: Jossey-Bass.

———. 2012a. "The Black Panthers' 'Militarist Error.'" *Waging Nonviolence* Blogs, Apr. 24. http://wagingnonviolence.org/feature/the-black-panthers-militarist-error/.

———. 2012b. "Did Civil Rights Need Deacons for Defense?" *Waging Nonviolence* Blogs. Apr. 17. http://wagingnonviolence.org/feature/did-civil-rights-need-deacons-for-defense/.

———. 2012c. "How to Create a Dilemma" *Waging Nonviolence* Blogs, Mar. 13. http://wagingnonviolence.org/feature/how-to-create-a-dilemma/.

———. 2012d. "Paradoxes of Protection" *Waging Nonviolence* Blogs. May 8. http://wagingnonviolence.org/feature/paradoxes-of-protection/.

———. 2012e. "The Right to Self-Defense." *Waging Nonviolence* Blogs, Apr. 10. http://wagingnonviolence.org/feature/paradoxes-of-protection/.

———. 2012f. *Toward a Living Revolution*. London: Peace News Press.

———. 2012g. "Who's Really Violent? Tips for Controlling the Narrative" *Waging Nonviolence* Blogs. http://wagingnonviolence.org/feature/whos-really-violent-tips-for-controlling-the-narrative/.

Lehman, Hannah. 2011. "Third Party Intervenes to Prevent Violence at Wounded Knee, South Dakota, 1973." *Global Nonviolent Action Database*. http://nvdatabase.swarthmore.edu/content/third-party-intervenes-prevent-violence-wounded-knee-south-dakota-1973.

Mahoney, Liam, and Luis Eguren. 1997. *Unarmed Bodyguards: International Accompaniment for the Protection of Human Rights*. Kumerian Press.

Moyer, Bill. 2001. *Doing Democracy: The MAP Model for Organizing Social Movements*. Gabriola Island, BC: New Society.

Nakhoda, Zein, and William Lawrence. 2011. "Egyptians Bring Down Dictatorship of Hosni Mubarak, 2011." *Global Nonviolent Action Database*. http://nvdatabase.swarthmore.edu/content/egyptians-bring-down-dictatorship-hosni-mubarak-2011.

Near, Holly. 1974. "It Could Have Been Me." *Holly Near, A Live Album*. Ukiah, CA: Redwood Records.

Ohrenschall, Rachel S. 2012. "Freedom Summer Campaign for African American Voting Rights in Mississippi, 1964." *Global Nonviolent Action Database*. http://nvdatabase.swarthmore.edu/content/freedom-summer-campaign-african-american-voting-rights-mississippi-1964.

Oppenheimer, Martin, and George Lakey. 1965. *A Manual for Direct Action*." Chicago: Quadrangle Books.

Palazzolo, Nick. 2013. "Third Party Intervenes to Support Domingo Laino's Return to Paraguay, 1986." *Global Nonviolent Action Database*. https://nvdatabase.swarthmore.edu/content/third-party-intervenes-support-domingo-laino-s-return-paraguay-1986.

Peace Brigades International–Canada. 2013. "Our History." Accessed Jan. 19, 2018. https://web.archive.org/web/20180119051754/http://www.pbicanada.org/index.php/en/about-us-2/our-history-2.

Phalen, Anthony. 2009. "Brazilian Priests Intervene Nonviolently to Prevent Violence, 1968." *Global Nonviolent Action Database*. http://nvdatabase.swarthmore.edu/content/brazilian-priests-intervene-nonviolently-prevent-violence-1968.

Polletta, Francesca. 2007. *It Was Like a Fever: Storytelling in Protest and Politics*. Chicago: Univ. of Chicago Press.

Sharp, Gene. 1973. *The Politics of Nonviolent Action*. 3 vols. Boston: Porter Sargent.

Sigmond, Carl E. 2012. "Quakers Fight for Religious Freedom in Puritan Massachusetts, 1656–1661." *Global Nonviolent Action Database*. http://nvdatabase.swarthmore.edu/content/quakers-fight-religious-freedom-puritan-massachusetts-1656-1661.

Sørensen, Majken Jul, and Brian Martin. 2014. "The Dilemma Action: Analysis of an Activist Technique." *Peace and Change* 39 (1): 73–100.

Tedla, Aden, and George Lakey. 2011. "Indians Campaign for Independence (Salt Satyagraha), 1930–1931." *Global Nonviolent Action Database*. http://nvdatabase.swarthmore.edu/content/indians-campaign-independence-salt-satyagraha-1930-1931.

York, Steve. 2001. *Bringing Down a Dictator*. Narrated by Martin Sheen. Washington, DC: York Zimmerman Inc., WETA-TV.

12

Rethinking Repression

Where Do We Go from Here?

Lee A. Smithey and Lester R. Kurtz

Drawing together the expertise of a global collection of social scientists and activists, we have interrogated a central dynamic of nonviolent civil resistance, the paradox of repression. Why and under what circumstances does repression against activists using nonviolent methods and tactics backfire, undermining the legitimacy of authorities and mobilizing greater participation in civil resistance? We also focus on the practical application of knowledge about repression and backfire by nonviolent activists. How can the paradox of repression be cultivated? How can activists prepare for, manage, and blunt the negative impact of repression?

Some readers may chafe at the lack of a unifying definition or theory of repression. We chose not to spend a great deal of energy on coming to a consensus among all of the volume's contributors about the parameters of "repression" (as opposed to oppression, suppression, etc.) so as to avoid cutting ourselves off from exploring fertile ground and important discoveries.

Some of our contributors define the paradox of repression as any unanticipated consequences of repression that authorities do not desire. Others complicate the concept of repression by delineating a range of repression types. We suggest in the introduction, further developed in chapter 8, that we consider repression along a continuum from overt violence, on one end, to hegemony (in which individuals self-censor)

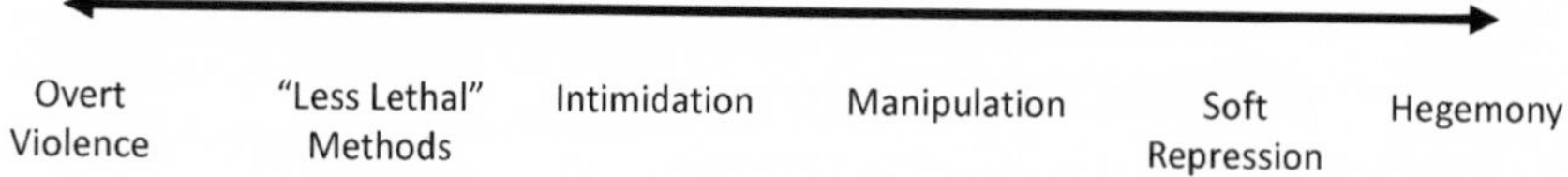

12.1. A Continuum of Demobilization (Source: Lee A. Smithey and Lester R. Kurtz)

on the other (see Figure 12.1). In a series of quantitative and theoretical overviews, as well as case studies from around the world, we have brought together insights from scholars and experienced activists to explore this crucial topic.

Issues and Themes

We believe that our approach has helped to generate exciting new insights and identified several important subdomains and avenues for further research. In this volume, we have explored a wide range of themes and issues around the paradox of repression, notably:

- the relational conception of power,
- agents of repression and the possibility of defections,
- strategic preparation for repression and overcoming fear,
- whether activists should deliberately provoke repression,
- the importance of mobilization,
- the role of external actors,
- cultural aspects of repression and its management,
- expanding frameworks for understanding repression,
- social psychological dimensions, and
- the role of the media and the issue of framing.

The Relational Conception of Power

In this volume, we focus on conflicts that are perceived as asymmetrical while at the same time suggesting that they are more symmetrical than they seem. The paradox of repression makes more sense when we understand that power is a relational social construct that emerges from negotiated interactions between people with different statuses, knowledge, and resources in a society. We discuss this at some length in the introductory chapter, starting with Simmel and Gandhi, and the feminist distinction between empowerment (power to) and domination (power over). In his seminal work on conflict, German sociologist Georg Simmel (1971) stresses the importance of understanding conflict as relational and interactional, an aspect of a struggle that is crucial to understanding the dynamics of repression and its backfire. Each party to a conflict is engaged in a meaningful exchange, according to Simmel, in which each responds to the actions and statements of the other, suggesting that power disparities are often not as severe as we might think.

Gandhi insisted, for example, that the British did not take India, but that the Indians gave it to them—after all, one hundred thousand soldiers could not control 350 million Indians unless the Indians cooperated with them. The apparent asymmetries of power can be profoundly affected when authority is abused or resisted. Moreover, as Arendt (1969, 1970) notes, violence does not create power; instead, it is used by people who lack power or feel it slipping away.

Furthermore, opponents in conflict are working to influence one another through planned or strategic moves, either persuading, coercing, or bargaining (Kriesberg 1982). Situations involving strategic nonviolent action are no exception. Understanding the most effective means of waging nonviolent resistance has been the subject of decades of research and is reflected in many of the chapters in this volume. However, if we are to truly understand nonviolent resistance as part of conflict, we must also understand it as an interaction of activists with authorities and even agents of repression.

Agents of Repression and Defectors

The decision-making processes among regime functionaries is crucial. Erica Chenoweth (chapter 2) shows that defections among security forces and elites are a crucial factor determining the outcome of nonviolent resistance campaigns, along with the level of movement participation (the most crucial factor) and withdrawal of support by foreign allies. In a backfire situation, when state repression increases, so does domestic condemnation of the regime; defections are more likely, however, with more media coverage. Moreover, it is possible that extremely intense repression can have a negative indirect effect on campaign success by reducing the size of subsequent campaigns.

The growing emphasis on defections means that we need further research on nonviolent struggle from the perspective of regimes and their agents, so we have incorporated that key aspect of repression in this book, even as it admittedly poses methodological challenges because of problems with access. We seem to know much more about the strategic efforts of social movement organizations than those of corporations, states, and other large institutions and their functionaries, although there are clues to the authorities' point of view and sometimes, as with Eric Nelson's (2013) "Subversion of Social Movements by Adversarial Agents," some responses to movement challengers are discussed openly in the strategic literature.

In chapter 4, Rachel MacNair explores the psychological costs to agents of repression in terms of what she calls perpetration-induced traumatic stress (see also MacNair 2002). Indeed, she argues, "the trauma of violence is actually more severe for perpetrators than victims." This psychological consequence of engaging in repression could potentially lead to defections by security forces, one of the factors that Chenoweth (chapter 2) found contributed to successful outcomes for an insurgency.

Agents of repression strategize about repression in order to maximize its demobilization effects and minimize its negative consequences, although most of the sociological research has interrogated the movement side of conflicts rather than exploring the role of repressive elites. That is the subject of our chapter on "smart" repression (chapter 8), in which we present the impulse of authorities to counterstrategize and develop tactics and methods intended to anticipate and create dilemmas for activists, much as activists attempt to do through their strategizing. Beyer and Earl (chapter 5) discuss how authorities not only try to block access to Internet sites but sometimes repress online activities offline. Two people were arrested during the G20 public protests in Pittsburgh, for example, because of their Twitter use regarding the actions, and authorities sentenced two young men for their Facebook posts following August 2011 riots in the United Kingdom, neither of whom had participated in the riots themselves (Bowcott, Siddique, and Sparrow 2011; Citizen Media Law Project 2010; Moynihan 2009).

In an effort to minimize backfire, authorities sometimes move away from overt violence to "less-lethal methods," intimidation, manipulation, and soft repression. The hegemonic strategies employed by political regimes are perhaps not entirely unlike the persuasive strategies developed by activists to encourage defections among police and the military, often by appeals to a common national or universal identity. Both sides try to choreograph the dance that adversaries share in movement-countermovement interactions.

One extreme case of this move away from violence was the Egyptian military's role in the Egyptian revolution of 2011, explored in chapter 9 by Dalia Ziada. Ziada notes that early on in the uprising, a triangle of actors emerged—the police, military, and protesters—and the nonviolent response of insurgents to police repression facilitated an emerging alliance with the military. Egyptian activists and military personnel engaged in mutual interaction, each trying to persuade the other. Eschewing their routine tactics of brute repression, the military first deployed "negative cooperation" by not shooting at demonstrators, eventually withdrawing their support from the Mubarak regime altogether and enabling his downfall, but eventually wresting control of the revolution away from organizers of the insurgency.

Ironically, the Egyptian military's success without violence underscores a fundamental principle of nonviolent civil resistance: power can be generated in multiple ways. As MacNair underscores, "power is not a physical property but a psychological experience" (chapter 4). Another powerful social psychological dimension of the repression dynamic is fear, the overcoming of which becomes a central aspect of strategic preparation, another prominent theme that emerged in these studies.

Preparing for Repression and Overcoming Fear

Preparation is one of the keys for a campaign to manage repression successfully and provoke its backfire against elites who try to demobilize a movement. Two of our authors who are also activists, George

Lakey (chapter 11) and Jenni Williams (chapter 6), emphasize the fear factor and the importance of strategic planning that addresses what happens before repressive events, how activists expect to respond when repression occurs, and how it is to be framed after the fact to highlight its injustice for a broader relevant audience. This work is especially important in managing fear.

Advance training of activists allows them to reframe repression meaningfully before and after it happens, such as tapping into the resonance of cultural themes of sacrifice. They can set in place structures like affinity groups that highlight the solidarity of common action. Organizers can choreograph actions so that they enhance the positive aspects of the repressive experience and make violent repression more difficult—like people kneeling to pray as the police attack rather than running away.

George Lakey (chapter 11) emphasizes the significance of "ways that activists have found to handle fear, make meaning of pain and suffering, and support risk-taking so violent repression will not shut down their movements." One such strategy is turning fear into excitement, taking the energy that fear generates and reframing it as an opportunity to act side by side with communities of like-minded, change-oriented people.

Jenni Williams (chapter 6) describes how Women of Zimbabwe Arise (WOZA) proactively replaced a culture of fear with one of resistance in order to move people from isolation to solidarity. She relates a story of being arrested at a march for leading a protest and those with her insisting that they be arrested with her. The culture of fear melted away as the police vehicle became so full of protesters she had to squeeze in and take her place among the others police arrested. The casting off of fear by WOZA members allowed them to undertake increasingly bold actions without inciting repression.

Provocation

When the civil rights campaign to desegregate public facilities waned in Birmingham, Alabama, some leaders wanted to organize a demonstration with willing young people because the leaders anticipated that repression of such a march would likely backfire. Others, including Dr. Martin Luther King Jr., at first objected to putting young people in harm's way. When they did eventually proceed with the Children's March, police attacked the teenage demonstrators with firehoses and dogs, producing widespread moral outrage (Oppenheimer 1995; Wicker 1963; Houston 2004). President Kennedy appeared on national television the following day telling the nation that it faced a "moral crisis," calling upon Congress to pass "sweeping legislation to speed school desegregation and open public facilities to every American, regardless of color" (Wicker 1963). This event was a classic case of the paradox of repression, but the question remains: is preparing strategically for repression tantamount to provoking it? The question has been a tender subject in the study of nonviolent civil resistance.

While Gandhi may not call for the provocation of opponents, he declares that nonviolence often involves taking on suffering rather than inflicting it. Whether that necessarily involves strategically provoking repression remains a matter for debate. Some feel that much of the power of nonviolent action lies in the purity of a nonviolent discipline that is easily contrasted with the brutality of open repression. In chapter 7, we argue that a fundamental goal of nonviolent resistance is to proactively heighten the contrast between the nonviolent discipline of activists and elite repression.

There may be a fuzzy line between preparing for repression to heighten backfire (knowing that it may work to a campaign's advantage) and actually provoking repression. In the 1970s, George Lakey ([1973] 2012), introduced the concept of dilemma demonstrations, in which activists develop actions that put authorities in positions where most or all their options might generate advantages for challengers (see also Sørensen and Martin 2014). This approach may include ensuring that any repression is certain to undermine authorities' legitimacy. However, Lakey warns against provoking repression because "provocation may alienate the revolutionaries from the people, brutalize the police, and even brutalize the demonstrators" ([1973] 2012, 144). Moreover, he argues that provocation is tantamount to a manipulation that risks disaffecting both the public and the rank and file of the movement.

"The organizers should never be in a position of depending on the authorities to react violently in order to make their point" (145).

Activists can be pleased when repression does not come, even if it could benefit the movement, but that does not bar them from optimizing backfire as a matter of prudence. Jenni Williams says that members of WOZA knowingly put themselves in situations that risked repression and that they took responsibility for being part of such a confrontational dynamic. Both Lakey and Williams stop short of calling for outright provocation of repression. In fact, in chapter 6, Williams describes how WOZA choreographs their marches proactively to avoid provoking repression. They stop after every city block to sit and recite their commitment to nonviolence before moving on.

Mobilization's Significance

The mobilization of many participants enhances both the paradox of repression and chances of a movement's success (see Chenoweth and Stefan 2011). Successful repression management requires mobilizing participants, bystanders, and even potential defectors from the forces of repression. Erica Chenoweth (chapter 2) found that the level of participation was a prime factor in determining the success of a movement and also in shaping backfire against repression. We speculate that wider participation means greater exposure to repression and thus a greater likelihood that those in victims' networks, and perhaps the broader public, would become outraged. Larger actions are also more likely to attract the domestic media attention that Chenoweth says is important, and are more likely to be diverse and thus include populations, such as women and children, that raise the potential cost of repression.

Moreover, when backfire occurs, it mobilizes more people to participate and to defect, as Doron Shultziner (chapter 3) notes was the case in the killing of a schoolboy in Soweto and the arrest of Rosa Parks in Montgomery. Such events radically change the political climate, transforming people within the movement and the broader society, inspiring people to act.

Jenni Williams approaches mobilization from the ground level of a movement organizer. In chapter 6, she relates how WOZA mobilized women to speak out, forging "a movement that opened up a new center lane in a highly polarized society." Their main strategy broke stereotypes about women as well as the hold of patriarchy on society, empowering women to build a culture of resistance that replaced the existing culture of fear and creating a climate in which mobilization could occur. Then, in a kind of reversal in the emerging cycle of repression and backfire, the women took advantage of their successful mobilization, forcing police to beg a large crowd of twenty arrested protesters and 180 of their supporters to leave the police station they had occupied—in a sense, "unarresting" them and capitulating to the growing power of WOZA.

External Factors

Although the civil resistance literature understandably focuses on the agency of nonviolent actionists, the role of external actors remains significant. The audience for insurgent actions is often not geographically present; indeed, the key actors in the paradox of repression are often in another part of the country or even the globe. Chenoweth's data reveals starkly the importance of regime allies and international media coverage of repressive events, which often erodes international support for a repressive regime. She finds that, once a regime ally withdraws support, the chances for success among the largest campaigns doubles; and when this is combined with "security force loyalty shifts and elite defections, . . . the chance of success rockets up to about 45 percent for the smallest campaigns and 85 percent for the largest" (chapter 2).

Doron Shultziner also identifies significant external factors in the creation of transformative events. Instances of repression and backfire can cascade into large-scale, system-shaking occurrences on the international stage that are not of the movement's making, causing transnational ripple effects. Backfire often occurs at other times and in other spaces than the repressive events themselves. Tunisia's rapid revolution, which was launched with a provocative act of self-immolation dramatizing injustice, inspired Egypt's, as Dalia Ziada notes (chapter 9), just as the massacre at Tiananmen Square in June 1989 shaped the trajectory of uprisings in Poland and Germany, as we point out in our introductory chapter.

In short, agency is enhanced by an understanding of "political opportunity structures," the configuration of factors constraining and favoring movement development. The campaigns most likely to take advantage of backfire may be those who recognize transformative moments of repression and how to strike the anvil when the fire is hot.

Managing Repression in the Cultural Domain

The paradox of repression is as much about culture as it is about politics, and it is often the more culturally creative strategies and tactics that shape political action rather than the other way around. Doron Shultziner's contribution to our understanding of backfire is, in large part, his understanding of repressive events as transformative because they resonate with a cultural context, disrupting and shaping it, and changing people and institutions in the process. As in anthropologist Victor Turner's (1967) concept of liminality, these iconic cultural moments turn the social world upside down. Such moments are often generated during rituals like the Mardi Gras parade during which the princess of spring dethrones old man winter. In the paradox of repression, the regime, whose legitimacy is usually taken for granted, suddenly becomes a monster slaying innocents and against which right-thinking bystanding publics should rebel.

Brian Martin, in his foreword to this volume, suggests that activists counter each one of the methods authorities use to reduce outrage in order to reshape the frame that the public uses to interpret repressive events: "exposing the action, validating the target, interpreting the events as an injustice, mobilizing support (and avoiding official channels), and resisting intimidation and rewards."

In chapter 10, Chaiwat Satha-Anand describes a "nonviolent explosion" of creative nonviolent actions across Thailand as a response to repressive violence. Nonviolent resistance became possible because of "how the political space left from repression interacted with alternative leadership from within the movement and a history of nonviolent resistance in Thai society." Culturally savvy leaders took advantage of a violent turn in the otherwise nonviolent Red Shirts movement, and the ensuing brutal repression caused the Red Shirts movement to collapse in May 2010. Protest leader Sombat Boonngamanong cried for days after the violent repression and channeled that energy into Facebook posts. Then, a new nonviolent resistance called Red Sunday challenged the emergency law prohibiting political gatherings; protesters tied red ribbons at the site of the demonstration that had been brutally repressed by the military. Rather than high-risk public demonstrations, the Red Sunday group held aerobic dances and used humor and cultural symbols to help people overcome the fear that the regime had promoted. Much of the struggle in Thailand was thus waged in the cultural and psychological arena.

Similarly, George Lakey (chapter 11) emphasizes the importance of the stories a movement's activists tell to themselves to make meaning out of the suffering they receive at the hands of those in power, often by refashioning ancient themes of suffering, martyrdom, and spiritual transformation in their cultural traditions.

Establishing meaning also figures prominently in our analysis of how a movement choreographs its acts of resistance, and the cultural contexts in which activists operate are always important, as we discuss in chapter 7. Insurgents thus generate frame resonance between movement goals and widely held cultural values to mobilize both potential participants in a movement and possible defectors from the power structure. Thus, Williams (in chapter 6) reflects on how WOZA participants transformed the authority of a traditional cultural role—that of the mother—into a vehicle for protest as they courageously scolded Robert Mugabe and the political elites for their unacceptable behavior as exploitative leaders of the country. In chapter 7, we apply the fundamental importance of framing and meaning-making to repression management and argue that the way activists "set the table" (culturally, through their tactical decisions) establishes crucial precedents for the interpretation of repression in their favor. The symbols resistors use and the narratives on which they draw prestructure the range of possible interpretations of moments of repression and enhance the perceptual contrast between the bullying tactics of opponents and the nonviolent discipline of activists.

Expanding Frameworks for Understanding Repression

Despite decades of theorizing and research into nonviolent civil resistance, the study of what has been called political jiu-jitsu (Sharp 1973), moral jiu-jitsu (Gregg 1938), backlash (Francisco 1995, 1996), or backfire (Martin 2007, 2012) remains relatively underdeveloped. As Beyer and Earl point out in chapter 5, there is a tendency to lump all forms of repression into one category, perhaps because methodologically it is easier to study spectacular and overt forms of physical repression that attract media coverage and generate moral outrage. However, as research progresses, we are bound to refine our study of nonviolent resistance, nonviolent organizations and movements, and the regimes and corporations that they challenge. This volume begins to outline the diverse types of movement and regime goals and actions that inevitably interact to generate various movement outcomes, including the paradox of repression.

Beyer and Earl take us into the burgeoning world of online activism that has a different set of ground rules (physics even) that govern the strategic interaction of opponents. They systematically enumerate different types of online resistance, such as denial of service attacks (often leading to arrests), networking, and information sharing. Likewise, they present alternative forms of repression most likely to be deployed against online activist strategies.

Observing a continuum of repression strategies that authorities employ to demobilize nonviolent movements, as we do in the introduction, enhances our conceptualization of repression by offering a higher resolution view of the concept (Figure 12.1), and Erica Chenoweth calls us to think more carefully about how the intentions of repressive actors may be difficult to discern as scholars try to reconstruct retrospective accounts of repression. Moreover, Dalia Ziada alerts us to the potential for multiple targets of repression. Simple dyadic models of regimes and dissenters may exclude repression against defectors and various resistance flanks.

Social Psychological Dimensions

Rachel MacNair's observation that power "is a psychological experience" (chapter 4) strikes us as a patently true but underestimated aspect of nonviolent strategic action. Like MacNair, Doron Shultziner focuses on transformative repressive events as psychological phenomena; chapter 3 hinges heavily on the mass perception that "'politics as usual' is suspended" and "the creation of new spaces and mass meetings inject new meaning, perspective, and points of reference to citizens' lives."

Fear emerges as one of the most fundamental psychological dynamics at play in nonviolent civil resistance. Gandhi wrote extensively about the importance of overcoming fear, arguing, "we cannot have too much bravery, too much self-sacrifice . . . I want . . . the greater bravery of the meek, the gentle and the nonviolent, the bravery that will mount the gallows without injuring, or harbouring any thought of injury to a single soul" (1967, see chapter 12 in "The Gospel of Fearlessness"). Gene Sharp (1973) has established overcoming fear as a fundamental principle of effective nonviolent resistance, noting that people obey authorities for a variety of reasons ranging from habit to fear, all of which can be helpfully studied through psychological lenses. Sharp points out that repression is not actually the generator of obedience, but the fear that repression creates. No regime can repress all of its people. It is the *threat* of repression that people fear, dissuading them from challenging injustices. Thus, overcoming fear is largely about altering perceptions. George Lakey explains how storytelling becomes a collective and therapeutic way of shifting perceptions of fear and managing repression. Similarly, Jenni Williams also relays the slow but intentional empowerment of women in Zimbabwe as a form of fear management.

In trying to expand frameworks for understanding repression, we must also strive to understand conflict from the perspective of agents of repression, as MacNair does in her chapter on how perpetration induced traumatic stress syndrome likely impacts many agents of repression and the likelihood that they may modify their repression, disobey orders, or even defect.

Framing and the Media

Because of the reciprocal nature of conflict, insurgent challenges and elite responses evolve into framing contests, with each party trying to mobilize support and resonate with significant themes within shared culture. These framing contests are profoundly shaped by the media, especially beyond a local level, where people do not experience them firsthand. How the media portrays their respective frames shapes the public's discourse about the issues at stake, a fact of which the various parties involved are usually quite aware. The media effect is embellished by the fact that repressive events are often the most newsworthy.

Chenoweth's (chapter 2) study of 323 campaigns for dramatic change, such as bringing down dictators or driving out occupations, concludes that the most significant processes leading to campaign success historically are "campaign size, loyalty shifts among regime functionaries, and the removal of support for the regime by an erstwhile ally." "For repression to backfire in any meaningful sense," she argues, "participation is crucial." One vital factor in mobilizing participation, especially on a broader geographical scale, is international media coverage, which raises awareness and pressures regime allies to withdraw support of the target regime.

Media coverage is not enough, however (surprisingly, domestic media coverage had no significant effect in Chenoweth's study); and we know from the extensive social movement literature that framing issues is one of the core tasks of social movements. We argue in chapter 7 that the framing contest between elites and movements must result in a shift in control of political discourse from elites to movement coalitions and that repressive events are critical sites of framing contention. Repression management to enhance backfire requires that insurgents' frames resonate with existing cultural norms and dispositions and that the careful choreography of strategic nonviolent action in the face of repression can go a long way toward ensuring that repression is more likely to backfire by boldly dramatizing the dissonance between authorities' repression and the nonviolence of disciplined activists.

Future Research

A number of the issues emerging in this volume have been inadequately studied or conceptualized and could be fruitfully explored. First, it would be helpful to have more focused case studies of nonviolent resistance under repression, on the one hand, and more big-picture explorations, either with quantitative data sets or conceptualizations, on the other. Case studies like those in this volume on Zimbabwe, the US civil rights movement, and the South African antiapartheid struggle, as well as movements for change in Thailand, Egypt, and online, provide in-depth insights into the actual processes set into motion by repressive events and movement responses to them. We need more on-the-ground case studies that focus specifically on repression to develop a better comparative historical basis for understanding which aspects of backfire are more general and which are more situation-specific.

Chenoweth's NAVCO data set[1] reveals a rich set of broad patterns regarding repression of particular types of campaigns (overthrowing dictators, removing occupying troops, and secessionist movements). Her new data set, NAVCO 2.0 (see Chenoweth and Lewis 2013) includes more cases and data that should give us further insights. It would be helpful to explore other large data sets in terms of repression issues and one such possibility is the *Global Nonviolent Action Database*,[2] which offers a growing selection of cases featuring the paradox of repression.

Conceptual issues in need of development and empirical investigation include the question of how the use of violence (regardless of by whom) actually undermines the legitimacy of the perpetrator among insider elites and within the broader population. Do non-state terror organizations suffer a loss of legitimacy when they use violent methods? If so, are they as great as those incurred by states and other authority structures?

1. This data set can be found at the NAVCO Data Project website (https://www.du.edu/korbel/sie/research/chenow_navco_data.html).

2. This database (nvdatabase.swarthmore.edu), housed at Swarthmore College, includes a selection of cases featuring the paradox of repression (bit.ly/pdoxrepgnad).

At the same time, we need research into the power elite side of framing contests. Most sociological studies of repression explore the social movement side of conflicts, paying less attention to the elite side, in part because of a lack of access to the latter. In our exploration of smart repression, we found some interesting research along those lines, and there is no doubt much more to be discovered.

MacNair's chapter on perpetration-induced traumatic stress suggests another crucial area, the psychological aspects of repression from the point of view of those actors attempting to demobilize a movement. Psychological costs may be associated with the use of violence that could be counted as part of the paradoxical nature of repression. Research into perpetration-induced posttraumatic stress disorder (Grossman and Siddle 2008; MacNair 2002) suggests that the relational nature of conflict can cause psychological distress among those who use violence. Future research should explore to what extent the use of violence carries psychological costs and whether and how those costs can be leveraged by others.

Both additional case studies and quantitative overviews might provide insights into the most successful tactics of repression management used by various movements for different kinds of change in particular sociocultural contexts. Indeed, one important issue often debated but inadequately researched is the relative impact of tactics on the one hand, and context, on the other, or what is sometimes called agency and structure. The nonviolence literature often emphasizes agency, while sociologists and many political scientists often see the structural constraints on action as more significant.

What are the key historical factors that have resulted in successful or failed attempts by movements to enhance the backfire effect of repressive events? It would also be helpful, as Beyer and Earl suggest in chapter 5, to learn more about the varying effects of repression on different levels, such as individuals, networks, SMOs, movements, and the public as bystanders.

Finally, a more in-depth understanding of the media's role in repression and its backfire would be an essential component of our effort to understand how the paradox of repression unfolds. Both the mainstream and alternative media, along with social media generally, are key sites for framing contests between elites and insurgents, and we get some insight into that from the chapter by Beyer and Earl. We look forward to other scholars and activists understanding and sharing how repression backfires and movements for change become empowered.

The paradox of repression is a major aspect of the power relationships between authorities and insurgents that has not been fully researched. In this volume, we have endeavored to present the theoretical foundations of the phenomenon and to investigate the way in which activists exercise agency by preparing for and managing repression. Careful nonviolent strategy can influence the course of a conflict by raising the costs of repression, although nonviolent activists and elites both think about and prepare for repression, choreographing their actions in relation to their opponents' actions.

We have joined our contributing authors to expand the frameworks for further scholarship on this topic by conceptualizing repression and the ever-changing terrain on which movements and authorities contend, technologically, politically, and culturally. Our contributors have confirmed that repression often backfires and has profound cultural and psychological underpinnings, including the fundamental generation of fear (which nonviolent activists work to overcome), the psychological costs of repression for perpetrators, moments of transformative awakening, and the many resources that movements and elites may draw on for hegemonic or liberatory purposes. We hope that this deeply collaborative process will help to generate ever more rigorous scholarship on the topics of repression and backfire, thus broadening and deepening the use of strategic nonviolent action as an alternative to more violent forms of conflict.

References

Arendt, Hannah. 1969. "A Special Supplement: Reflections on Violence." *New York Review of Books* 12 (4). http://www2.kobe-u.ac.jp/~alexroni/IPD%202015%20readings/IPD%202015_8/A%20Special%20Supplement_%20Reflections%20on%20Violence%20by%20Hannah%20Arendt%20_%20The%20New%20Yor.pdf.

———. 1970. *On Violence*. Orlando: Harvest Book, Harcourt.

Bowcott, Owen, Haroon Siddique, and Andrew Sparrow. 2011. "Facebook Cases Trigger Criticism of 'Disproportionate' Riot Sentences." *Guardian*, Aug. 17. Accessed Nov. 15, 2012. http://www.guardian.co.uk/uk/2011/aug/17/facebook-cases-criticism-riot-sentences.

Chenoweth, Erica, and Orion A. Lewis. 2013. "Unpacking Nonviolent Campaigns Introducing the NAVCO 2.0 Dataset." *Journal of Peace Research* 50 (3): 415–23. doi:10.1177/0022343312471551.

Chenoweth, Erica, and Maria J. Stephan. 2011. *Why Civil Resistance Works: The Strategic Logic of Nonviolent Conflict*. New York: Columbia Univ. Press.

Citizen Media Law Project. 2010. "United States v. Madison." Jan. 10. Accessed Mar. 13, 2018. https://web.archive.org/web/20120317071256/http://www.citmedialaw.org/threats/united-states-v-madison.

Francisco, R. 1995. "The Relationship between Coercion and Protest: An Empirical Test in Three Coercive States." *Journal of Conflict Resolution* 39: 263–82.

———. 1996. "Coercion and Protest: An Empirical Test in Two Democratic States." *American Journal of Political Science* 40: 1179–204.

Gandhi, Mahatma. 1967. "The Gospel of Fearlessness." In *The Mind of Mahatma Gandhi*, edited by Ramachandra Krishna Prabhu and U. R. Rao, chap. 12. Ahmedabad: Navajivan Publishing House. http://www.mkgandhi.org/momgandhi/chap12.htm.

Gregg, Richard Bartlett. 1938. *The Power of Non-Violence*. Ahmededabad: Navajivan Press. https://archive.org/details/mkbook080omkga.

Grossman, Dave, and Bruce Siddle. 2008. "Psychological Effects of Combat." In *Encyclopedia of Violence, Peace and Conflict*, 2d ed., edited by Lester R. Kurtz, 1796–805. Amsterdam: Elsevier.

Houston, Robert. 2004. *Mighty Times: The Children's March* (short documentary). https://www.youtube.com/watch?v=5c113fq3vhQ.

Kriesberg, Louis. 1982. *Social Conflicts*. Englewood Cliffs, NJ: Prentice Hall.

Lakey, George. [1973] 2012. *Toward a Living Revolution*. London: Peace News Press.

MacNair, Rachel. 2002. *Perpetration-Induced Traumatic Stress: The Psychological Consequences of Killing*. New York: Praeger.

Martin, Brian. 2007. *Justice Ignited: The Dynamics of Backfire*. Lanham, MD: Rowman & Littlefield.

———. 2012. *Backfire Manual: Tactics against Injustice*. Sparsnäs, Sweden: Irene Publishing.

Moynihan, Colin. 2009. "Arrest Puts Focus on Protesters' Texting" *New York Times*, Oct. 4, A19. http://www.nytimes.com/2009/10/05/nyregion/05txt.html.

Nelson, Eric L. 2013. "Subversion of Social Movements by Adversarial Agents." *International Journal of Intelligence and CounterIntelligence* 26 (1): 161–75.

Oppenheimer, D. 1995. "Kennedy, King, Shuttlesworth and Walker: The Events Leading to the Introduction of the Civil Rights Act of 1964." *University of San Francisco Law Review* 29 (645): 645–999.

Sharp, Gene. 1973. *The Politics of Nonviolent Action*. 3 vols. Boston, MA: Porter Sargeant.

Simmel, Georg. 1971. *On Individuality and Social Forms: Selected Writings*. Edited by Donald Nathan Levine. Chicago: Univ. of Chicago Press.

Sørensen, Majken Jul, and Brian Martin. 2014. "The Dilemma Action: Analysis of an Activist Technique." *Peace and Change* 39 (1): 73–100.

Turner, Victor. 1967. *The Forest of Symbols: Aspects of Ndembu Ritual*. Ithaca: Cornell Univ. Press.

Wicker, Tom. 1963. "President in Plea: Asks Help of Citizens to Assure Equality of Rights." *New York Times*, June 12.

Contributors

Index

Contributors

Jessica L. Beyer is a lecturer in the Henry M. Jackson School for International Studies at the University of Washington. Her current research focuses on cybersecurity issues, particularly non-state actors and social spaces online. Her past research explored political mobilization emerging from highly populated online communities and focused on actors such as Anonymous and other hacktivists, the Pirate Parties, and digital pirates. In 2012, she won the Association of Internet Researcher's Dissertation Award. Her book *Expect Us: Online Communities and Political Mobilization* was published by Oxford University Press in 2014.

Erica Chenoweth is a professor and associate dean for research at the Josef Korbel School of International Studies at the University of Denver, where she teaches courses on international relations, terrorism, nonviolent resistance, and contemporary warfare. Previously, she was an associate senior researcher at the Peace Research Institute of Oslo (PRIO) and an assistant professor at Wesleyan University, and she has held visiting appointments at Harvard University's Kennedy School of Government, Stanford University, UC-Berkeley, and the University of Maryland. Her book, with Maria J. Stephan, *Why Civil Resistance Works: The Strategic Logic of Nonviolent Conflict* (Columbia University Press, 2011) won the 2012 Woodrow Wilson Foundation Award, given annually by the American Political Science Association in recognition of the best book on government, politics, or international affairs published in the United States in the previous calendar year. Chenoweth has presented her research all over the world at various academic conferences, government workshops, and international governmental organizations. From 2008 to 2017, she served on the Academic Council for the International Center on Nonviolent Conflict. She is currently a research fellow at the One Earth Future Foundation and a term member at the Council on Foreign Relations.

Jennifer Earl is a professor of sociology and (by courtesy) of government and public policy at the University of Arizona. She is director emeritus of the Center for Information Technology and Society and director emeritus of the Technology and Society PhD Emphasis, both at University of California, Santa Barbara. Her research focuses on social movements, information technologies, and the sociology of law, with research emphases on Internet activism, social movement repression, and legal change. She is the recipient of a National Science Foundation CAREER Award for research from 2006 to 2011 on web activism. She is coauthor, with Katrina Kimport, of *Digitally Enabled Social Change* (MIT Press, 2011), which was awarded Honorable Mention for the Communication and Information Technologies Section of the American Sociological Association's (ASA) Book Award in 2013, and she is the winner of a career achievement award from the same ASA section for her research on Internet activism.

Lester R. Kurtz is a professor of public sociology at George Mason University, where he teaches peace and conflict studies, comparative sociology of religion, and social theory. In 2018, he taught at Mason-Korea in South Korea. He holds a master's degree in religion from Yale University and a PhD in sociology from the University of Chicago. He is the editor of the three-volume *Encyclopedia of Violence, Peace and Conflict* (Elsevier, 2008) and *The Warrior and the Pacifist* (Routledge, 2018), and is coeditor of the two-volume *Women, War and Violence* (Praeger, 2015), *Nonviolent Social Movements* (Blackwell, 1999), and *The Web of Violence* (University of Illinois Press, 1997), as well as author of books and articles, including *Gods in the Global Village* (Pine Forge/Sage, 2015), *The Politics of Heresy* (University of California Press, 1986), *Evaluating Chicago Sociology* (University of Chicago Press, 1986), and *The Nuclear Cage* (Prentice-Hall, 1988). He is currently working on a book on Gandhi and has taught at the University of Texas-Austin, the University of Chicago, Northwestern University, and Tunghai University. He has lectured in Europe, Asia, Africa, and North America, and he has served as chair of the Peace Studies Association and the Peace, War, and Social Conflict Section of the American Sociological Association, which awarded him its Robin Williams Distinguished Career Award. In 2014, the Association for Applied and Clinical Sociology awarded him the Lester F. Ward Distinguished Contribution to Applied and Clinical Sociology Award. He is a distinguished research fellow at the Institute of Nanjing Massacre History and International Peace in Nanjing, People's Republic of China.

George Lakey, a former Lang Visiting Professor of Issues for Social Change at Swarthmore College (2007–2009), has been a leader in the field of nonviolent social change since the 1960s and has published extensively for both activist and academic readers. He is the founder and executive director of Training for Change, a Philadelphia-based organization known internationally for its leadership in creating and teaching strategies for nonviolent social change. Lakey has worked in the United States with mineworkers, steelworkers, and civil rights leaders, and internationally with South African antiapartheid activists, Cambodian human rights organizers, and many others. Lakey is the author of numerous book chapters, pamphlets, and articles on social change, and his work has been translated into at least six languages. His books include *A Manual for Direct Action* (Quadrangle Books, 1964), *Toward a Living Revolution* (Wipf & Stock, 2016), and *Grassroots and Nonprofit Leadership: A Guide for Organizations in Changing Times* (Daniel Hunter, 2016). His teaching includes stints at the University of Pennsylvania, Haverford College, and Temple University. George Lakey is formerly a research associate at the Lang Center for Civic and Social Responsibility and a faculty member in the Peace and Conflict Studies Program at Swarthmore College.

Rachel MacNair is a member of Penn Valley Meeting in Kansas City, Missouri. She is the author of *The Psychology of Peace: An Introduction* (Praeger, 2003) and *Perpetration-Induced Traumatic Stress: The Psychological Consequences of Killing* (Praeger, 2002) and the editor of *Working for Peace: A Handbook of Practical Psychology* (Impact Publishers, 2006). She is director of the Institute for Integrated Social Analysis, the research arm of the nonprofit organization Consistent Life. She also coaches dissertation students on statistics. She graduated from Earlham College with a bachelor's degree in peace and conflict studies, and she received a PhD in psychology and sociology from the University of Missouri at Kansas City.

Brian Martin is emeritus professor at the University of Wollongong, Australia. He is the author of seventeen books and hundreds of articles on nonviolence, whistleblowing, scientific controversies, information issues, democracy, and other topics. He is vice president of Whistleblowers Australia and runs a large website on suppression of dissent. His PhD is in theoretical physics from Sydney University. He has taught a wide range of subjects including communication studies, environmental issues, peace studies, and the politics of technology. He has undertaken many community research projects with the group Schweik Action Wollongong.

Chaiwat Satha-Anand has been a pragmatic peacemaker in Thailand, engaging policymakers and military and civil society forces to stem violence and address conflict, particularly in the country's south. He was appointed to lead Thailand's National Reconciliation Commission and has championed the mainstreaming of peace education in Thai schools. A globally renowned scholar of Islam and nonviolence, Dr. Satha-Anand has pioneered the view that Islamic practices and values like fasting, daily prayers, self-discipline, and spiritual reflection are conducive to successful nonviolent conflict resolution. Internationally, he is recognized for such influential works as "The Nonviolent Crescent: Eight Theses on Muslim Nonviolent Action" (in *Arab Nonviolent Political Struggle in the Middle East*, Lynne Rienner Publishers, 1990). He is founder and director of the Peace Information Centre at Thammasat University in Bangkok, the Foundation for Democracy and Development Studies, and Thailand Research Fund. He is also the founder and chair of the Strategic Nonviolence Committee (SNC), located first within the Royal Thai Government's National Security Council and now a freestanding policy institute. Chaiwat Satha-Anand received the 2012 El-Hibri Peace Education Prize.

Doron Shultziner was born in Haifa in 1975. He holds a bachelor's degree in political science and Middle Eastern studies and a master of arts degree (Summa Cum Laude) in political science, both from the Hebrew University of Jerusalem. His doctoral degree is from the University of Oxford. He was a fellow at the Institute for the Study of Modern Israel in Emory University, and then held post-docs at the Hebrew University of Jerusalem and Tel Aviv University. He is now head of the Politics and Communications Department at Hadassah Academic College Jerusalem. His research interests cover various topics, focusing on social movements, media, and comparative democratization.

Lee A. Smithey serves as coordinator of the Peace and Conflict Studies program at Swarthmore College in Swarthmore, Pennsylvania, and he directs the Global Nonviolent Action Database (http://nvdatabase.swarthmore.edu). He is an associate professor of peace and conflict studies who investigates social conflict and social movements, especially ethnopolitical conflict and nonviolent conflict methods. He has focused much of his work on conflict transformation in Northern Ireland. His book, *Unionists, Loyalists, and Conflict Transformation in Northern Ireland* (Oxford University Press, 2011), was launched at the Northern Ireland Assembly and won the 2012 Donald Murphy Book Prize for Distinguished First Book from the American Conference for Irish Studies. He is a co–primary investigator of the Mural Mapping Project, a longitudinal and geospatial study of murals and public art in West Belfast and the Shankill Road area. He has served as chair of the Peace, War, and Social Conflict section of the American Sociological Association.

Jenni Williams is the founder and inspirational leader of WOZA (Women of Zimbabwe Arise), one of the most active civil society organizations in protesting government abuses in Zimbabwe. Ms. Williams has suffered arrest, harassment, and physical abuse. By uniting women in Zimbabwe of all races and ethnic backgrounds to advocate for issues directly affecting them, she has brought social, economic and political issues to national attention. Ms. Williams and WOZA lead annual peaceful marches on Valentine's Day and Mother's Day to promote peace and development. These marches have led to the mass arrest of peaceful women who are seen as threatening to the government of Zimbabwe, but the women remain undeterred. Ms. Williams and the organization she founded have provided an example of courage and leadership by working for change through peaceful and nonviolent means.

Dalia Ziada is the founding director of the Liberal Democracy Institute of Egypt and member of the Foreign Affairs Committee at Egypt's National Council for Women. In recognition of her continued work advocating and promoting women's rights, civil freedoms, and liberal democracy in the Middle East, she has received several international and regional awards. She was named by *Newsweek* for two years in a row (2011–12) as one of world's most influential and most fearless women, named by CNN as one of the Arab world's eight agents of change (2012), named by *Time* magazine as women's rights champion (2009), and selected by *Daily Beast* as one of the world's seventeen bravest bloggers (2011). She received the Tufts University Presidential Award for civil work (2011) and the Anna Lindh Euro-Mediterranean Journalist Award for her blog (2010). Dalia Ziada holds a master's degree in international relations from Fletcher School of Law and Diplomacy, Tufts University with a special focus on civil military relations in times of social and security crises.

Index

Italic page numbers denote illustrations or tables.